Also by Tony Wagner

How Schools Change
Making the Grade
Change Leadership
The Global Achievement Gap
Creating Innovators

Most Likely to Succeed

PREPARING OUR KIDS
FOR THE INNOVATION ERA

Tony Wagner
and Ted Dintersmith

SCRIBNER

New York   London   Toronto   Sydney   New Delhi

SCRIBNER
An Imprint of Simon & Schuster, Inc.
1230 Avenue of the Americas
New York, NY 10020

First Scribner hardcover edition August 2015

SCRIBNER and design are registered trademarks of The Gale Group, Inc.,
used under license by Simon & Schuster, Inc., the publisher of this work.

For information about special discounts for bulk purchases,
please contact Simon & Schuster Special Sales at 1-866-506-1949
or business@simonandschuster.com.

The Simon & Schuster Speakers Bureau can bring authors to your live event.
For more information or to book an event contact the Simon & Schuster Speakers Bureau
at 1-866-248-3049 or visit our website at www.simonspeakers.com.

Manufactured in the United States of America

1   3   5   7   9   10   8   6   4   2

Library of Congress Control Number: 2015008645

ISBN 978-1-5011-0431-2
ISBN 978-1-5011-0433-6 (ebook)

To America's teachers   .

There are no two ways about it—teaching is demanding. We're counting on our teachers to shape and transform our next generation, but we pay them salaries comparable to that of someone who works at a rental car counter. We expect them to deal with learning, family, motivational, and life issues for hundreds of students yet decide that they are so untrustworthy that we need to hold their feet to the fire with nonsensical standardized tests. We blame them when things don't go exactly the way we want—with a given child, class, school, or national cohort—yet we do next to nothing to support them. Yet they persevere, and come to school every day committed to helping our kids become better people. So, to our teachers, we say thank you, and hope that this book, and the documentary *Most Likely to Succeed*, will help you in your important mission.

CONTENTS

INTRODUCTION

This book is a product of an unlikely collaboration that began with a breakfast in Cambridge, Massachusetts, on a snowy day in early 2012.

We come from very different worlds. Tony Wagner has spent his career in the world of education. He taught English for more than a decade, ran a school, got a doctorate from Harvard's Graduate School of Education, started an education-related nonprofit, is a frequent keynote speaker at major conferences around the world, and has written five books on education. His body of work points the way toward a completely reimagined education system, one optimized for a world of innovation and the complexities of twenty-first-century citizenship. His two most recent books, *The Global Achievement Gap* and *Creating Innovators*, have sold almost a quarter of a million copies, received widespread critical acclaim, and have been translated into more than ten languages.

Ted Dintersmith spent his career in the world of technology and innovation. He got his PhD in Engineering from Stanford and then ran a start-up making the semiconductors that helped enable the digital revolution. The majority of his career has been in the field of venture capital, as a senior partner with one of the nation's top-tier early-stage venture firms, Charles River Ventures. He's been on the board of directors of the National Venture Capital Association, championed their national competitiveness initiative, and was ranked by Business 2.0 as the top-performing venture capitalist in the United States during the period 1995–1999.

A few years ago, Ted began directing more of his focus toward education. As a father of two school-aged children, he was concerned by what he saw as a disconnect between schools and an increasingly innovative world. He knew that rapid advances in innovation were eliminating traditional jobs from the economy. Workers performing routinized tasks were becoming an endangered species. Companies wanted to hire creative problem-solvers able to continually invent ways to add value to their organizations, but found few of them graduating from our schools. Alarmingly, the schools he visited seemed intent on crushing the creativity out of students—erasing the very skills that would have allowed them to thrive.

Ted began meeting with education experts to learn more. These meetings were highly informative, but they often ended with, "Well, the person you really need to meet is Tony Wagner." After reading Tony's books, Ted sent him a blind email, asking him to get together on one of Ted's upcoming trips to Boston. Tony agreed, and a one-hour breakfast turned into a three-hour discussion about how our obsolete education system was stymieing the innovation crucial to success in today's economy.

By the end of the breakfast, the two of us found that, despite vast differences in professional backgrounds, we shared convictions that could be distilled to these points:

- Rapid advances in innovation are eliminating structured routine jobs from our economy, leaving millions of young Americans at risk;
- The critical skills young adults need in the twenty-first century for careers in the world of innovation, and for responsible citizenship, are the very skills the school years eviscerate;
- The education policies our country is pursuing to "fix" schools only serve to harm students and disillusion teachers;
- While education credentials were historically aligned with competencies that mattered, they have become prohibitively expensive, emotionally damaging, and disconnected from anything essential;
- Unless we completely reimagine school, the growing divide between the haves and have-nots will threaten to rip civil society apart; and,
- We have an urgent obligation to speak out, since we know what our education system needs to do to give every student a fighting chance in life.

That initial three-hour breakfast conversation subsequently blossomed into a daily collaboration. The two of us have worked closely with award-winning documentarian Greg Whiteley on a feature-length film on education, *Most Likely to Succeed,* which premiered at the prestigious Sundance Film Festival in January 2015. The documentary has served as the foundation for a broad and ambitious initiative we are launching to help schools move forward. Together, the documentary, the outreach initiative, and this book provide a framework for reimagining school.

What Mattered to You

When we talk to people, we always find it revealing to inquire about their school experiences; we've all been students. For starters, we thought it might help if we provide a bit of context on our own school experiences.

Tony hated school, had average SATs, and went to two nondescript colleges before finally earning his BA degree at what was then one of the most experimental (but equally anonymous) undergraduate programs in the country. He went on to earn a Master of Arts in Teaching and a Doctorate in Education at Harvard University, where he found himself to be a complete outlier. While at the Harvard Graduate School of Education, Tony was almost constantly at odds with the mainstream of education, and he developed his views despite what was covered in classrooms. Tony is an example of someone who survived the education system and went on to have a successful career as an author, speaker, and consultant. And he'll be the first to admit that a doctorate from Harvard has a sort of "Wizard of Oz" benefit—the credential is important largely because everyone thinks it's important.

Ted has an innate ability to do simple math problems quickly. While this skill is of limited value in life, it was his best friend in school. He never missed a point on a standardized math test, and excelled at his math and physics courses. Only when he went to Stanford for graduate school did he realize that what is required to be a great physicist has almost nothing to do with what is required to be a great physics student. Fortunately for his career prospects, after earning an MS in Applied Physics and a PhD in Engineering from Stanford University, he switched out of physics into technology and innovation, where he experienced considerable success. He is now an active education philanthropist, providing guidance and funding to several high-potential organizations seeking to move education into the twenty-first century.

The authors went to school in the 1960s and '70s, a period that stands in stark contrast to today's pressure-packed school years. Back then, there was dramatically less competition to get into colleges. The concept of test preparation wasn't on the radar screen. Kids didn't do activities simply for the sake of building the perfect college application. Instead, they had ample time in their childhoods to explore, create, and develop passions. And no matter what your education level was when you entered the workforce, entry-level jobs were relatively easy to secure. For children in America today, those days are long gone.

Whether over the dinner table or in large auditoriums, we have found it invaluable in setting the tone for a discussion about education to ask participants to reflect on their school years. Specifically, we ask them to describe what aspects of their education had a profound positive impact on them: experiences in and out of the classroom, teachers, mentors, coaches, et cetera. The sharing of these results is revealing, and it gets everyone energized to think hard about what really matters in education.

We'd like to encourage you to take a few minutes to reflect on the most transformational aspects of your education—experiences that took place either inside or outside the classroom. You can jot them down on a piece of paper or in the margin of this book (assuming it's not an e-book!).

We've asked this question to thousands of people and received a wide range of responses. People describe participating in an after-school club; leading a committee; designing and completing an ambitious project; being inspired by a teacher with an infectious love for a given field; hearing from an adult who believed in them; practicing and playing on an athletic team; failing at something and recovering. Not a single person we've asked has responded, "Well, there was a lecture class with multiple-choice quizzes that really changed me."

In case you're curious, here's who each of us would like to thank:

Tony: I changed schools in the twelfth grade, and sadly I cannot recall the name of the teacher who made the greatest difference for me in high school. I've tried to track him down, but the school I attended then has since closed its doors.

I was a late starter as a reader, but I grew to love the beauty and evocativeness of words and stories. I devoured great novels and began writing stories of my own in ninth grade. I wanted to be a novelist. Unfortunately, my English teachers throughout high school were of no help. To the extent that we received any classroom "instruction" in writing, it consisted of lessons in grammar—subject-verb agreement, the proper use of commas, dangling participles, split infinitives, and so on.

The few papers my teachers assigned were usually essays, where the purpose of the paper was to repeat the teacher's interpretation of the book we'd "discussed" in class. (The teachers did all the talking!) And they'd spend an inordinate amount of time spilling red ink all over our papers. We, like most students today, would glance at the grade, ignore the corrections, and toss the papers in the trash on the way out the door.

The twelfth-grade English teacher at my new school was the same as the rest, but there was another English teacher at the school, a kindly and soft-spoken British gentleman, who seemed different. I don't know why but for some reason—maybe desperation—I mentioned my interest in writing to him and asked if he could help me. "I'd be delighted" was his reply. At his suggestion, we'd meet once a week, and he encouraged me to experiment with a different kind of writing or genre for each meeting. One week he'd say, "Why don't you try writing a dramatic scene with just dialogue." The next week he might say, "How about writing a humorous story this week." Or, "Give a childhood reminiscence a try." Or, "Have you seen any good movies lately? How about trying a review?"

He'd read each piece as I sat beside him, and he'd make just a few comments. He'd pick out a word choice or a metaphor that he thought was especially effective. Or he'd comment on the evocativeness of a particular scene or the persuasiveness of a paragraph. He'd also often suggest things I might want to read: novels, short stories, poems, or essays that were examples of the genre I was playing with in my writing that week.

And "playing" was really the operative word. Years later, I realized that these weekly assignments were the equivalent of artists' sketches—ways to train the eye (or ear, in this case) and free up the hand. His comments were intended to highlight what was my best writing so that I had a sense of what to strive for.

The effect on me was profound. I couldn't stop writing—and still can't. I did far more work for this noncredit activity than I'd ever done for any of my required classes. And years later when I began to teach writing to a wide variety of high school students—from kids at risk in an alterative public school to privileged kids attending an elite private school—I used the same method of instruction: I had kids experiment with a new writing genre each week, met with them individually to go over a piece of work, and then encouraged them to polish pieces they especially loved.

Ted: Jim Canavan taught me Spanish in high school. He was charismatic, inspiring, and passionate about the Spanish language. What was so unusual about the way Mr. Canavan taught is that it was all about fun. In his class, multiple laugh-filled conversations took place simultaneously. For the entire fifty-minute class period, we'd talk—entirely in Spanish—about school, current events, sports, or funny things that happened in our lives. I can still remember his telling us how his Pontiac Firebird caught fire in his driveway, and the irony of the car's name!

Mr. Canavan didn't stand at the front of the class—his back to the students—writing vocabulary words or verb conjugations on the blackboard. His focus was leading and coaching a great conversation in Spanish—with vigorous class participation. At the end of each class, though, he would say, "*Vaya, y si usted quiere la clase de mañana sea aún más divertido, es posible que desee aprender algunas palabras del vocabulario y los verbos de esta noche en casa, y el uso de ellos mañana.*" Or, in English, "Gee, and if you want tomorrow's class to be even more fun, you might want to learn some vocabulary words and verbs tonight at home, and use them tomorrow." And we all did, enthusiastically.

By the end of his course, we were all conversationally fluent and learned the language in a way that would be retained for life. I've traveled extensively in Spanish-speaking countries, and forty-five years later can still navigate my way around. In contrast, the two years of French I was required to take in college disappeared completely from my mind seconds after the final exam.

In a field where the prevailing (and failed) way to teach a language is a death march through memorization, Mr. Canavan was an outlier. Shortly after I graduated, he gave up the teaching profession. I have tried a few times to find him to say, "Thanks for inspiring all of us, and showing that meaningful learning and fun aren't mutually exclusive," but I haven't been able to track him down. I hope, wherever he is, he reads this book, and gets my thank-you.

This exercise highlights an irony of our education system. For the last century, the classroom experience for most students has revolved around lectures, note-taking, recall-based tests, and grades. Clubs, sports, and social interaction were regarded as providing a welcome break from the intense learning process. We will see, however, that most lecture-based courses contribute almost nothing to real learning. Consequential and retained learning comes, to a very large extent, from applying knowledge to new situations or problems, research on questions and issues that students consider important, peer interaction, activities, and projects. Experiences, rather than short-term memorization, help students develop the skills and motivation that transforms lives.

In this book, we will explore the contradiction between what students must do to earn a high school or college degree versus what makes them most likely to succeed in the world of work, citizenship, and lifelong learning. We'll also show what can and must be done to transform education for the twenty-first century and provide examples of best practices in high schools and colleges around the country. And we'll emphasize the urgency of effecting change. In coming chapters, here's what we'll cover:

Our beginning chapter, *Our Education DNA,* delves into why society places such outsized value on academic credentials—associating them with a person's intrinsic "quality," not just with skills that have been acquired. We have been conditioned to view some types of credentials as being marks of outsized distinction, and certain types of "learning" (e.g., Latin conjugations) as vastly superior to more base endeavors (understanding how a piece of machinery works). Education credentials are our country's caste system.

Given this obsession with education credentials, people repeatedly follow the assertion that "education is key" with the concern that "our schools need to do much better." But few can answer the overarching question: "What is the purpose of education?" Few can define what constitutes real learning. And few can articulate a direction forward for our schools. We will in chapter 2, *The Purpose of Education.*

As our education system muddles along with unclear purpose, the stakes couldn't be higher. Chapter 3, *What's at Stake?,* argues that not only are millions of young lives on the line, but our social fabric is at risk. As tens of millions of young adults exit our education system destined for chronic unemployment, the growing divide between the rich and the rest will broaden. Civil society faces the real prospect of being ripped apart.

Our frenzied chase for the college credential adversely affects all aspects of K-12 education. Chapter 4, *The Formative Years: K-12,* will show how the academic priorities of colleges, coupled with the hypercompetitive admissions process, have outsized influence on secondary (and increasingly primary) school. The net result is that we're letting our entire education system become intense yet vapid, setting our students up for failure.

Chapter 5, *The Gold Ring: The College Degree,* examines what's taken as a given in our society—that college is the key to preparing kids for life. Our colleges, despite exorbitant tuition levels, are failing to produce graduates prepared for careers or citizenship. In many cases, students graduate with alarming debt levels and no real improvement in the minimal skills they were taught in high school.

Testing is a prerequisite for gaining education credentials, but these tests are antithetical to meaningful learning. Increasingly, we rely on flawed assessments to gauge student—and with Race to the Top, teacher—performance. Chapter 6, *Teaching, Learning, and Assessing,* examines the trade-offs between scale and authenticity in ways to assess student achievement.

Chapter 7, *A New Vision for Education,* outlines key elements of a systemic strategy for the creation of an education system that can meet the needs of the twenty-first century. We will discuss the need for both a top-down and bottom-up strategy for systemic change and outline a framework for an accountability system that measures what matters most, incenting powerful teaching and learning. We will outline the ways in which education, community, and business leaders must work together to advocate fundamental change.

Unbeknownst to many, there are incredibly exciting things happening in many schools and school districts around the country. We view much of this work as "educational R&D" that points the way toward a radically different education system. We will showcase some of this work and discuss what parents and community members can do to advocate for change.

Finally, we will describe exciting new initiatives being built around the acclaimed documentary film *Most Likely to Succeed.* The film was originated and funded by Ted, directed by Greg Whiteley, and relied heavily from strategic advice from Tony. We will highlight available resources for effecting change in your school, and show how our readers can play a key role in improving the life prospects of the children in their lives.

Ultimately, we hope that our readers will benefit from what we believe has been a vibrant melding of our careers in the worlds of education and innovation. As you consider the points we make, we anticipate that you may be impressed by our credentials from two of the world's finest universities. Don't be. We're here to tell you that credentials are increasingly a sucker's game. We hope you'll benefit from this book, despite—not because of—our five graduate degrees from Harvard and Stanford. If you find this book useful, it will be because we understand the dynamic forces profoundly reshaping our society and the role education needs to play in preparing our students to succeed. These insights come from a combined eight decades of real-world experience, not from a few years of advanced education that, in hindsight, taught us little of relevance to our careers or the world we live in.

Our bottom line? Our nation continues to plod away with incremental fixes to an obsolete education system, as innovation races ahead. Our world continues to place outsized weight on education credentials, despite skyrocketing financial and emotional costs and considerable data that the value proposition behind most credentials is empty. For the millions of Americans charting the education waters today, the stakes couldn't be higher. Today's youth live in a world brimming with opportunity. Some will create, catalyze, and capitalize on a dynamic world hungry for innovation. Others will be left behind. Students who only know how to perform well in today's education system—get good grades and test scores, and earn degrees—will no longer be those who are most likely to succeed. Thriving in the twenty-first century will require real competencies, far more than academic credentials.

During my years in school, the mentor who had the biggest impact on my life trajectory was _____ because_____.

PART I

MILLENNIAL INTERVIEWS
(with Tamara Day)

JACOB

Jacob grew up in an affluent neighborhood in Southern California. He was a popular child, curious and creative, who loved figuring out how things work. A self-described "tech nerd," he spent his time outside of school exploring a multitude of hobbies: tinkering on the computer, playing video games, making music. He eventually taught himself coding and, in seventh grade, started a web design business with friends. "The Internet was so new, and I spent so much time playing games and then time on the Internet looking for info about the games, it was only a matter of time before I started thinking, why couldn't I make a site? Six months into it, I realized, I had built a site, module by module. Eventually I stopped using the templates and just started from scratch. Coding is like language. I never sat through a traditional coding class. It was a really organic process that came from asking myself, how can I figure this out?"

Jacob attended the local public high school, where he excelled academically. He got good grades, was involved in extracurricular activities, and took all but two of the AP courses his school offered, ten in total. College was always a priority—to both him and his parents—and he saw it as the first step to the life path he had clearly marked out.

Despite his entrepreneurial spirit, his plan for the future was clear and predictable: work hard in high school, get into a good college, study

finance, and get a job in banking. From there, he would make a successful career, earn lots of money, and, for all intents and purposes, be living
the dream. Finance was the safe choice and the sure bet, something he
believed he could count on to lead him to the successful and lucrative
lifestyle he envisioned. He described an exercise from his senior year of
high school that encapsulates his thinking at the time: "In our senior
English class, we were talking about boiling literary works down to their
one truth, and that all of these authors have one truth that they want to
communicate. Our teacher asked us, if you could boil down your one truth,
what would it be? I, being seventeen and super naive, wrote up on the
whiteboard, *Money CAN buy happiness.*"

After working hard in high school, earning a 3.7 GPA, and getting a
1340 on his SATs, Jacob was accepted to the University of Washington.
He was starting three quarters ahead from all of the AP credits he had
racked up. As an incoming freshman in 2005, he felt himself one step
closer to realizing the bright future he envisioned. The only problem, in his
own words, was that "the world doesn't work in straight paths anymore."

Jacob graduated in 2009, a year after the financial crisis, with a bachelor's degree in Finance. The industry that once seemed like the safe bet
was suddenly in turmoil. "We were studying the impending collapse before
it happened," he said. "Then it happened and our professors were like,
'Well, we were hoping this would hold until after you graduated, but it
didn't.'" Not surprisingly, the job climate, especially for a recent graduate, was grim.

The university's Career Center mostly focused on placing graduates at
large local companies: Microsoft, Boeing, Amazon. So on his own, Jacob
attended job fairs, contacted banks and other financial institutions, and
searched the Internet looking for positions in his field. Nothing panned out.

Not one to give up, he adjusted his plan and decided to move back to
Los Angeles and find a job in entertainment. His uncle was in the industry
and he thought he might have better luck there. He leveraged every tech
listing service he could find: LinkedIn, Indeed, Career Builder. He emailed
friends, cross-referenced mutual contacts and alumni networks, and spent
days searching Craigslist and job boards. He pictured getting his foot in the

door with a junior position and then working his way up through the ranks, just the way he'd heard a career trajectory was supposed to work. Despite his efforts, though, finding even an entry-level position proved to be incredibly difficult. Two of the top talent agencies had just merged and there was an abundance of talented people with years of experience looking for work. He considered going back to school in order to postpone the job hunt for a few more years, but his parents wouldn't pay for it. Not wanting to take out loans, Jacob accepted an unpaid internship and moved back home.

After nine months of internships, during which time his parents generously supported him, Jacob finally got a break, even if it was not the one he had been waiting for: He took a job delivering mail at a talent agency for $7 an hour. The college degree, which had once seemed like the key to his success, was beginning to seem more like a joke.

Five years out of college, Jacob has worked his way up from the mailroom and is now a successful talent manager in Los Angeles. He has changed jobs a few times, making his way laterally to different positions within the industry and figuring out how things work along the way. Just as in his earlier days of coding, he never formally studied the work he does but rather picked it up by an organic process of trial and error. He attributes his success to grit and perseverance, and his willingness to work hard. He observed, "It's interesting because our parents, and this is the first time in history really, had no business whatsoever giving us advice. And they didn't know this and were trying their best, but the world has changed so much. We were really guinea pigs and the last generation that can remember life before the Internet."

We asked Jacob if he ever uses the skills he learned in college in his current job. "I have used my degree skills exactly once, when creating a funding proposal for a film." More often, he said, he utilizes his natural creativity and entrepreneurial skills. Reflecting on his course of study and degree, he told us, "I have a very expensive degree from a pretty great university that I use as a coaster. I had a horrible time finding a job in my degree field, and eventually went into entertainment, where my degree is absolutely useless."

Ironically, he had briefly considered majoring in film in college, but after enrolling in a film course and realizing that it was all theory and that he would never get to make an actual film, he decided to stick to finance. Jacob told us, "I'd 100 percent have *not* gone to college if I could do it all over."

That's not to say that he didn't find certain aspects of his college career valuable. The socializing in particular was important to him, and he made sure to stress that he is a supporter of his university and believes he got a good education. But his experiences have made him question just what exactly it was he went to college for.

We asked him if he values the credential of a college degree in others. He told us it depends. "USC has one of the only master's programs in the country for film producing. It's called the Peter Stark Program. It's very prestigious, very difficult to get into. If I meet someone who's twenty-three and never worked a day in the industry and they're in the Peter Stark Program, to me that's code for unemployed: 'I finished undergrad, I couldn't find a job, so I went to film grad school.' That's great, but there are so many better ways to learn about film producing, like mainly going out and producing a film. But on the other hand, I just got a director yesterday who's twenty-three years old who's in the Peter Stark Program and has managed a budget and crews of up to thirty people, and to me that's super impressive."

Today, Jacob adheres more to a "learn by doing" philosophy that harks back to his earlier days of tinkering on the computer and making music. We asked him, if he could give advice to his younger self, what his formula for success would look like. He said that he no longer believes there is a set formula that will allow someone to succeed. He would simply recommend a "balance of hard work and socializing, with a little more emphasis on socializing. Knowing thyself." Instead of rushing to check boxes, he loves the idea of taking a gap year. "Go and expand yourself. Travel, sign up for volunteer programs, something like that. Really get out into the world and figure out . . . your passion. When you have to stop and think about those things it's impossible, but when you come across something, if you find that thing where you can lose hours in it, that's your passion. Go for it."

Jacob wishes that his formal education had focused on more practical areas like financial education, writing skills, and computer skills, things he uses at work every day. He is at the same time both skeptical about the value of his college degree and loyal to his alma matter and his own college experience. He also knows how fortunate he was to have parents that were able to support him financially, something that is not true for many of his friends.

He reflects on education and his own experiences a lot, and believes something needs to change: "In finance, you are taught to value things in concrete terms based on what you can measure. When people talk about the value of a college degree, they are really talking about all of these other things like 'success' and 'your future.' They are really asking, how much is your future worth? Of course the answer is an infinite amount, so people will pay an infinite amount of money for it. But how high can tuition get before people start to say it's not worth it anymore? This is not a hit on my school. I'm a supporter of my university and think I got a good education. This is a systemic issue. This is an America issue."

CHAPTER 1

Our Education DNA

We worship at the altar of academic credentials. We live in a society obsessed with people's degrees. Do they have their high school diploma? What were their SAT scores? How many AP courses did they take, and how many 5's did they get on the AP exams? Did they earn a college or advanced degree? How exclusive was the college they attended? What was their GPA? How about their GMAT scores? We ask these questions as if the answers provide critical insight into a person's intrinsic value. We also spend increasing amounts of time and money to obtain these credentials, whether in the form of rising K-12 costs, college tuition levels, time spent in school, amount of homework, tutoring fees, number of standardized tests, or the booming test prep industry.

But something is seriously amiss. Despite our enormous investment in education, the majority of our students lack the skills necessary to get a good job, be an informed citizen, or—in some way that defies crisp definition—be a good and happy person.

The data are alarming. A recent Gallup poll found that just 11 percent of business leaders think colleges satisfactorily prepare students for success in the workplace.[1] Even more alarming, of recent college graduates, over half are either unemployed or holding a job any high school grad could fill. Yet, despite this glaring mismatch, some 94 percent of U.S. adults still believe a college degree is critically important to career prospects. Our beliefs haven't yet caught up with the reality of the world we live in.

We also count on our education system to prepare our youth to be responsible, informed citizens. Sadly, we're failing at this objective as well. A recent poll by Just Facts, a nonprofit research and educational institute, concluded that even our most engaged voters are uninformed.[2] Of twenty questions (involving things like government spending, income distribution, and climate change), the majority of "engaged voters"—people who actually vote most of the time—managed to correctly answer just 20 percent of the questions. And the most recent Civics Assessment conducted by the National Assessment of Educational Progress revealed that twelfth graders' civics knowledge and skills actually declined between 1998 and 2010.[3] We live in a country where young adults know and care more about Beyoncé than Boehner. More about LeBron James's contract size than the cost of the Iraq War. More about *Duck Dynasty* than our national debt.

When we ask parents what they most want for their children, they answer, almost without exception, "I just want my child to be happy." Yet the way parents and schools work with kids is, in too many cases, completely counterproductive. We test our kids on criteria that have very little to do with life skills, and tell most of them that they're not cutting it. We tell our kids that they will be abject failures without a high school diploma, but fail to provide them with relevant or engaging challenges during their four years in high school. We engrain in kids that the key to success in life is getting into a great college, but then parents are amazed when their child feels completely inadequate after a few rejection letters. Look no further than teen suicide rates. Since 1950, college-age suicides in the United States have doubled, while high school–age suicides have tripled.[4]

We live in an innovation economy. In this new world, the skills necessary to do well professionally have converged with the skills needed to be an effective citizen. Fifty years ago, before the Internet, it made sense for schools to teach kids "just facts." But in today's world, there is no longer a competitive advantage in knowing more than the person next to you because knowledge has become a commodity available to all with the swipe of a finger. Now, adults need to be able to ask great questions, critically analyze information, form independent opinions, collaborate, and communicate effectively. These are the skills essential for both career and citizenship.

Yet developing these is precisely where our schools fall so short. As we churn out millions of kids each year from an education system that teaches and tests them on narrow aspects of content retention that any smartphone can handle, we set them up for failure, unhappiness, and social discontent. We are, in every important sense, educating our way to national demise.

A Whirlwind Tour of the Entire History of Education

To understand the growing divide between credentials and competence, we need to go back in time. Way back. Back to before the printing press was invented. Before the wheel. All the way back to cavemen. This brief history will help explain exactly why credentials—not competence—hold the upper hand in today's society.

From their earliest origins, humans invented, learned, and adapted. And then shared their know-how. In a primitive version of cave-schooling, cave parents would pass important discoveries about survival on to their children—effective ways to work together to hunt for food, to defend against approaching threats, or to deal with harsh winters. Cave parents also taught their children how to get along with others in their family or clan. As basic as it sounds, cave people understood the core purpose of education: teach the next generation the lessons needed to survive and thrive.

As civilization advanced, a set of specialized tradesmen and craftsmen emerged: farmers, blacksmiths, cobblers, seamstresses. Concurrently, an effective form of education developed: the apprenticeship model. Aspiring artisans learned by studying under the tutelage of a master. They learned by doing. They remained in apprentice mode until achieving mastery. For thousands of years, apprenticeships formed the educational backbone of society's primitive economy, enabling essential skills to be passed down from generation to generation.

As society evolved from roving packs of savages to more hierarchical structures, an elite ruling class emerged alongside a class of artisans and tradesmen. Tradesmen, educated as apprentices under the tutelage of a master, formed the backbone of emerging economies. Those lucky enough to be born into the aristocracy were "above" learning a trade. Instead, they were immersed in ideas, the fine arts, and rhetoric—skills perceived to be important for the ruling class—in an education process orchestrated by respected tutors.

In ancient Greece, for instance, boys in wealthy families studied reading, writing, singing, and playing a musical instrument. A student learned by watching his mentor give speeches, helping the elder perform public duties, and attending symposia with him. The richest—not the best—students went on to study with famous teachers, at places like the Lyceum of Athens. The reputation of the mentor was the credential earned by the student.

Whether you were an apprentice or an anointed member of the ruling class, education has historically been linked to a meaningful credential. And the credential you earned was aligned to what you would do in life. For the anointed, your credential came from your bloodline and from the cachet of your tutors. For apprentices, your credential came from studying under a respected master. There was no fixed timeline for mastery—apprentices progressed at varying paces, getting individualized guidance and assignments. The master's reputation, in turn, depended on the success of her or his protégés. These educational methods, in place for thousands of years, were effective, but with a major limitation: They couldn't scale to keep up with an exponentially increasing population.

THE MODERN APPRENTICESHIP MODEL

Consider the exacting craft of making fine furniture, which requires great handwork, patience, and artistry, as well as a mastery of aspects of mathematics, materials science, and chemistry. How does someone become a master furniture-maker? Well, we spoke at length to Tim Philbrick, one of our nation's top furniture-makers, with pieces on display at leading art museums across the country including Boston's Museum of Fine Arts, the

Renwick at the Smithsonian, the Rhode Island School of Design, and the Philadelphia Museum of Art. Tim grew up in a family with deep academic roots, including a father who taught English at Brown University. But his father also had a real appreciation for hands-on learning and accomplishment. After high school, Tim pursued a real passion for making beautifully crafted furniture. Instead of spending four years in college in the 1970s, he found and arranged a four-year apprenticeship with Johnny Northup, a master furniture-maker who actually paid Tim $80 a week to learn how to make world-class furniture. Tim recalls the reaction of some of his relatives when he opted to pursue a path different from the normal college track. While some were aghast at a career path that they viewed as "blue collar," others were highly supportive. He fondly recalls his grandmother saying, "It takes a lot of brains to work with your hands."

While there are academic programs that teach the craft of fine furniture, Philbrick explained, "I felt I learned so much more working as an apprentice in a shop like Northup's. In a traditional course, I might have spent a semester doing something like dovetailing, over and over. My hands-on apprenticeship required me to take on a range of complicated, ambiguous challenges. I did a lot of furniture repair, learning what doesn't work. And I got the best of all feedback on my progress—the work I completed." So Philbrick, in essence, created his own mastery-driven "undergraduate experience," without a tuition bill.

After his four-year apprenticeship (and lacking a formal undergraduate credential), Philbrick was accepted as a graduate student at Boston University, where he studied artisanry and earned a certificate of mastery in Wood Furniture Design. He also pursued American Studies, focusing on the history of fine furniture. To earn this certificate, he needed to complete a body of master-level work, which was judged by professional furniture designers. It was, in Tim's words, "a practice straight from the medieval guild system." And Tim has never looked back, establishing himself as one of the world's top furniture-makers.

The apprenticeship model evident in Philbrick's story was, for centuries, the source of "credentials" for aspiring young artisans, who would work closely with an expert in a given field until mastering the craft. When historians refer to Paul Revere's silversmith credentials, they note that he apprenticed under John Coney. Claude Monet studied under Eugène Boudin. Frank Lloyd Wright apprenticed under Joseph Lyman Silsbee. Rachmaninoff studied under Zverev. And on and on. It's all about who they apprenticed under, not what school they attended. It's quite striking that, almost without exception, the great contributors to civilization were educated as apprentices, not as note-takers.

The impetus for our current education system came some seven centuries ago, as demand arose in religious society for copies of the Holy Bible. A set of Latin grammar schools emerged to train monks and priests for the exacting task of transcribing the Holy Bible—word for every Latin word. Each new copy had to be indistinguishable from its predecessors. These grammar schools revolved around four core educational principles: standardization, time efficiency, minimization of error, and intolerance to accidental or—God forbid—creative departures from the norm. Sound familiar?

As Bible replicas worked their way into society, the Latin grammar school model was also replicated. Early British boarding schools trace their roots to these Bible-copying factories of schooling. This model shaped education throughout Europe, the United States, and ultimately the rest of the world. Its guiding principles remain with us to this day.

In the eighteenth century, innovation in education came from an unlikely source: the Prussians. Devastated by a military defeat at the hands of Napoleon, they introduced a compulsory eight-year regimen of primary education that focused on reading, writing, and arithmetic. They invented the idea of grades, classes, subjects, and controlling teachers instead of master advisers.[5] They tailored the school experience to impart, on a scalable basis, the skills needed in an early industrial economy. The model spread rapidly through Europe.

In 1843, a man by the name of Horace Mann visited Germany and brought the Prussian system back to America. Mann was instrumental in getting Massachusetts to adopt tax-supported elementary public education, and set the stage for the scaling of a new kind of education in the United States. At the end of the nineteenth century, America needed to educate large numbers of immigrants and refugees from farms for basic citizenship and for jobs in a growing industrial economy. As work-flow experts like Frederick Winslow Taylor formulated efficient means of production, the level of expertise of workers in the production chain narrowed. The economy needed single-task interchangeable employees, not skilled artisans.

And we needed schools to teach the surging numbers of factory workers the basic skills needed for jobs in our emerging cities—to follow orders, be punctual, and perform rote tasks. We also wanted these future trained laborers to have basic citizenship literacy skills (the so-called three R's). The individual tutors and one-room schoolhouses, the hallmarks of nineteenth-century education, were suddenly obsolete.

An "assembly-line model of education" emerged at the turn of the twentieth century that could batch-process far larger numbers of students. It excelled at what it was designed to do: train millions of young adults to perform repetitive tasks quickly, retain modest amounts of content, and keep errors to a minimum. The results in the first half of the twentieth century were spectacular. The U.S. education system rose to the challenge of meeting the needs of the rising industrial economy and enabled the United States to gain world economic dominance.[6]

As the twentieth century rolled forward, the fundamentals of our economy changed. Midway through the last century, our industrial base began to contract, and low-wage routine jobs moved offshore. As growth in manufacturing jobs stalled, millions of new white-collar jobs for "knowledge workers" (a term coined by Peter Drucker in 1959) were created, fueling the next phase of U.S. economic growth and creating a robust middle class. The economic landscape was dominated by large organizations hungry for mid-level knowledge workers to produce, refine, and manage information.

To keep pace with these changes, Americans put increasing priority on education, largely by extending the number of years students spent in school. The number of high school and college graduates soared. With some tweaks (such as including a college prep track in public high schools), the core of the Prussian-American education model—the transfer of basic literacy and numeracy skills and content knowledge from teachers to students—remained effective in preparing students for knowledge-worker jobs. Our education system and economy maintained their productive alliance.

As we moved into the 1980s, a handful of people began voicing concerns about the state of education in the United States. They cited data questioning the international competitiveness of our students, reflected in lackluster performance on standardized tests. They expressed a concern that our slow-moving education system was incapable of adapting to a changing world. The prescient *A Nation at Risk* report, issued over thirty years ago, noted: "If an unfriendly foreign power had attempted to impose on America the mediocre educational performance that exists today, we might well have viewed it as an act of war."[7]

As our nation headed into the twenty-first century, we faced an existential choice. We could completely redesign our education system—the position advocated by leaders like Ted Sizer, founder of the Coalition of Essential Schools in 1984—or we could push our existing system harder for incremental improvements and rely on policies calling for curriculum homogeneity, more pervasive standardized testing, and teacher accountability tied to student test score performance.

The United States made the exact wrong bet, choosing to double down on our obsolete education system. Bad went to worse when President George W. Bush and Senator Ted Kennedy teamed up to enact the No Child Left Behind Act into law in 2002. This legislation put the standardized testing of students into hyperdrive. Then, in 2009, Barack Obama and his Secretary of Education, Arne Duncan, unveiled the Race to the Top initiative, effectively bribing states to implement programs to hold teachers accountable on the basis of their students' performance on standardized tests. By Obama's second term, "teaching to the test" was firmly established as the center of our education universe. And despite this all-in bet on prepping our students for standardized tests, test scores stayed stubbornly flat.

In short, the United States picked the wrong goal and failed at it. We opted to chase South Korea and Singapore on standardized test performance (a race we never had a chance of winning against children who spend every waking hour cramming for the tests) instead of educating our youth for a world of innovation and opportunity (a race that plays to our strengths). As Gallup has found in its polling, the United States is paying a very high price for this choice. Student and teacher engagement levels have plummeted in the face of a steady diet of test prep. While nearly 80 percent of fifth graders report being engaged at school, that number drops to only 40 percent by the start of high school. And according to Brandon Busteed, executive director of education at Gallup, "Teachers are dead last among all professions Gallup studied in saying their 'opinions count' at work and their 'supervisors create an open and trusting environment.'"[8]

Even if the world had stood still, the U.S. education bet would have been a colossal mistake. But the world raced forward. As we moved into the twenty-first century, the Internet exploded, changing our society and challenging our education system in profound ways. Pre-Internet, we lived in a world of knowledge scarcity. The best sources of information were schools and libraries. But with ubiquitous interconnectivity, knowledge became a free commodity—like air or water—available on every Internet-connected device. You no longer needed a teacher or librarian to provide you access.

In the span of a decade, the role of content knowledge has moved from the front to the back of the bus. Since information is readily available to everyone, content knowledge is no longer valued in the workplace. What matters most in our increasingly innovation-driven economy is not what you know, but *what you can do* with what you know. The skills needed in our vastly complicated world, whether to earn a decent living or to be an active and informed citizen, are radically different from those required historically.

Quite simply, the world has changed, and our schools remain stuck in time. "Knowledge workers" have become obsolete. What the world demands today are "smart creatives," the term that Eric Schmidt and Jonathan Rosenberg use to describe the kind of people Google needs to hire in their book *How Google Works*.

In our efforts to "fix" education, we've taken a course of action that extirpates the creative spirit and confidence from our youth while drilling them on frivolous things, like memorizing the definition of *extirpate* for the SAT verbal exam. Over and over, in classroom after classroom, on assignment after assignment, we condition kids to look for *the* right answer, instead of encouraging them to come up with multiple creative approaches. When they ask, "When will I ever use this?" we respond, "Trust me. This will come in handy down the road." Except it won't, and they know it. And so kids treat school as a set of hoops to jump through, instead of a vehicle for developing the skills and resources needed to accomplish their dreams. The worst part is, we set these creativity-killing priorities in a world that is screaming, "We need creative problem-solvers!" But our education system has deaf ears.

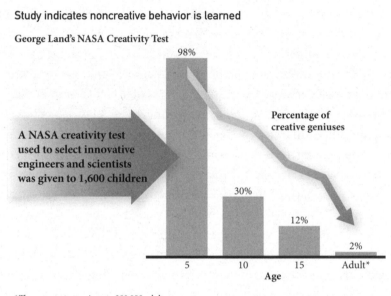

Study indicates noncreative behavior is learned

George Land's NASA Creativity Test

A NASA creativity test used to select innovative engineers and scientists was given to 1,600 children

Percentage of creative geniuses

98%

30%

12%

2%

5   10   15   Adult*

Age

*The same test was given to 280,000 adults.
Source: *Breakpoint and Beyond: Mastering the Future Today* by George Land; A.T. Kearney analysis

Riding a Bicycle

Imagine if we relied on our schools to teach kids how to ride bikes. Teachers would lecture and assign reading from bicycle textbooks. Students would stay up late at night memorizing the names of the various components of a bike. They would be marked down on tests—and lose self-confidence—for misspelling *derailleur*. Some students would excel; others would struggle. None would ever ride a bike.

Students would take lots and lots of standardized, multiple-choice tests of their bicycle knowledge. Because there are so many of these tests, and the stakes are sky-high, the tests would have to be "objective" and cheap. And the tests would have to produce a perfect bell-curve distribution of scores, so that we could rank every single child in America, to the decimal point, relative to others in bicycle "aptitude."

We would constantly remind our high school students that the key to being an outstanding cyclist goes beyond their high school experience. They would need to get accepted to an elite bicycle college, and the BAT (Bicycle Aptitude Test) would weigh heavily in the process. Students would spend nights, weekends, and summers preparing for the high-stakes BAT. Wealthy families would spend tens of thousands of dollars on BAT test prep. Some educators would finally receive respectable compensation—not for inspiring a joy of learning in students, but as BAT test tutors commanding more than $500 per hour in well-off communities.

A High-Stakes Bicycle Aptitude Test (BAT)

1. If the front gear of a bike has three levels and the rear has nine levels, how many total possible gear combinations are there?
   - a. 6
   - b. 12
   - c. 18
   - d. 27
   - e. None of the above

2. What component of, or accessory for, a bicycle is optimized to accommodate the needs of the ischial tuberocities?
   - a. Pedal
   - b. Handlebars
   - c. Height of the frame
   - d. Seat
   - e. Helmet

3. The shift levers that mount in the ends of the handlebars so you can shift without removing your hands from the bars are called:
    a. Stream-lined shifters
    b. Merckx shifters
    c. Bar end shifters
    d. Hands-on shifters
    e. Turbo shifters

4. In what year was the Campognolo Bicycle Company formed?
    a. 1745
    b. 1867
    c. 1896
    d. 1917
    e. 1933

5. How many teeth are on the front ring of a typical racing-bike crank-set?
    a. 7
    b. 9
    c. 13
    d. 39
    e. 53

Now content to rest on their laurels, the Bicycle College Board adds the Bicycle Advanced Placement (B-AP) test to its suite of offerings. This test requires students to memorize the English and Latin name for every component of unicycles, bicycles, and tricycles. This challenging AP credential reflects an advanced understanding of the fundamentals of biking and is revered by college admissions officers. It also adds a significant revenue source to the nonprofit College Board's annual billion-dollar top line.

Over time, competition for admission into elite bicycle colleges reaches a frenzy point. Millions of students spend their teenage years crafting the perfect application, hoping for the chance to earn acceptance into an esteemed bicycle college. They know their life prospects hinge on securing this credential. And they believe, as do their parents, that through their coursework they are becoming highly qualified bike riders.

While America's leading bicycle universities are the envy of the rest of the world, there are troubling signs that our K-12 system is falling behind. Our students can't seem to break away from mediocre BAT scores, even though test prep has become all-consuming. Countries like Singapore and South Korea put us to shame with exceptional test scores (even though they have yet to produce any great bike riders). With considerable alarm, we realize that if we don't close the "bicycle achievement gap," we risk becoming a second-rate nation.

In response to this crisis in bicycle education, our education leaders launch a bevy of education reforms supported vigorously by business leaders. Their Bicycle Education Reform Agenda includes:

- An extended school year, since kids forget so much during the summer
- Weekly standardized bicycle tests
- Making satisfactory test scores a requirement for high school graduation
- Holding teachers accountable for making their students improve on bicycle test scores
- Cutting back on electives to focus entirely on bicycle test prep

Schools serving disadvantaged students struggle to make "adequate yearly progress" on test scores. Policy pundits blame the teachers and castigate their unions, while ignoring the 22 percent childhood poverty rate in America, and the fact that few inner-city kids can afford even a junkyard bike. There's a general assumption in the country that inner-city kids just aren't cut out to ride bikes.

The net result of these enlightened policy moves?

Well, for starters, kids end up hating all aspects of riding a bike. Teachers dread coming to work, and our best leave the profession. The joy of riding a bike gets lost in the grind of schooling. When these kids get to college, it's more of the same: lectures, cramming, and tests of memorized content. When they graduate, most struggle to find a job, since the workplace doesn't value expertise in bike trivia. When "top" graduates do start work, their bosses say, "Gee, after all this time and money spent earning an amazing credential, this kid has no clue how to ride a bike. Something doesn't make sense here." And, nationally, we keep "cycling through" the same failed set of initiatives, with no discernible progress.

Thankfully, we don't rely on schools to teach kids how to ride a bike. Kids learn by doing. They struggle to master the technique. They fail, fall off, and get back up. They persevere until they achieve competency and eventually mastery. Oh, and if they take time away from their bike (for five months here in Boston during the long, cold winters!), they hop right back on the bike afterward, without missing a beat. We can assess, based on observation and evidence, whether a child is a beginner, intermediate, or accomplished bike rider. What we can't do is assign children a precise score on a scale of 200–800 through multiple-choice questions that correlate with competence.

U.S. education is failing, in large part, because of the misguided belief that it's imperative to test on a massive scale. To test millions of students every year is expensive in terms of time, money, and opportunity cost. With the goal of rank-ordering millions of test-takers, assessment inevitably gets reduced to simple multiple-choice quizzes, even though there's a complete disconnect between what is easy to test and what really matters.

But back to the bike. We assess aspects of "learning" that have nothing to do with riding a bike. Somewhere along the way, Education PhDs have done studies that demonstrate a high correlation between the ability to spell *derailleur* and to ride a bike competently. They espouse the view that our "standardized bike test" measures something of consequence. No one notices, let alone objects, that our students spend all of their time memorizing low-level content (which they quickly forget), instead of actually learning how to ride the bike. Since we've always done it that way, it must make sense.

A Modern Caste System

We promised this history-based chapter would help explain the educational mess we've gotten ourselves into. So here goes:

We've formed stereotypes over thousands of years about different forms of education. Hands-on, or learning-by-doing, education is associated with the trades (lower class). Education centered on abstract ideas is for the gifted (upper class). If you don't believe this prejudice exists, ask yourself which of these professionals you hold in higher regard:

Category 1	Category 2
Physicist with Princeton PhD	Master electrician
Chemist with Harvard MS	Master chef
English professor with Stanford PhD	Superb eighth-grade English teacher

The market salaries for each pair are comparable, so our economy doesn't favor Category 1 over Category 2. But if you're like most people, you hold Category 1 in much higher esteem.

It's human nature to want the best for your children. So we, as a society, have pushed emphatically for our kids to have an "elite" white-collar education based on abstraction and symbolic manipulation, with the goal of earning esteemed academic credentials. These priorities permeate the choices we make and the values we hold. We've largely removed hands-on activities from the K-12 curriculum. For instance, almost all kids are now pushed into college tracks in high school, while almost no schools still offer shop, even though it's a powerful way to learn and apply math. Vocational education, in the eyes of many middle- and upper-class parents, is one step removed from juvenile delinquency. Instead, students spend years studying things like the proper placement of French accent marks, the capital of North Dakota (or, in more advanced schools, Kenya), the Avogadro constant, factoring polynomials, or conjugating gerunds—none of which they'll remember or need as an adult.

> Both Tony and Ted have visited and delivered talks in Finland—a country that has developed what most people consider the best education system in the world. One of the things they learned is that, in tenth grade, students in Finland choose between an academic track and a career/technical education (CTE) track that has been developed in close collaboration with businesses and leads directly to good jobs after high school. Forty-five percent of kids choose the CTE track. Recently, Tony was discussing the Finnish education system with a group of fifty twelfth-graders in an upper-middle-class public high school in the United States. He asked how many planned to go to college, and every hand in the room went up. But when he asked how many would have chosen a CTE track had it been available in their school, half the hands in the room were raised.

So what's in America's education DNA? We're a hypercompetitive society that loves rankings and numbers. We have inherited an education system designed by business and education leaders, well over a century ago, to train workers for manufacturing jobs. We have been conditioned to think an education that involves memorizing Coulomb's law and conjugating Latin verbs is superior to one that focuses on understanding the home electrical system or learning to love reading through Harry Potter books. And we place more importance on the college sweatshirts people wear than what they've accomplished with their own sweat and tears.

CHAPTER 2

The Purpose of Education

What is the purpose of education?

The question seems innocuous enough. But thoughtful people disagree, at times vehemently, when taking it on. As important as this question is, it is rarely addressed in a meaningful way. Instead, it simmers beneath the surface of our education system, shaping operational decisions and policies at every level. If you review school mission statements, statements by school leaders, or relevant books and articles, you'll observe that this debate centers around a few key priorities, reflected in the question below:

> **The Purpose Question:** The overarching purpose of education is to:
> a. teach students cognitive and social skills.
> b. prepare students to be responsible, contributing citizens.
> c. build character.
> d. help students in a process of self-discovery.
> e. inspire students through the study of humanity's great works.
> f. prepare students for productive careers.

In most circumstances, this question demands added context before it can be answered. For example, most would agree that the purpose of a kindergarten is quite different from that of a graduate school. Most educators consider all of these goals to be important, and do their best to help students in every dimension. But few schools are operationally clear on their priorities, and even fewer have consensus across faculty members. If you want to see sparks fly, just put on the next faculty meeting agenda a question like, "Should the next teacher our school hires be for our English Department or our Computer Science Department?" Or, "Should we offer a course on practical job skills?" Or, "Should we stop making foreign language study a mandatory graduation requirement?" Any experienced school leader will tell you that questions like these can dominate faculty lounge conversation for weeks or even months.

Before proceeding in this chapter, we encourage you to take a couple of minutes to consider the following questions about schools that you know well:

1. If you were able to set priorities for the high school you last attended, its overarching purpose would be to:
    a. teach students cognitive and social skills.
    b. prepare students to be responsible, contributing citizens.
    c. build character.
    d. help students in a process of self-discovery.
    e. inspire students through the study of humanity's great works.
    f. prepare students for productive careers.

2. If you were able to set priorities for a college you care about, its overarching purpose would be to:
    a. teach students cognitive and social skills.
    b. prepare students to be responsible, contributing citizens.
    c. build character.
    d. help students in a process of self-discovery.
    e. inspire students through the study of humanity's great works.
    f. prepare students for productive careers.

The question of purpose comes up at every level of education. Placing more emphasis on one dimension (e.g., developing cognitive skills) almost always means less emphasis on others (e.g., building character). It's hard for anyone, let alone a school leader, to accept that there are inevitable trade-offs implicit in what a school can do. But trade-offs are made daily, whether explicitly or tacitly.

Even with a clear sense of purpose, a school faces challenges in aligning its classroom experiences with its purpose, and in assessing progress. Ask, "Do you think it's important for your school to _____?" (insert any one of the above goals here), and schools jump to say yes. Then ask, "And exactly how do you do that, and how do you know if you're making progress?" Most schools struggle mightily with the follow-up—where the rubber meets the road.

A colleague of ours has been a longtime board member of an Ivy League college. She relates that the administration regularly informs the board that the college excels at teaching critical thinking. For years, she has asked the obvious follow-up question: "How do we know?" She consistently gets the same response: "Well, we just know we do. It's integral to our culture here." We find this pattern at almost every school we visit. A school head will go out of her way to tell us she places high priority on a goal like helping students discover their passions, but when we talk to the students, they tell us, "You're kidding. We're so busy here we never have time to explore." These same schools often have policies in direct conflict with stated goals (e.g., they claim to support a process of self-discovery for students but offer few or no opportunities for independent study, since it's "impossible" to cut back on the required course load).

A July 2014 *New Republic* article by William Deresiewicz, "Don't Send Your Kids to an Ivy League College," summarizes his excellently titled book *Excellent Sheep* and shows the level of violent disagreement that the topic of education's purpose can spark. The author argues that the main purpose of college should be to help students in "building a soul." This article generated over two million online hits and more readers, comments, and controversy than any article in the *New Republic*'s one-hundred-year history. *New York Times* columnist David Brooks was compelled to weigh in on the debate, offering the view that moral education is "largely abandoned ground" as universities focus on career and cognitive issues. Brooks's column received six hundred reader comments, reflecting a level of emotion more often associated with debates on gun control than education.

One fact that often remains unstated in these debates is that many schools seem to be hopelessly lost when it comes to their overarching goal. Consider the kindergarten that canceled its school play to devote more time to preparing its six-year-old students for college and the workplace.

Elwood Public Schools
Harley Avenue Primary School
30 Harley Avenue, Elwood, NY 11731-4900

Phone (   )   -   Fax (   )   -

Peter C. Scordo	Ellen Best-Laimit, Ed. D.
Superintendent of Schools	Interim Principal

April 25, 2014

Dear Kindergarten Parents and Guardians:

We hope this letter serves to help you better understand how the demands of the 21st century are changing schools and, more specifically, to clarify misconceptions about the Kindergarten show. It is most important to keep in mind that this issue is not unique to Elwood. Although the movement toward more rigorous learning standards has been in the national news for more than a decade, the changing face of education is beginning to feel unsettling for some people. What and how we teach is changing to meet the demands of a changing world.

The reason for eliminating the Kindergarten show is simple. We are responsible for preparing children for college and career with valuable lifelong skills and know that we can best do that by having them become strong readers, writers, coworkers, and problem solvers. Please do not fault us for making professional decisions that we know will never be able to please everyone. But know that we are making these decisions with the interests of all children in mind.

Sincerely,

Ellen Best-Laimit

Angela Casano

Keri Colmone

Martha DeMartini

Stefanie Gallagher

As this "truth is stranger than fiction" example painfully illustrates, schools can enact policies that reflect a hopelessly misguided sense of purpose.

Aspiration versus Reality

Albert Einstein, who had his share of struggles with school, said, "The formulation of a problem is often more essential than its solution." As administrators, faculty, boards, and parents debate strategic goals, they generally dive into issues around the importance of the goals listed in Question 1 above and the precise wording of their mission statement. In so doing, they skip over a more fundamental step in the process: Is our teaching approach one that actually helps our students to learn? If Einstein were observing one of these debates, he might note that the trade-offs posed by the purpose question are, for many schools, strictly theoretical, since their pedagogy is obsolete. A question that aligns more with the reality of schools' decisions would be the following:

> **The Mission Statement Question:** Our school's overarching
>   priority is to:
>   - a. cover content.
>   - b. help students discover their passions and purpose.
>   - c. help students develop cognitive and social skills.
>   - d. help students form character and be responsible citizens.

As we visit schools and classrooms, we find a consistent pattern. School leaders articulate a mission statement that reflects a combination of b, c, and d, but never a. However, when we observe the way students are taught and evaluated, their school's unequivocal priority is to cover meticulously specified content. Classes and report cards are organized by subject. Tests revolve around content recall. Kids cram for days (or months, in the case of high-stakes SOLs, SATs, or APs) for tests that call for them to regurgitate content, which they quickly forget.

This emphasis on content coverage is hardly surprising. As we saw in chapter 1, our education system was designed around the model of content coverage. In 1893, Charles Eliot of Harvard and the Committee of Ten partitioned the world into five distinct subject areas: math, science, English, history, and foreign languages. Over the last century, the meager changes we've made in pedagogy have revolved around refining these five departments into subclumps (e.g., biology, chemistry, and physics), and assigning subclumps to grade levels. It's shocking that the typical student day in 2015 is eerily similar to what it was at the beginning of the twentieth century.

Nationally, we have somehow convinced ourselves that if a child in America went the entirety of K-12 without covering important content (e.g., the Crimean War), that child would suffer irreparable harm. Or, just as bad, if a child moved from Nebraska to Illinois and ended up covering the Crimean War twice, our education framework must be fundamentally flawed. And now the "Common Core" wants to standardize curriculum broadly, trying to ensure that the same content is taught in the same sequence across the country, and that all students are "college ready."

If school is mostly about memorizing and recalling content (and that's the case for almost all of the schools we visit), the debate about Question 1 is moot. The problem is poorly formulated. If students learn almost nothing in a process of memorizing and cramming, it's pointless to debate the relative priorities of what they will soon forget. These students will be poorly educated whether they spend their school days memorizing and forgetting Plato's categorization of the three parts of a human's soul, the definition of the Cost of Goods Sold, the date the U.S. Constitution was written, the rivers shaping commerce for the Mesopotamians, the chemistry equation determining how 2,3-dibromobutane is formed, or the definition of the quadratic equation.

To put it another way, suppose you went to a foreign country and visited hundreds of colleges, high schools, middle schools, and elementary schools. Suppose that, in classroom after classroom, the students were memorizing phone books. Some schools wanted career-ready graduates, so their students would memorize the yellow pages. Some schools wanted to make sure their students were educated to be responsible citizens, and had their students memorize the phone book of government employees. Some schools wanted their students to become more complete adults by immersing them in the classics, and had their students memorize phone books from Athens and Rome—in Greek and ancient Latin, no less. In all cases, students spent long and pointless days memorizing low-level content.

And suppose these students were assessed on the basis of how many entries they could recall precisely in timed exams. Those that were good at memorization and facile recall would be labeled as academically "gifted" and on life's fast track. The rest, no matter how remarkable their talents or character, would be labeled "ordinary" or even "remedial," and face a lifetime of societal biases and obstacles.

It's tempting to believe that the textbooks students memorize are far more valuable than phone books. But, if all we demand of a child is to memorize and recall a narrow set of content, it really doesn't matter whether it's from a biology textbook, an AP exam flash card, or a phone book. An ineffective education is still ineffective, irrespective of its purpose.

The Lawrenceville School is consistently rated as one of the very best of U.S. elite private high schools.[1] A decade ago, it ran a fascinating experiment with students taking core science courses. When students returned after summer vacation, they were asked to retake the final exam they had completed three months earlier. Actually, it was a simplified version of the final, as the faculty eliminated any detailed questions that students shouldn't be expected to remember a few months later. The results were stunning. When students took the final in June, the average grade was a B+ (87%); when the simplified test was taken in September, the average grade was an F (58%). Not one student retained mastery of all important concepts covered by the course. Following this experiment, Lawrenceville completely rethought the way courses were taught, eliminating almost half the content to emphasize deeper learning. When it repeated the experiment in subsequent years, the results were far more satisfactory.[2]

This Lawrenceville experiment is something more schools should do. If most students who get A's in June have retained almost nothing by September, what did they really learn? And if the carry-over from year to year is minimal (biology to chemistry to physics, algebra to geometry to calculus, U.S. history to ancient history to civics, etc.), meaning the content covered in one year *never* gets revisited, what exactly has the year of study done for the student? And is that why so many people, when asked what really made a difference to them in school, talk about out-of-classroom experiences or teachers—but never conventional courses?

If this experience is happening over and over in schools (which we believe is the case), then the bulk of U.S. education is a largely hollow process of temporarily retaining the information required to get acceptable grades on tests. If schools were helping kids to learn in a meaningful way, students would pick up almost where they left off a few months earlier (as someone who learns how to ride a bike, or how to write well, or to master scientific inquiry does), not return to square zero (as would be the case if you memorized parts of a phone book).

Our country needs to bring clarity to the fundamental goals of education. These goals need to reflect the changing realities of our surrounding world. They need to give every child in America a fighting chance in life. It's neither moral nor pragmatic to reject a thoughtful set of goals just because they differ from goals set 125 years ago.

A Starting Point for Defining Purpose

Each school is its own community, with a unique context. The goals, aspirations, and talents of its students, teachers, and surrounding community shape its purpose. If we want our education system to be dynamic and innovative, we need to respect each school's distinct nature, and give schools the trust and support to determine how best to formulate and achieve a well-thought-out purpose and set of goals. We need to embrace and encourage—not seek to eliminate—local differences in our approach to educating students. That said, we need clarity for the overarching purpose of education, irrespective of local context, and a foundation for putting our students in a position to succeed in life.

History gives us a starting point for thinking about education's core purpose. If you go back to 1893, when our current school system was defined, educators and industrialists had clear goals for education: prepare youth for manufacturing jobs by providing them with an education that emphasizes routine tasks, with minimal errors and no creative variations. These goals were perfect for most of the twentieth century and served our nation well. The Committee of Ten would have been clear:

The purpose of education is to teach students low-level cognitive skills, train them to perform repetitive tasks quickly and error free, and eliminate all traces of creativity and innovation.

Over the course of the twentieth century, that goal has been somewhat modified with the expectation that public schools, and not just private schools, should prepare more students for white-collar professions and for the "knowledge economy." A college education was assumed to be required for both. But, as we will see, the nature of the education that students receive in many colleges today does nothing whatsoever to prepare them for the innovation economy that has emerged in the last two decades.

Today's world is different. Routine tasks are being automated. Content is ubiquitous. Even many of the tasks required in a knowledge economy—collection, transmission, and processing of information—are increasingly handled by computers. White-collar professions are being profoundly disrupted. Take law, for example. It used to be one of those professions that many parents wished for their children, white collar—a safe bet. No longer. Law firms have drastically cut back on hiring because the routine work of young lawyers can now be automated, outsourced, or done by paralegals.

To have good prospects in life—to be most likely to succeed—young adults now need to be creative and innovative problem-solvers. In the increasingly innovative world our kids will live in, the purpose of education set out in 1893 by the Committee of Ten couldn't be more damaging. Subsequent tweaks, such as the addition of college tracks in high schools and now the Common Core, do not begin to address the need to educate students in profoundly different ways.

We believe that the starting point for taking on the fundamental question of "What is the purpose of education?" is that education needs to help our youth discover their passions and purpose in life, develop the critical skills needed to be successful in pursuing their goals, be inspired on a daily basis to do their very best, and be active and informed citizens. Without this foundation, schools will continue to fall short.

1893 Model	21st-Century Model
Jump through hoops	Discover passions and purpose
Cover content	Develop critical skills
Sort and weed out	Inspire

If the Committee of Ten were reconvened, we hope that their reimagined statement about the purpose of education would read something like the following:

The purpose of education is to engage students with their passions and growing sense of purpose, teach them critical skills needed for career and citizenship, and inspire them to do their very best to make their world better.

These twenty-first-century goals are conspicuous for their failure to make content coverage a priority. We can hear critics objecting, "How can you say children in America are educated if they never learn about Abraham Lincoln, or Shakespeare, or Newton's Laws of Motion?" Or, "It's absurd to have education goals that don't ensure that every student has core competence in literacy and numeracy."

We agree that our students need to master some level of content and fundamentals, but disagree with how to integrate this mastery into a child's educational experience. Clearly, we want every child by a certain grade level to be an adept and passionate reader, to be proficient (without a calculator) at core math operations (e.g., division, fractions, estimation, and financial literacy), and to be able to communicate well. Mastering these foundational building blocks requires repetition and practice. But the real question is how we help our students to master these core skills in a way that reflects real learning and retention.

Case Study: NBA Math Hoops

Khalil Fuller is an unusual young man. He grew up in a tough neighborhood of Los Angeles, earned a scholarship to Brown University, and started an amazing nonprofit as an undergraduate. Khalil is passionate about helping kids in America develop a mastery of core math operations: addition, subtraction, division, multiplication, decimals, percentages, fractions, and probability. His organization has developed a game called NBA Math Hoops, which inspires kids to get really good at math in the context of playing a board game (and now a smartphone app) of virtual basketball. In the 2013–2014 school year, some 35,000 kids in several inner cities used his game, and most advanced several grade levels in math proficiency. Most importantly, Khalil recognized that the key to learning core skills is not a steady diet of in-class drills, but to give kids a reason and motivation for learning.

We fully recognize the importance of having young adults be familiar with important concepts and historical figures and events. Ron Suskind's book *A Hope in the Unseen* describes an inner-city kid starting his college experience at Brown University who is immediately lost in a dinner conversation when classmates talk about Freud and Einstein. To our knowledge, though, no one has come up with a rubric for determining what content knowledge is essential. To provide a concrete example of the inextricable link between teaching pedagogy and lasting impact, a recent survey found that some 70 percent of U.S. adults don't know what our Constitution is.[3] For certain, every one of these adults was required to "learn" about the Constitution in school, and tested on facts about its details and mechanics. Yet content vital to informed citizenship, while "covered," has been long forgotten by most of our electorate.

Tony's two most recent books, *The Global Achievement Gap* and *Creating Innovators*, have reached a wide audience. *The Global Achievement Gap* identifies seven survival skills—the core competencies any young adult needs in order to do well in our dynamic and innovative world. *Creating Innovators* explores the role of play, passion, and purpose in helping parents and educators preserve and further develop the innovative and creative capabilities of the children in their lives. These works lay the foundation for addressing the question that confronts us in this chapter: What is the purpose of education in the twenty-first century?

Discover Passions and Purpose

We live in a world that is globally competitive, that rewards excellence and punishes mediocrity. Young adults pursuing a career for which they have no real passion will almost certainly be unhappy, unsuccessful, or both. The primary goal of education at all levels should be to expose students to a wide array of pursuits and help them find what they love spending time on. It's a rare five-year-old that doesn't demonstrate real joy for things in his or her life. Our preschool kids, across all geographies and demographics, are full of passion, curiosity, and exploration. But it's a rare high school senior who demonstrates any joy for something related to his or her education. And that's the issue. A young adult just going through the motions at school is a young adult who isn't learning or developing skills.

If you doubt this proposition, we have a short film for you to watch. Scarsdale High School is one of the most prestigious public schools in the country, with some 60 percent of its graduates securing admission to our nation's most elite colleges. In recent years, the district has pursued important changes—including the elimination of Advanced Placement courses. But these changes have come a little too late for Rachel Wolfe, who attended Scarsdale Public Schools for twelve years and graduated from

Scarsdale High in 2014. Before going off to Haverford College, she made a movie entitled *Losing Ourselves* about her—and her fellow students'—experiences in school. The title says it all. It is a compelling account of the loss of purpose, passion, and curiosity as students move from elementary school through high school. This half-hour documentary can be viewed at http://rachelbwolfe.wordpress.com/2014/06/26/losing-ourselves/.

Parents and teachers can play an invaluable role in helping a child sustain current passions, discover new passions, and—most importantly—use those passions as a means to help that student develop critical skills. An engaged student who feels there's a purpose to his or her school day is invariably a student who is learning and retaining factual information along the way. The early passions of children—for animals or sports, for building things, for drawing or singing, for asking and absorbing—all too often dissipate without leading to lifetime competencies. That's precisely where our educators can be so pivotal. Can a passion for sports blossom into an expertise in statistics? A love of drawing lead to becoming a gifted architect? A passion for Legos develop into a love of engineering? A love of asking questions inspire a child to become a teacher? Or even an "addiction to video games" (a phrase we often hear from concerned parents) lead to expertise in computer programming?

Develop Critical Skills

Imagine what would happen if a student's report card were organized by critical skills, not subject matter. Students would be assessed on their progress on the "Seven Survival Skills" that Tony described in *The Global Achievement Gap*:

- Critical thinking and problem-solving
- Collaboration across networks and leading by example
- Agility and adaptability
- Initiative and entrepreneurship
- Effective oral, written, and multimedia communication

- Accessing and analyzing information
- Curiosity and imagination

And imagine if schools had a clear set of achievement standards and ensured that each student reached a certain level of mastery for each critical skill. Even better, imagine if the school looked for skills where a student could achieve excellence, and then set out on a path to create definitive life advantages for that student applicable across a broad range of careers. Imagine that each student's progress was regularly evaluated and assessed, with informed and constructive feedback (not by dumbed-down bulk multiple-choice tests). Finally, suppose subjects and content were a means of enabling students to make progress on critical skills—with appropriate steps taken to make sure each student covered, at some point, important areas of content—instead of an end.

While these goals may seem too ambitious to be achievable, we have visited schools across the country, in a wide range of geographies and socioeconomic strata, that are producing spectacular results. What's striking about these schools, some of which will be highlighted in chapter 7, is that their guiding principles are all based on engaging students in challenges that align with their passions, and prioritizing the school experience around developing critical skills. While students may cover less content than at a traditional school, they retain what they cover. They are getting an education that prepares them for careers, citizenship, and life. They are learning how to learn. Just because the students may be having fun at school shouldn't cause us to conclude that they're not learning. It is, in fact, possible for students to experience a real joy of learning in a way that reinforces—not comes at the expense of—developing critical skills.

With these "survival" skills, any young adults can make their way in the world, no matter how challenging their environment or economic circumstances. But we can do more. If we help kids grow their passions into competencies, they can thrive. We need to help students develop *decisive life advantages*—things they are so good at, and so passionate about, that they stand out in adding value to their employer or community. The fact is that any young adult leaving our education system without decisive life skills is likely to be left behind economically, since it's easy to replace a mediocre worker with an outsourced or automated solution.

Case Study: The Future Project

Imagine a student like Zaire O'Neil, who at a young age shows a real gift for speaking in front of groups. Today's school system doesn't include courses on public speaking, and it rarely gives students feedback or encouragement on their public speaking skills. In ordinary circumstances, one of Zaire's potential decisive life skills (the ability to be a compelling public speaker) would be ignored throughout her education. She was lucky enough, though, to attend Malcolm X Shabazz High School in Newark, New Jersey, and got real mentorship from Divine Bradley. Divine is part of The Future Project, a national nonprofit initiative working to revolutionize high schools, and was Zaire's Dream Director at Malcolm X Shabazz. Divine recognized that this young woman had enormous potential as a public speaker (in addition to being captain of the undefeated women's basketball team!) and helped her develop her public speaking skills. Whether Zaire, who is now at Georgia Tech, goes on to play in the WNBA or pursues a different career path later in life, she'll bring her speaking skills with her as a decisive life advantage.

Inspire

Our world is surrounded by "amazing." We are fortunate to live in a world full of natural beauty and remarkable human achievement. It's odd, though, that somehow much of this surrounding inspiration never makes its way to our students. Many students take an art or music appreciation class, which all too often devolves into memorizing facts about the works. Ditto for history classes, where some of civilization's greatest accomplishments are lost in a sea of definitions and dates. Amazing discoveries of science and mathematics, or stunning innovations, never reach students who are taught and tested on cookbook formulas. The natural beauty of our planet gets lost in a maze of memorized chemistry equations or biology definitions.

An overarching goal of education should be to immerse students in the beauty and inspiration of their surrounding world. We keep looking for a school that offers an "Appreciating Greatness in Our World" course. We'd venture to say that this type of course, which could be repeated multiple times throughout a student's education with progressing degrees of intellectual challenge and rigor, would be a powerful force in preparing any student for life.

Conclusion

To make real progress in preparing all students to succeed in the twenty-first century, schools need to tap into the passions of students, help them develop critical skills and decisive life advantages, and inspire them. Engaged students and motivated teachers are capable of making stunning advances—in critical thinking and creative problem-solving, in citizenship preparation, in character development, and in career readiness. Each school community can make meaningful decisions about the relative priorities they set among these transformations. But if a school's foundation is in decay, the school will fail its students—no matter how many times we test the students and how accountable we hold the teachers.

Since *The Global Achievement Gap* was first published in 2008, Tony has spoken in front of audiences many hundreds of times. To date, not a single audience member out of an estimated *fifty thousand* has voiced an objection to the vision he articulates in his talks about how our education system needs to change.[4] And when he asks how many in the audience believe our current school reform efforts are successfully addressing the problems of education in the twenty-first century, no more than one or two hands have been raised. There is universal agreement that our education system is failing our kids, that our current efforts are not addressing this problem, that the very skills they need to do well in life are being ignored, or even trampled, by our school system, and that we're educating our way to catastrophe. Yet the pace of change in adapting our education system to a new reality is glacial.

One obvious reason for the lack of progress in moving our schools forward is the inertia inherent in large, bureaucratic entities. Our education system includes some 130,000 schools, 4 million teachers, 1 million administrators, 83 million students, over 100 million parents, and a vast, installed base of textbooks and tests.[5] So it's hardly surprising that a system so big, with deeply entrenched practices, will be slow to change.

What's holding education back far more than inertia, though, is an acute lack of inspiring direction, amidst a set of loud, misguided voices. Our "leaders"—on both the left and the right side of the aisle—continue to claim that our schools are failing and in need of reform while, in reality, our education system is obsolete and needs reimagining. Our education policy leaders, at all levels of government, are hell-bent on eking out marginal improvements from an obsolete system, and rely on empty metrics to gauge progress. The Department of Education's Innovation Grant initiative channels its funds to the safest "scale-ups" of our existing model. The total amount spent in the United States on education research and development is less than what we spend on staplers. Our politicians offer timid endorsements of the importance of education, but not one has the insight or courage to say, "We need an education strategy that matches the core strengths of our nation. We will educate our kids to help them to be as innovative, creative, and entrepreneurial as humanly possible. We are going to stop chasing South Korea and Shanghai in the standardized test race, and focus on winning the innovation race. That's the only race that will matter in the century ahead."

The perspective of so many of our business leaders reflects an infatuation with data and a strong antipathy to tenure and unions. Billionaire philanthropists channel their money into initiatives seeking to hold teachers accountable to stale metrics and to unleash the power of the free market on reforming schools. They assume that the biggest problem in education today is an education monopoly and a tenure system protecting teachers they label as lazy and incompetent. Yet their initiatives and the majority of charter schools they have funded have not produced any significant improvements in students' learning, as we'll see, and they have only served to polarize our education debate.

Mission statements and websites notwithstanding, most of our schools adhere to education priorities that are counterproductive. The strategic issue dragging down U.S. schools isn't one of the wrong choice or emphasis among Question 1's priorities. What is destroying our education system is that schools are forced to focus on a far less uplifting set of daily objectives. A process that seeks to prepare our youth for a lifetime gets bogged down with monthly measurements. Teachers, in spite of their best instincts, are required to implement a daily agenda they don't believe in. Our schools don't have the latitude to focus on the aspirational aspects of Question 1. Instead, our centralized policies, and our wealthy philanthropists, drive our schools to make choices reflected by this cynical question:

> **The All-Too-True Question:** While we wish this weren't the case, the overarching goal of education at our school is to:
>   a. boost standardized test scores.
>   b. get students through the process to have acceptable graduation rates.
>   c. get students into colleges that please their parents.
>   d. sort and rank-order kids with a meaningless bell curve.
>   e. All of the above

CHAPTER 3

What's at Stake?

M illions of Americans sense that something is terribly wrong with
our education system. Few would disagree with Harvard's 2011
"Pathways to Prosperity" report, which stated, "The American system for
preparing young people to lead productive and prosperous lives is clearly
badly broken."[1] And just as we know that education is broken, we instinctively recognize that the stakes are very high.

But what really is at stake?

There are two prevailing, but off-target, views of what's at stake in our
education crisis. The first is that the United States is falling behind other
countries in educational performance. We're on the path to becoming a
second-rate nation, eclipsed by test-taking superpowers like South Korea,
Singapore, and—most frighteningly—China. The second prevalent view
is that our education crisis resides largely in our low-performing inner-
city and rural schools. If only we had the guts to enact hard-nosed education reforms, we could provide economically disadvantaged kids with the
education they need to pursue the American Dream.

The reality is that obsolete and ill-conceived education priorities
impair the prospects of almost *all* young adults, irrespective of socioeconomic class. Education in the United States is an equal opportunity abuser.
What's at stake in educating our youth is whether we help launch them on
creative, innovative, and successful lives or allow our education system to
continue to play its leading role in deepening the divide between the rich
and the rest.

Myth #1: We're falling behind other countries

Over and over, we read about how poorly the United States performs compared to other nations on international standardized tests, most notably the Organisation for Economic Co-operation and Development's PISA (Programme for International Student Assessment) test. As our students turn in another round of underwhelming results that lag far behind two dozen other nations, alarm bells sound. As though it's breaking news, the media reports that U.S. students are squarely in the middle of the pack internationally, often adding a snarky aside that at least we edged out Lithuania and Croatia. The story line continues that if we continue to wallow in mediocrity, we're headed for national demise. Unable to close the global test performance gap, the United States will be run into the ground by high-scoring Asian nations.

Pure myth.

The United States has *always* performed poorly in international test ratings. We compete against nations that take test prep for kids so seriously that teen suicides are rampant. There is also evidence that many of these countries limit their sample size to better-prepared students.[2] The PISA test, while better than most bulk tests, addresses only a sliver of what it means to be educated or prepared for a successful career; it doesn't assess creativity, collaboration, innovation, grit, resourcefulness, or ethics. Education expert Yong Zhao calls PISA "one of the most destructive forces in education today. It creates illusory models of excellence, romanticizes misery, glorifies educational authoritarianism, and most serious, directs the world's attention to the past instead of pointing to the future."[3]

None of this is to say that we can't learn important education lessons from abroad. Finland's education system, for example, is an inspiring model for preparing kids for a world that values creativity and innovation. Finnish students spend almost no time on test prep or homework and are largely responsible for their own education agenda. They have fifteen minutes of recess for every hour of class, and arts and crafts are a regular part of their school day. Teachers are respected, in part because the nation's graduate schools of education are prestigious. In Finland, vocational education is also a respected path to adulthood. For a great look at Finland's education, watch the documentary *The Finland Phenomenon*, produced by our friend Bob Compton, and narrated by Tony.[4] Or read Pasi Sahlberg's excellent book *Finnish Lessons*. But make no mistake. While the Finnish educational system is laudable, it would be silly to think the future of our children will be severely impaired because Finland will drive the U.S. economy into the ground.

And what about those formidable Asian education systems? Are their leaders thrilled with how it's going? Well, no. Their leaders are deeply concerned about the lack of creativity and innovation in their graduates. Chinese education leaders frequently come to meet with education leaders in the United States, such as Larry Rosenstock, CEO of High Tech High, one of the best K-12 networks of schools in the world. The Chinese, as well as education leaders from all over the world, come to learn from the extraordinary work being done there. Larry told us, "The Chinese are asking themselves, 'Why do we find ourselves only as the manufacturers of other people's innovations? What can we do about our schooling so that we can be manufacturing our own innovations?' They appear to be recognizing that their schooling is an important place to start, so they are limiting direct instruction and mere recitation of facts and are looking for innovative pedagogies that encourage students to design and make things." Yong Zhao elaborates on this point, asserting that "the West is where China is working to find the inspiration for the new education it desperately needs because its exam-oriented education does not work for the new world."[5]

By focusing on our international test score performance, we buy into the wrong framing of the education problem, accepting standardized tests as the metric that matters most. We accede to turning U.S. education into one long test-prep death march; this is the mindset that has led magazines to put failed educators like Michelle Rhee on their covers. We sign up for a race we will never win, and that we shouldn't be running in the first place. Zhao sums this up perfectly, writing, "What . . . admirers ignore (about China's education system) is the fact that such an education system, while being an effective machine to instill what the government wants students to learn, is incapable of supporting individual strengths, cultivating a diversity of talents, and fostering the capacity and confidence to create."[6]

Let Singapore, Shanghai, and South Korea drill the hell out of their kids and deal with off-the-chart dysfunction and the workforce of robotic clones that ensues. In a world that increasingly values the core innovative strengths of our nation, it is pure folly to obsess about the global standardized test race.

	U.S.	China	Japan	India	Korea
Nobel Prizes[7]	353	8	21	11	1
100 Most Innovative Co.'s[8]	38	6	7	4	0
Patents (last 5 yrs.)[9]	619K	21K	240K	7K	66K

Myth #2: If only we could fix our underperforming schools

The second prevailing view about what's at stake in our education crisis is that our real issue lies in problematic bottom-tier schools; many believe that the way to reform these schools is to apply lessons learned from our business economy. A particularly compelling illustration of this point of view is the documentary *Waiting for Superman*. We loved the drama of the film, but its message left us cold. This film's thesis is as follows: Millions of kids (almost all disadvantaged, inner-city, African-American) are stuck in failing schools with lazy, lousy teachers protected by teachers' unions. The ray of hope is a new wave of innovative charter schools that offer superb educations and—it just so happens—shake off the hold of those pesky unions and bureaucratic public school officials. Since admissions spots for charter schools are extremely limited, applicants enter a lottery for admissions that leaves their future up to pure chance. If only every child in America could "win" the school lottery, the thinking goes, all would be well.

Successful businesspeople live and breathe the free-market economy. They respond to unions the way a starving wolf goes after raw meat.

They are certain that if offered options, parents will choose good schools, causing bad schools to close for lack of "customers." Even though these business-oriented reformists generally send their own kids to expensive private schools that the majority of Americans can't afford, they feel that the very least they can do for the disadvantaged is to help our nation unleash the power of the free market to reform the public school system.

Unfortunately, charter schools don't perform better on balance than other public schools. The most recent report from Stanford's Center for Research on Education Outcomes shows that as many charters (31%) underperform public school comparables in math as outperform (29%). The numbers were slightly better for literacy scores, but the bottom line is that the majority of charter schools are no better or worse than their public school counterparts.[10] We aren't big believers in this study's measure of performance—standardized test scores—but experienced observers of charter schools characterize charter schools as a mixed bag at best. Deborah Stipek, dean of Stanford's School of Education, notes that "charter schools provide the space for innovation, but because their success is measured entirely by traditional achievement tests, they feel pressed to focus almost exclusively on the basic skills that the tests assess. As a result, they are no more likely than noncharter public schools to engage students in meaningful learning that whets their intellectual appetites. Most that are considered successful in low income communities rely substantially on young, missionary-like teachers who are willing to work long, exhausting days until they burn out. It is not a solution that can go to scale because we do not have an endless supply of selfless teachers."[11]

Some charter schools have had extraordinary success in getting their students into top colleges. But, as Paul Tough chronicles in *How Children Succeed*, getting a student into college is an incomplete measure of success. For instance, the highly touted KIPP network of charter schools had great college placement success, but realized that only a tiny fraction of its graduates were completing college.[12] To its credit, it's reshaped key aspects of its program, but the lesson KIPP learned, and one the rest of us need to heed, is that just because you drill a kid on the definition and spelling of *tenacious* doesn't make the kid tenacious. Drilling kids on solving simultaneous equations does nothing to help them learn how to solve complex problems in life.

There are millions of kids in our country growing up in incredibly challenging circumstances. We're saddened that our country, the richest in the world, tolerates a childhood poverty rate of 22 percent.[13] Most lower-income schools are unacceptably under-resourced compared to schools in tony neighborhoods. Lots of well-off businesspeople are generous and effective with their philanthropy. We also know that some teachers' union leaders have been significant obstacles to innovations and improvements in education in the past, and that tenure agreements make it very difficult to fire incompetent teachers.

But, and this is a very big *but*, the crisis in education doesn't lie just in our bottom quartile schools, and teachers' unions aren't the main problem. You don't find better teaching in schools that have no unions or in right-to-work states. The crisis is ubiquitous. Every child in America is at risk. Student after student, in school after school, spend their school hours bored, covering irrelevant material, doing mindless tasks, taking far too many ill-conceived standardized tests, and having the creativity and innovation schooled out of them. Our focus shouldn't be to give all kids equal access to the same bad education experience. We need to reinvent education and give all kids a fighting chance in life.

The Reality: America at the Inflection Point

Years from now, historians will point to this period as an inflection point for the United States. They'll write about how the core structure of the global economy changed in the blink of an eye. The creative force of innovation erased millions and millions of routine jobs and eroded the power of large, bureaucratic organizations. As those economic dinosaurs died off, they were replaced by countless opportunities for the innovative, for the creative, for the nimble. And this was a time when our nation struggled to preserve a functioning democracy, when we were challenged by the fracturing of news sources, ever more complex policy issues, and citizens (including elected officials) lacking the basic skills needed to deal with complex challenges. When our government was brought to a standstill by gridlock, and no progress was made to solve essential crises.

Historians will go on to write that the single most important issue that determined the future of the United States wasn't foreign policy, tax policy, healthcare, or terrorism. It was education.

Perhaps our country will step up and make wholesale changes in how we educate our kids. We'll empower our youth to capitalize on their creativity and entrepreneurship, help them develop the skills needed for meaningful careers, and give them the tools to be responsible citizens. We will move ahead in a way that educates to our strengths, creating a vibrant economy where success embraces a broad base of citizens. We'll trust our teachers more, and use measures of accountability that are rational and professional. As millions of young graduates help create a robust and expansive economy, social mobility will become more accessible, and the middle class will stage a rebound. Once again, our nation will inspire the globe.

But, perhaps not. Our country may continue to stumble from education reform to education reform like a drunken sailor. In the process, we'll continue churning out millions of students each year with no real skills and no fighting chance in life. We'll prioritize measuring irrelevant things and drill the innovation and creativity out of our youth. A small number of our most talented will escape the damage of school and go on to create successful new companies and unimaginable wealth. Our wealthiest parents will continue to get their kids into top colleges, arrange the "right" internships, and—despite education's failings—help their advantaged kids pull ahead. The rest will plod through enervating school years, leave with abysmal career prospects, and have citizenship skills no better than mob psychology. As the ranks of chronically unemployed youth swell, the rift between the unrelenting rich and the disenfranchised rest will rip our society apart. We will fail as a country, not because other nations defeated us, but because we defeated ourselves.

The Economic Stakes

To understand what's at stake economically, we need to examine the fundamental changes that are occurring in our labor markets. Throughout most of the twentieth century, the U.S. economy expanded rapidly, "lifting all boats." Almost all job-seeking parents got a job, moved up the ranks, provided for their family, and lived to see their children "do better." The American Dream became broadly available and realized.

The twentieth-century economy was shaped by companies like AT&T, U.S. Steel, and GM—massive organizational pyramids. At the top were a few positions requiring high-order skills. But for every high-skill position, there were thousands of jobs in the middle and bottom of the pyramid, where employees performed structured tasks defined by rigid job specifications. These were both blue-collar and rote white-collar (processing claims, handling customer inquiries, or typing memorandums) jobs, requiring the basic skills our education system excelled at providing.

Entry-level positions were abundant in the twentieth-century economy. Motivated people could get their foot in the door, whether as a bricklayer's helper or mailroom clerk, and then work their way up. Career strategy? Get a job, learn the ropes, perform your tasks responsibly, and advance through the labor grades. The bottom rungs of the economic ladder were easily reached, and the doors to "a better life" were generally open.

In many ways, the typical life for an American was like riding on a conveyor belt. Get on in first grade (kindergarten and home school were rare), and ride it for sixty years through retirement. There were a few branch points along the way. After high school, you could get a job, join the military, or go to college. Select your profession sometime between ages eighteen and twenty-five. Perhaps change companies every decade or two, but never change careers. This economy was marked by stability, order, and defined paths of advancement. Our assembly-line model of education was a perfect match for this economy. Young Americans of all income brackets got an education that prepared them for what they were expected to do in the workplace: understand and retain the facts of the job, and execute defined tasks on a daily basis. In an economy aching for millions of workers, our education system rose to the occasion.

Americans in the last century accomplished remarkable things, with courage and determination. Many were part of The Greatest Generation, and deserve every credit for building our great nation. This was a century when our workforce excelled at "getting the job done," generally within large private- or public-sector organizations. Our nation rose to the top of the international economic, education, military, and citizenship ladders.

Toward the end of the last century, though, international competition grew, and our economy changed profoundly. The Internet went from being a communications protocol used by a handful of labs to a force reshaping every aspect of our world. Today, more than a billion people have instant access to resources beyond the imagination of twentieth-century science fiction. Books have been devoted to chronicling these changes (most notably our friend Thomas Friedman's outstanding *The World Is Flat*).

This convergence of technology means that everyone has access to resources beyond what even the most powerful organizations could draw on just three short decades ago. In a very real sense, each of us is now supported by our own personal supercomputer, thousands of software developers, millions of personal research assistants, experts in every domain, and instant access to virtually any essay, article, book, or video ever made.

As technology transformed productivity, it changed our economy's structure. Jobs that were the backbone of the old economy (assembly-line jobs, office administrators, information processors) have vanished and been replaced by automated or outsourced solutions. Top technologists anticipate an ever-accelerating pace of innovation, as robotics, artificial intelligence, nanotechnology, and personal genetics advance and become mainstream. We live in a time when our most talented engineers and entrepreneurs are developing stunning innovations that bring radical improvements to business productivity. But as a productivity tool is deployed, it decimates any structured job in its path.

Ted remembers vividly the day he realized the scale of impact that innovation would have on the economy. A friend in venture capital told him about a recent investment his firm had made in a company that designs, manufactures, and sells robots and software that would replace the hourly workers who move plants around in landscape nurseries. It was a wake-up call for Ted—no routine job is safe in the twenty-first century.

Technology is turning our economy upside down. The bulky organizational pyramids of the last century are being replaced by millions of tiny inverted pyramids—small, agile organizations consisting almost entirely of innovative, creative employees. These agile organizations draw on employees and outsourced partners spread around the globe. Some of these organizations hire a few low-skilled workers; many hire none. With the proliferation of these companies, career options for creative problem-solvers will become ever more abundant, while options for hoop-jumpers will be dismal.

Ted is on the board of a fast-growing start-up called Xamarin, which makes software for creating mobile applications. Its employees live in twelve different countries, and are all adept at collaborating virtually. There isn't one position in this 300-person company that could be characterized as "routine."

As our economic supertankers break apart, there will be far fewer employment situations with built-in career progression. Few, if any, large organizations will offer hand-holding training programs for entry-level employees. Entry-level jobs will be much harder to come by, a phenomenon familiar to parents of children now returning to live at home after graduating from college. The conveyor belt of the last century is gone. Lifetime employment with a large company is increasingly unlikely; individuals will change jobs, companies, and even professions many times in their lifetime. In today's world, if you can't invent (and reinvent) your own job and distinctive competencies, you risk chronic underemployment.

In the new economy, some new companies will take off, shape our economic and social landscape, and create jobs and enormous wealth. What will be different, though, is that the new-era companies will be far more productive than last century's counterparts, and these successful companies will offer little opportunity for the unskilled. While the Intels, IBMs, and Genentechs of the last century employed hundreds of thousands (the majority of whom were low- and middle-skilled workers), the Googles, Facebooks, and Twitters of the twenty-first century will employ an order of magnitude fewer employees. Almost all of them will be creative problem-solvers.

For a good example of how the innovation economy is upending traditional models, check out Elance, a rapidly growing online service that enables entrepreneurial freelancers to earn income in hundreds of ways, including as editors, graphic designers, creative writers, software developers, and researchers. Need your logo designed? Go to Elance. Need careful research about an article? Go to Elance.

Elance is hardly unique. Millions of people are generating income through the online microeconomies of sites like Care.com, Freelance .com, eBay, oDesk, TaskRabbit, Uber, Airbnb, Lyft, Teachers Pay Teachers, iTunes, Kickstarter, and on and on. These marketplaces represent the wave of the future, where anyone can:

- reach lots of customers readily.
- build an online reputation through customer feedback and examples of work.

- succeed in a world where customers don't care about education credentials or standardized test scores.
- thrive in an economy that values skills (liberal arts as well as STEM) that matter.

It turns out that even our military now needs innovators. While researching his last book, *Creating Innovators,* Tony interviewed the current chairman of the Joint Chiefs of Staff, General Martin Dempsey, who was head of the U.S. army's Training and Doctrine Command from 2008 to 2011. Dempsey spearheaded a complete overhaul of all training programs in the army in order to make every soldier an innovator, believing that with the right training, "[A] second lieutenant in a mountain pass in Afghanistan can often do more to advance the mission in a very strategic way than can a four-star general in Kabul." He went on to tell Tony that traditionally, West Point cadets wanted "to know what the answer is, what you are looking for." Now, the aim is to graduate cadets who can think strategically.

A dozen emerging innovations that will send tremors through our labor force:

- Driverless cars are now three times safer than vehicles operated by careful human drivers.
- Software applications can take raw data and write newspaper stories or business reports indistinguishable from those of journalists or analysts.
- Personal robots are replacing healthcare providers on hospital floors, in nursing homes, and even in private residences.
- Robotics and software are replacing construction workers and architects.
- Self-service tablets and mobile robots will replace waiters.

- Self-service checkout, robotics, and online vendors will replace retail clerks.
- Drones and robots will replace much of our military personnel.
- Self-service software is replacing workers in banking and insurance.
- Watson-based software will replace doctors, both general practitioners and specialists.
- Robots, drones, and driverless trucks will replace workers in waste management and disposal.
- Advances in artificial intelligence and smart outsourcing are replacing lawyers at all levels.
- Intelligent robots are replacing workers in facilities and grounds maintenance.

Added side note: If you are an educator, and you view your teaching role as delivering lectures and administering multiple-choice quizzes, then you, too, are a sitting duck in the very near future. But if you offer informed guidance and support to students to help them develop skills that matter, you remain indispensable.

All economies around the globe will likely see a steady erosion of large, bureaucratic companies, with job creation coming from our "inverted triangle" gazelles—small, nimble companies with lots of creative and innovative workers. The real question for our country is, "How well are we preparing our youth to succeed in this new economic reality?" If we do a great job (which requires the wholesale reinvention of education), fabulous companies and jobs will be created here. If we continue to drill the innovation and creativity out of our students, we face the chilling prospect of having tens of millions of young adults without the skills necessary to participate and succeed in this new world.

Are young students up to this challenge? Absolutely. We have seen many inspiring examples of kids, at impressively young ages, creating and innovating at levels unimaginable two decades ago. Teachers often mention to us in passing, "Gee, it's amazing how quickly any kid can become an expert on something they're interested in." Our follow-up question is always, "Do you think that has profound ramifications for how we educate our youth?" All too often, the rejoinder is, "Hmmm . . . Interesting question. Let me think about that."

As the innovation era collides full force with our education system, there is an urgent need to effect broad change. Depending on the choices we make, our country could experience two very different futures. Within the next two decades, it's entirely possible that the United States will have an ever-widening inequality gap that makes Occupy Wall Street look like an early tremor foreshadowing a massive earthquake. Or, it's entirely possible that millions of kids will leave school able to fully capitalize on the productivity advantages offered by a globally connected world, define their own dreams, and live happy, productive, self-sustaining lives. These millions of innovative successes will create new jobs that benefit society broadly, narrowing income inequality and reducing poverty levels.

The Stakes for Civil Society

For much of our nation's history, we functioned with an effective citizenship model. Our society had a small number of information sources that were shared broadly across the population. Our limited information sources served to focus the attention of citizens and their representatives and ensured, generally for the good, a shared set of assumptions in making policy decisions. There were high barriers to obtaining and sharing information that supported a nonmainstream point of view. We were represented by elected "citizen volunteers" who were committed to moving the country forward through creative problem-solving, collaboration, and compromise. We had a population with the skills needed to perform the basic duties of citizenship.

Profound change in our civil society and economy began in the late 1990s; the Internet's impact was far, wide, and deep. Our historic citizenship model was replaced by a completely new, and vastly more complicated, twenty-first-century model. Today, we get our news from a multitude of sources ranging from cable news stations with audiences of millions down to microbloggers and Facebook updates. News sources today are driven not by civic responsibility to report the news accurately, but by the need to build an audience, to find a receptive niche, and to appeal to emotions rather than reason. It's telling that the popularity of MSNBC and Fox News has soared, while balanced sources struggle to hold an audience. News is delivered in entertaining, attention-grabbing sound bites—140-character tweets instead of thoroughly researched articles. Every citizen selects and controls the news he or she receives, and we all gravitate toward comfortable, predictable sources that reflect our own beliefs.

Until quite recently, our representative democracy functioned on a foundation of bipartisan respect and friendship. Politicians recount how, as recently as the 1990s, Democratic and Republican senators and congressmen would dine together, play sports together, and even room together. These elected representatives were committed to progress, civility, collaboration, and compromise. Our population generally trusted and respected these officials and had confidence that they would act in the best interests of our country.

As the Internet fragmented our sources of news, it polarized our electorate and destroyed any semblance of cohesion on Capitol Hill. Elected officials know full well that the average voter hasn't figured out that his or her vote carries far more weight in a primary than in a general election. The zealous extremists and special interest groups capitalize on this voter ignorance and dominate the primaries, ensuring that only the most extreme candidates survive to run in the general election. Voters, largely unable to connect the dots, wonder why their moderate views aren't represented by either candidate in the general elections, and choose between the "lesser of two evils" or sit out the election entirely.

Our elected officials today are held in shockingly low regard and are no longer trusted to do what's best for our country. These same officials are safe in their elected position as long as they placate special interests and the zealots within their party. The biggest threat to holding your seat is losing in the primary to a more extreme candidate. The 2014 primary defeat of House Majority Leader Eric Cantor underscores this point. With a lifetime approval score of over 95 percent from the American Conservative Union, and with enormous clout for his district, Cantor appeared to have the safest seat in the House, in his conservative district.[14] Yet despite a 26-to-1 advantage in campaign funds,[15] Cantor lost in a primary to an unknown extreme-right candidate who attacked him for a couple of statements hinting at the possibility of modest immigration reform. This unseating never would have happened in the past.

The complexity of today's civil society places extremely high demands on citizens. If our democracy is to hold together with any hope or prospect for pragmatic alignment of interests and actions, we need a citizenry with a strong base of essential skills: critical analysis, communication, collaboration, and creative problem-solving. But, as we will see in the next two chapters, few of our graduates are receiving an education equipping them with the skills needed for effective citizenship.

Case Study: Climate Change

Scientists widely agree that climate change is real. Every credible science-based organization has issued a statement that climate change is almost certainly caused by the activities of humans and poses a threat to the future of the planet. The conclusions of a 2006 report by the American Association for the Advancement of Science are representative of the views of our science community: "The scientific evidence is clear: global climate change caused by human activities is occurring now, and it is a growing threat to society."[16]

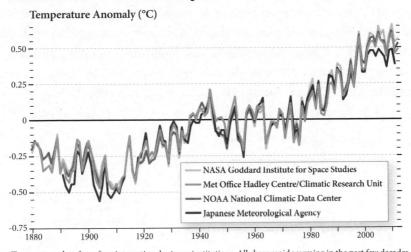

Temperature data from four international science institutions. All show rapid warming in the past few decades and that the last decade has been the warmest on record.

Within the United States, Gallup tracks the opinions of adults on global warming and climate change. In a recent poll, Gallup concludes, "More Americans believe increases in the Earth's temperature over the last century are due to pollution from human activities (57%) than to naturally occurring changes in the environment (40%)."[17] So our population, while more evenly split, is in general agreement with scientists on this issue.

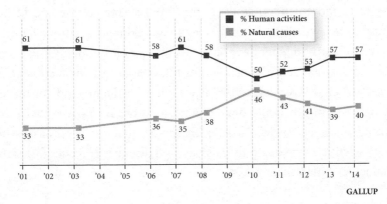

Things get particularly interesting when we look at the relationship between party affiliation and views on science. Sharp differences across party lines about what policies, if any, are appropriate to deal with climate change are understandable. But do political views determine one's interpretation of scientific evidence? Apparently, yes, as Pew's research has determined. By an almost two-to-one margin, Democratic voters are more likely to agree with scientific consensus than Republican voters.[18]

Across Party Lines, More Say There Is Evidence of Warming

% saying there is solid evidence of warming

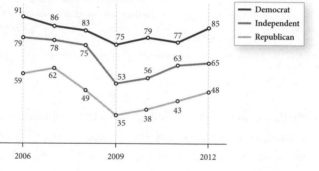

PEW RESEARCH CENTER Oct. 4–7, 2012

Consider the role our education system plays in preparing citizens to analyze climate change issues. For starters, even high school AP biology and chemistry courses don't spend time on climate change.[19] When it comes to more general skills, high school science classes do little or nothing to help students learn how to weigh evidence, critique scientific research, or form independent opinions on complex issues. Only a small percentage of our high school students take statistics. Most people take it in stride when a U.S. senator builds an igloo on the grounds of the U.S. Capitol, asserting that one big snowfall in February proves that global warming is a hoax.[20] And we seem okay with living in a country where climate scientists face death threats[21] as civil discourse recedes faster than glacial ice in Antarctica.

Case Study: Future Financial Obligations

At the federal, state, local, and private-sector levels, our society has large pools of collective funds in complex vehicles such as state and local pension funds, federal entities (Social Security, Medicare, and our national debt), or corporate pension funds. The aggregate amount of capital in such pools across our country approaches some $50 trillion.

A vitriolic controversy rages in our country about the fiscal sustainability of these funds. We have prominent political figures calling them "Ponzi schemes"[22] and other political influencers calling them the financial equivalent of the Rock of Gibraltar.[23] Analyzing the financial footing of any of these large pools of money, including realistic estimates of future in-flows and out-flows, is a numbers-driven exercise. Determining under what circumstances a given pool will remain financially solvent shouldn't be determined by political party affiliation. Yet, as our parties have become more polarized, we see a sharp partisan divide on the issue of financial reality.[24]

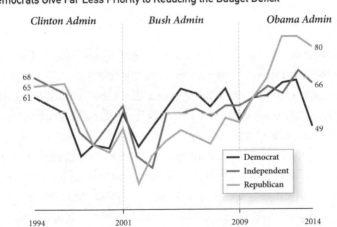

Survey conducted Jan. 15–19, 2014. Percent rating reducing the budget deficit as a top policy priority.

PEW RESEARCH CENTER

71

While we wouldn't use the ethically charged term "Ponzi scheme" to describe the financial underpinnings of these pools, it is quite clear that many of these vehicles are ticking financial time bombs. Despite overwhelming evidence that our future generation is being handed a huge financial mess, our civil society is stuck in the mud in making progress on reform. Each year of delay only makes the ultimate challenge more difficult to overcome.

Young Americans are the ones who will have to deal with the consequences of this mess, but most don't have the general skills, or domain-specific context, to understand financial issues ranging from personal finance to national debt. The overwhelming majority of our high school graduates have been required to take a variety of advanced math classes as a requirement for graduation, but they have no understanding of the statistics they read or hear about every day. Nor are they able to understand the terms of their college loans, let alone explain the difference between simple versus compound interest. Why is this so, you might ask. Well, it turns out that while we insist that high school students take two years of algebra, neither financial literacy nor statistics are required subjects in high school.

Case Study: "Jury Ready"

In a 2006 *Education Week* commentary, "Rigor on Trial," Tony wrote, "Imagine, for a moment, that you were accused of a serious crime you did not commit and were on trial for your life. How confident would you be of getting a fair trial if the members of your jury had merely met the intellectual standards of our college-prep courses as they exist today? Certainly they would know how to memorize information and perform on multiple-choice and short-answer tests. But would your jurors know how to analyze an argument, weigh evidence, recognize bias (their own and others'), distinguish fact from opinion, and be able to balance the sometimes competing principles of justice and mercy? Could they listen with both a critical mind and a compassionate heart and communicate clearly what they understand? Would they know how to work with others to seek the truth?"

We continue to observe that the majority of high school students—even those who are studying the new Common Core curriculum—are not graduating "jury ready." Why? Because the skills described above aren't being tested or assessed in any way. And in our country, what gets tested is all that gets taught.

We are not the first or only authors to worry about our young people's lack of preparation for citizenship. Deborah Meier, a MacArthur Award winner and one of the great education pioneers of the twentieth century, has written extensively about how to prepare high school graduates for citizenship. At the heart of what they need is mastery of what she calls the "Five Habits of Mind"—the habits of asking the right questions. In her powerful 2009 essay "Democracy at Risk," she presents the best definition we've seen of what is often vaguely referred to as "critical thinking," described concisely as:

- *Evidence:* How do we know what we know, and what's the evidence?
- *Viewpoint:* Could there be another point of view?
- *Connections/Cause and Effect:* Do you see any patterns? Has this happened before? What are the possible consequences?
- *Conjecture:* Could it have been otherwise? If even just one thing had happened differently, what might have changed?
- *Relevance:* Does it matter? Who cares?[25]

No matter what kind of education system our nation has, it won't in and of itself mean that there will be widespread agreement on important issues. In any complex society, differences of opinion are inevitable. But consider how differently our country might approach these problems if most citizens were equipped with the ability to critically analyze, collaborate, communicate, and creatively solve problems. The discussion about climate change might go from "Is it or isn't it a hoax?" to "What are creative ways to reduce carbon emissions while stimulating the economy?" The debate about the impact of overcommitted pension/retirement funds might go from "Do they or don't they exist?" to "How do we work together to introduce near-term adjustments to help ensure long-term solvency?" And we might, just might, have an engaged voting citizenship that would seek out candidates who were somewhat objective and realistic about the issues, with the skills and commitment to forge compromise in our democracy to move our country ahead.

PART II

MILLENNIAL INTERVIEWS
(With Tamara Day)

JAIME

Jaime knew from an early age that he was destined to succeed. He grew up in a rough neighborhood in East Los Angeles where poverty and violence were rampant. Despite this rough environment, his mother was a shining example of the value of education and hard work. She had immigrated to the United States from Mexico, where she used to be a teacher. Her degree was not recognized in the United States, however, so, in addition to working a series of jobs and raising Jaime and his brother on her own, she was also studying to get her GED, BA, and eventually her MA degree. She was an overachiever who instilled in her boys the importance of working hard and giving back. "I was always so proud of her," Jaime told us.

As a young boy, Jaime dreamed of going to UCLA and then joining the Peace Corps. He also wanted to be a teacher, like his mother, and believed in the power of education to make a difference in the world. In his neighborhood, college was not the natural assumption, and success was usually defined in more practical terms like making money or owning a business. He said, "Being in a lower-income community meant that a lot of people didn't go to college. Most of us probably did not go to college." But for Jaime, college was central to his vision for the future. "We had a lot of teachers that definitely encouraged us to go to college and my mom was a college graduate, so that was part of the way that we grew up. College was something that you did and something that you had to do. It was part of what made you successful as a person."

Jaime attended a public high school where teachers took a special interest in him. Of the more than 2,400 students at his school, he was part of a select minority who were viewed as college-bound. "You knew who they were because there were not that many. And we all knew each other because we were in all of the AP courses and the honors classes. We were a very small group of kids."

Jaime and his brother were almost constantly at work. "I don't remember ever having a free summer or vacation, because we were always in school, always doing some school-related thing. That was my mom's way of keeping us out of gangs and out of trouble. We never needed tutoring, and because we didn't, we were encouraged to be tutors. It was her strategy for keeping us not just good students, but keeping us out of the very real danger of the community." There were also environmental factors that Jaime believes allowed him to excel academically. "We came in at the right moment. It was the end of the '90s; the gang violence had gone down, or was at least in a dip. There were a lot of antibullying movements, and people were becoming more accepting of things like sexual orientation. It was a changing society." As for pursuing passions or creative interests outside of academics, not only was there little time, but there were other constraints to consider. "We were limited by economics. Being on the wrong side of the tracks kind of things. I would have loved to further pursue a music interest. I would have loved to further pursue other kinds of arts interests, but the reality is that we didn't live with the economics that would have made it easy for us to pursue creative outlets."

Despite external challenges, Jaime finished high school with flying colors. He earned over a 4.0 GPA and posted high SAT scores. When he found out that he had received a full scholarship to UCLA, it seemed like all of his dreams were coming true.

The reality of school proved to be different from what he had expected. Jaime had a difficult first year at UCLA. He found that in addition to academic rigors, college life was filled with high stakes and high expectations. He struggled at first to adjust to the new environment and dealt with emotional issues tied to personal identity. The content in his classes seemed light-years away from the things he was dealing with in real life, and he had difficulty staying focused. "You have to be ready for college. It's a big commitment of time, academics, effort. I learned to become prepared, but I wish I could have taken more time to make the most of it," he said. "At the time, I just wasn't academically inclined."

After the first semester, his grades started to slip. "I depended a lot on UCLA counseling. I was part of the Academic Advancement Program, which was for students who come from low socioeconomic areas in California. And I was extremely grateful for the counseling I received." But the extra support wasn't enough. Jaime's grades continued to fall and by the end of his first year, he lost his scholarship. Jaime made the difficult decision to take a year off from college to reassess his priorities.

During his time off, Jaime got a job teaching in the local community he came from. It was great. He found his passion reignited and loved working with students. But even though he felt professionally fulfilled, he felt that in his mother's eyes, and in his own, if he didn't finish school, he would always be a failure. "I think every mom wants their child to succeed, to be better, to do better than they did. No one has a perfect vision. Sometimes they confuse things they want for themselves and project it onto the child. The gist of her desire was that we had more peace of mind than she had."

After a year off, Jaime reenrolled at UCLA. Since he had lost his scholarship, he was forced to take out a large amount of federal and private student loans in order to finance his education. He received no advice from his college about alternative options or from the bank about the responsibilities of what he was signing on for. "The only time I remember getting some kind of education regarding economics was one time in elementary school, which was sort of an introduction to people doing business: *What is money?* And then in middle school we studied the Depression and FDR and what the stock market was. And there was literally never any other conversation in school about real economics. It was always theoretical. It wasn't practical economics, the everyday economics of your pocketbook." But Jaime wasn't thinking about any of those things. He was determined to finish school and prove that he could succeed, no matter the cost.

Jaime graduated from UCLA with a BA in English. Shortly after graduating, he was accepted to the Peace Corps, another lifelong dream fulfilled. He deferred his federal loans and his mother agreed to pay his private loans while he was away. He left for two years of service in Nicaragua believing everything was taken care of.

After two years abroad, Jaime returned to the United States to find his credit cards canceled and creditors coming after him. He looked into the situation and discovered that his mother had been paying an old invoice on his private loans that was $18 per month less than it should have been. He had never been notified and, in the meantime, the interest rates and his principal balance had skyrocketed.

Under the burden of mounting debt, Jaime moved back home with his mother for the first time since high school. He took a job as a recruiter with the Peace Corps, something he found through a Listserv for recently returned volunteers. He still believes his calling is to be a teacher, but said that with the amount of debt he has, he can't afford to teach. His lenders refuse to lower his monthly payments, so the majority of his paycheck each month goes toward paying those. He told us, "My student debt really puts a large load onto the things that I am able to do that aren't work."

Jaime said he takes full responsibility for his situation, but wishes someone had taken the time to educate him on loans or discuss other options for funding college. He wonders if he would have made the same decision if he had been aware of the implications or alternatives. He also thinks that if he had taken time off before starting college, he might have been better prepared and been able to take advantage of it in a way he just wasn't ready to do at eighteen.

Still, Jaime has hope that his degree will pay off. He said, "I don't regret it one bit. I do believe it is an investment. In energy, in *a lot* of money, but education no matter the cost is important." An education, particularly a public education, is central to his values in life. "I think getting a public education and encouraging public education that is free or almost free is really part of my system of social beliefs. Education should be accessible. The caliber of education should not be dependent on the amount of money you can pay for school."

The last time we talked with Jaime, he shared that he had recently decided to move back to Nicaragua. "I took a calculated risk to get paid a slightly lower salary than what I was making, with a much lower cost of living so I can pay my debt." He is currently in the process of applying for jobs and waiting to hear back.

His advice for current high school students? "I don't think any piece of advice is going to make a person who isn't adequately prepared to take that piece of advice succeed. You can't just give advice to any high school student. You have to know what this person's goal is. What this person's desire is. Does this person even want to go to college? Does this person already know that saving is a smart thing to do? Does this person know that there are federal programs to help you pay for college?" Instead of giving advice to the student, his advice would go to the people who surround the student. "How to make a student more successful takes a team. Including their parents and society at large."

Jaime shared that he no longer believes in a single definition of success. In speaking about his mother, he said, "She climbed her way up to the thing she wanted to do. Not because of the money but because it was her desire. It was always her desire to be a teacher." His brother has an amazing job at a defense company that contracts with the government. He owns a big house and has three cars, beautiful kids, and a dog. "For him, that looks like success. But for me, that's not my version of success. And that tells me that there are a lot of versions of success. And mine is to do something that I love and not to be just on survival mode my whole life. My goal is not to be the richest man in the world. I love being part of the middle class and growing that middle class of people who enjoy the parity of being the peer of someone else. When I think about my students, I treat them with love and respect. To me that is also a kind of success."

CHAPTER 4

The Formative Years: K-12

Each year, our nation spends a trillion dollars, and our kids spend a billion hours, on K-12 education.[1] These children will be adults in a world that's dynamic, globally and ruthlessly competitive, and replete with opportunity and challenge. In an ideal world, schools would be riveted on preparing our kids for life, helping them learn and develop essential skills and character traits. Assessments would reinforce the goal of helping students master what matters most. College admissions processes would have thoughtful criteria aligned with kids' long-term interests. And we'd periodically review historic practices, keep those of enduring merit, drop what's obsolete, and innovate.

But when it comes to education, we don't live in an ideal world. Instead, the forces that determine what gets taught in our K-12 schools are largely:

> What's been done historically
> High-stakes tests
> College admissions

What's important in life is, at best, an afterthought. In our K-12 curriculum, especially in grades seven through twelve, life preparation is a distant fourth. Educrats, business leaders, and often parents set a hollow agenda for our schools, encumbering our teachers. And while powerful voices advocate for the test/data/accountability status quo, our nation lacks strong voices calling for reimagined priorities. The net result: Our kids spend their formative years preparing for tests, not for life.

Let's face it. Our education system is plagued by inertia—lots of it. Multiple constituencies need to buy into change before it can happen. Schools are surrounded by a hardened infrastructure. Public schools adhere to local, state, and national directives. Private schools often carry a legacy of success that inhibits change. And a school's future is tied to an entrenched present, embedded in curriculum, texts, tests, lesson plans, and existing faculty. Much like the QWERTY layout of a typewriter (introduced in 1873 to purposely *slow down* typewriters, to avoid mechanical jams), our education model has a hard time moving past its nineteenth-century roots.

There are more than 100,000 K-12 schools in the United States, no two alike. Nor should they be. Each one has its distinct set of teachers, students, surrounding community, and aspirations. In a country where innovation is built into our gene pool, every school should seek creative ways to engage and educate their students and to prepare them for fulfilling lives. When we visit schools, we find stunning variation on many dimensions, but we find stunning similarity on two fundamental issues:

Lots of Variation	Lots of Similarity
Geographical setting	What we teach our kids
Quality of the physical plant	How we teach and test our kids
Per-student budget	
Parent affluence and involvement	
Teacher expertise and engagement	
Expectations for the students' career and college placement	
Size of school and classes	
Student culture	
Reputation	
Test scores	
Quality of after-school programs	

In this chapter, we focus on the first issue in the right-hand column: what gets taught. And we direct most of our attention to grades seven through twelve. Why just these grades? Over the years, we've seen many outstanding examples of excellent preschools and elementary schools with education practices influenced by the best research. Since the days of Maria Montessori, educators have had a growing understanding of what excellent elementary schools should look like. More recent work that's been done in Reggio Emilia and Waldorf schools has added to the richness and variety of the education models that exist at the elementary level.

The *Wall Street Journal* recently reported on several of our country's most successful innovators: Jeff Bezos (founder of Amazon), Larry Page and Sergey Brin (founders of Google), Julia Child, Jimmy Wales (founder of Wikipedia), and Sean "P. Diddy" Combs. The article suggested the Montessori School experience was the most important aspect of these influencers' education, setting them on a life path of creativity, passion, self-direction, and comfort with failure and ambiguity. The Google founders were featured on a Barbara Walters/ABC special. When asked if having college professors as parents was important to their success, they said it wasn't. Page explained, "We both went to Montessori school and I think it was part of that training of not following rules and orders, and being self-motivated, questioning what's going on in the world, doing things a little bit differently."[2]

The Montessori experience resembles what adults do in innovative organizations. Montessori emphasizes collaboration, communication, self-direction, and risk-taking. There are no grades or tests, but teachers and other students give informed feedback. Kids take the lead in defining their goals, exploring passions, and learning about the world. It's an environment of discovery, of inquiry, of working on something for long blocks of time instead of shifting gears every forty-five minutes. And kids are encouraged to take chances, fail, and iterate to an end goal of importance.

The problem in elementary education today is test prep—plain and simple. Increasingly, what happens in preschool is determined by the need to get kids ready for their first major high-stakes state accountability test in third grade. Educators in pre–K-5 classrooms have a wealth of knowledge and exciting examples of truly excellent schools at these grade levels. The need to prepare kids for new accountability tests is preventing educators from doing what they know is right.

Many of our schools teaching grades seven through twelve don't look very different from the ones kids attended fifty years ago. Until the founding of the Coalition of Essential Schools in 1984, one would have been hard pressed to find any interesting experimentation going on at these middle-school levels. One big change—increasing amounts of time spent preparing for new state accountability tests—harms our middle and high schools, but you could wave a magic wand and make these tests disappear tomorrow, and little would change in most classrooms. When it comes to what is taught in grades seven through twelve, college is the 8,000-pound gorilla.

Most U.S. high schools are focused exclusively and obsessively on two things: college preparation and teaching to the state tests. Driven by an ambitious parent community, affluent schools for decades have defined their value in terms of test scores, AP courses, and matriculations to elite colleges. Schools with high dropout rates and few college placements (synonymous, tragically, with our lower-income communities) are now forced to emulate their more affluent cohorts, as the mantra of "all kids, college ready" has, in effect, become national education policy. The impact of college admissions criteria reaches beyond high school, as middle schools must now work to prepare students for high schools.

This chapter covers the five core subjects established by the 1893 Committee of Ten—subjects that still define the school day in grades seven through twelve. We will also have some things to say about the arts and interdisciplinary courses near the end of the chapter. For math, English, history, science, and foreign languages, we explore:

- the traditional curriculum arc
- a reimagined experience
- the skills students need to succeed for each model

In taking on the five core K-12 subjects, we start with math and English for two reasons: their importance in life and their importance in standardized testing.

Young adults in our country who struggle to read, write, or perform simple math operations are screwed. They're of little interest to employers, and jobs will be increasingly hard for them to land and hold. Even worse, they won't be able to learn on their own. Young adults can do just fine without chemistry or French, but it's "game over" if they can't read, write, or do basic math.

There's a second reason why grades seven through twelve focus on math and verbal performance. Math and verbal test scores are the backbone of high-stakes tests, used to gauge the performance of students, teachers, schools, districts, states, and nations. These scores get reported to newspapers, influencing school budgets, community property values, and the public perception of the quality of schools. They can prevent a child from graduating. Math and verbal test scores measure our kids and communities, and shape their futures.

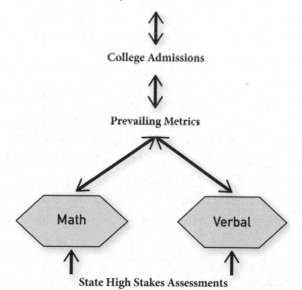

After a detailed exploration of math and English, we discuss more briefly other core subjects. We'll discuss the opportunity costs of our current education agenda. Curriculum is, after all, an exercise in strategy; more time spent on one thing means less time on everything else. Finally, we'll make the case that the biggest price we pay for an obsolete education curriculum is what our kids don't have time to learn.

Math

Math is a body of logic that brings clarity to a complex world. Basic math proficiency permeates professional, civic, and social interaction. Math is a powerful and creative way to gain insight into real-world phenomena. The field of mathematics has changed lives, has formed the basis for transformational companies and industries (electronics, search engines, biogenomics), and is the conceptual foundation for our deepest scientific breakthroughs. And math is crucial in everyday life. A lack of financial literacy can lead to heartbreaking personal distress—even for our most educated.

Let's start by reviewing what a student does to excel at K-12 math. In the early grades, students are drilled on core math operations: addition, subtraction, multiplication, division, percentages, fractions, and decimals, with problems like:

$$4 + 9 = \underline{\hspace{1cm}} \qquad 5 \times 7 = \underline{\hspace{1cm}} \qquad 12 \div 4 = \underline{\hspace{1cm}} \qquad 3 \div 11 = \underline{\hspace{1cm}} \%$$

Students are graded on accuracy and speed of execution. Those who perform these operations quickly with few errors are labeled as "gifted." Those less facile are "normal" or "remedial."

As students progress, math gets symbolic and abstract—moving to variables, expressions, and systems of equations. Students solve equations ranging from

$$2x + 7 = 13$$

to:

Factor: $x^3 + 7x^2 - 9x - 62$

Again, students are tested on their ability to do these operations quickly, error free, and under time pressure.

Advanced high school math students take calculus, performing tasks like computing closed form integrals:

$$\int 7x \sin^5 x^2 \cos x^2 \, dx.$$

For problems like these, students will do categories of problems in class (e.g., integration by parts), reinforced by homework assignments. They succeed on exams if they can recognize which category the problem belongs to, recall the procedural steps required to solve it, and carry out the computation. The integral above certainly looks hard, so it's natural to assume that someone who can solve it by hand has learned something important.

Occasionally, students will take on a problem that goes beyond what an adept math student (or a computer) can do in a few seconds. Word problems, though, show up in the context of Maisie and Jamaal going to the market to buy roses and tulips with $1.20 and not getting change back. Almost always, these problems are contrived, matching a procedure rather than engaging students on relevant, important, or conceptual challenges.

Some of you thrived on this arc of tasks and were viewed as math superstars. Others got the message along the way that you're "not good at math." You probably ended up being at least proficient at core math operations (+, -, ×, ÷, fractions, decimals, percentages)—an invaluable lifetime skill. But for most of you, the years studying math in middle and high school have become a speck in life's rearview mirror (unless called on to help a child with math homework).

For the nineteenth and most of the twentieth century, the skills below were the right priorities for the era. They were needed for numerous professions—surveyors, furniture-makers, architects, merchant marine officers, military personnel, scientists, and engineers—that were vital to our nation's economy and security. And in some situations, lives depended on the ability to perform low-level operations quickly, error free, under immense time pressure.

20th-Century Model:
Math Skills Needed to Succeed

Memorization of low-level procedures

Pattern recognition

Ability to perform calculations by hand

Speed

Accuracy

Ability to perform well under time pressure

Our present-day math curriculum was established during the heyday of the slide rule. Invented by Reverend William Oughtred four hundred years ago, this device enables a slide rule whiz to perform multiplication, division, exponentials, logs, and trig functions on hairy numbers. It takes weeks to learn how to operate a slide rule and years to master it. This curious contraption had a 350-year run as the computational workhorse of science and engineering, and was widely used as recently as the 1970s.

While the slide rule spared people from messy computations, it had limitations. Slide rules couldn't simplify complicated polynomials, solve simultaneous equations, simplify trig expressions, or perform calculus mechanics. If you couldn't do these by hand, your recourse was a reference guide like the spellbinding *Tables of Integrals, Series, and Products*, written by two Russian math freaks. It paid to be able to perform operations by hand, since the alternative was thumbing through 1,200 pages of this!

45. $\int_u^c \sqrt{\dfrac{c-x}{(a-x)(b-x)^3(x-d)}}\,dx = \dfrac{2}{a-b}\sqrt{\dfrac{a-c}{b-d}}\left[F(\gamma,r)-E(\gamma,r)\right]$

$$\left[a>b>\mathrm{c}>u\geq d\right] \qquad \text{BY (254.08)}$$

46. $\int_c^u \sqrt{\dfrac{x-c}{(a-x)(b-x)^3(x-d)}}\,dx = \dfrac{2}{b-a}\sqrt{\dfrac{a-c}{b-d}}E(\delta,q)+\dfrac{2}{a-b}\sqrt{\dfrac{(a-u)(u-c)}{(b-u)(u-d)}}$

$$\left[a>b\geq u>c>d\right] \qquad \text{BY (254.08)}$$

47. $\int_u^a \sqrt{\dfrac{x-c}{(a-x)(x-b)^3(x-d)}}\,dx = \dfrac{2}{a-b}\sqrt{\dfrac{a-c}{b-d}}\left[F(\mu,r)-E(\mu,r)\right]+\dfrac{2}{a-b}\sqrt{\dfrac{(a-u)(u-c)}{(u-b)(u-d)}}$

$$\left[a>u>b>c>d\right] \qquad \text{BY (257.10)}$$

48. $\int_a^u \sqrt{\dfrac{x-c}{(x-a)(x-b)^3(x-d)}}\,dx = \dfrac{2}{a-b}\sqrt{\dfrac{a-c}{b-d}}E(v,q)$

$$\left[u>a>b>c>d\right] \qquad \text{BY (258.01)}$$

49. $\int_u^d \sqrt{\dfrac{a-x}{(b-x)^3(c-x)(d-x)}}\,dx = \dfrac{2}{b-c}\sqrt{\dfrac{a-c}{b-d}}\left[F(\alpha,q)-E(\alpha,q)\right]+\dfrac{2}{b-d}\sqrt{\dfrac{(a-u)(d-u)}{(b-u)(c-u)}}$

$$\left[a>b>c>d>u\right] \qquad \text{BY (251.12)}$$

50. $\int_d^u \sqrt{\dfrac{a-x}{(b-x)^3(c-x)(x-d)}}\,dx = \dfrac{2}{b-c}\sqrt{\dfrac{a-c}{b-d}}E(\beta,r)-\dfrac{2(a-b)}{(b-c)(b-d)}\sqrt{\dfrac{(u-d)(c-u)}{(a-u)(b-u)}}$

$$\left[a>b>c\geq u>d\right] \qquad \text{BY (252.09)}$$

51. $\int_u^c \sqrt{\dfrac{a-x}{(b-x)^3(c-x)(x-d)}}\,dx = \dfrac{2}{b-c}\sqrt{\dfrac{a-c}{b-d}}E(\gamma,r)$

$$\left[a>b>c>u\geq d\right] \qquad \text{BY (253.01)}$$

52. $\int_c^u \sqrt{\dfrac{a-x}{(b-x)^3(x-c)(x-d)}}\,dx = \dfrac{2}{b-c}\sqrt{\dfrac{a-c}{b-d}}\left[F(\delta,q)-E(\delta,q)\right]+\dfrac{2}{b-c}\sqrt{\dfrac{(a-u)(u-c)}{(b-u)(u-d)}}$

$$\left[a>b>u>c>d\right] \qquad \text{BY (254.06)}$$

53. $\int_u^a \sqrt{\dfrac{a-x}{(x-b)^3(x-c)(x-d)}}\,dx = \dfrac{2}{c-b}\sqrt{\dfrac{a-c}{b-d}}E(\mu,r)+\dfrac{2}{b-c}\sqrt{\dfrac{(a-u)(u-c)}{(u-b)(u-d)}}$

$$\left[a>u>b>c>d\right] \qquad \text{BY (257.08)}$$

54. $\int_a^u \sqrt{\dfrac{x-a}{(x-b)^3(x-c)(x-d)}}\,dx = \dfrac{2}{b-c}\sqrt{\dfrac{a-c}{b-d}}\left[F(v,q)-E(v,q)\right]$

$$\left[u>a>b>c>d\right] \qquad \text{BY (258.08)}$$

Ted was a calculus animal in high school, nailing the AP calculus exam. And he used what he learned in calculus for a college honors thesis in physics. He developed a mathematical model of low-energy atomic collisions that required integrating a hairball expression by hand. He eventually derived a closed form expression, relying heavily on the Gradshteyn and Ryzhik manual (see page 91). Ted keeps this book on his desk to remind him to be thankful that messy integrals can be done computationally today.

The slide rule shaped history. It was essential for bombardiers and navigators in World Wars I and II, for the Manhattan Project team, for the astronauts on *Apollo* space missions, for the crew of the *Enola Gay*, and for designers of tanks, planes, ships, and rockets. Alex Green argued in "How Slide Rules Won a War" that the slide rule played a decisive role in defeating Germany and Japan in World War II.[3] In a real sense, the slide rule—in the hands of people trained to perform low-level tasks under enormous pressure—preserved the free world and propelled us to global leadership.

For well over a century, the U.S. math curriculum was in harmony with the world around it. Math educators identified the skills young adults needed. They took advantage of available, albeit primitive, technology. With clear goals, they trained future generations of scientists, engineers, craftsmen, surveyors, and military officers. Nothing less than national security was at stake.

Those who devised the nineteenth-century math curriculum could not have known they were helping to launch the standardized test industry. First administered in 1926, the SAT is chock-full of short, low-level math questions that are easy to generate, have an unambiguous answer, and test whether a student can replicate procedures taught in school. Using these types of questions, Princeton statisticians can deliver an inexpensive test that produces the desired bell curve of results. Test scores correlate with other consequential factors (such as college GPA), lending assurance that these tests measure something important. From their launch in 1926, multibillion-dollar industries grew up around these tests. These tests now shape how we teach our kids, and how we measure their worth.

But, today, these tests require students to master skills that are obsolete.

A recent survey found that some 80 percent of U.S. adults never use any math beyond decimals, fractions, and percentages.[4] Think about that. Four out of five adults never use math beyond what sixth graders do well. Of those using "higher" math, blue-collar workers are the most likely to use it—for welding, machine tooling, construction, drafting, and repair. Regrettably, schools have largely eliminated "making things" (shop, sewing)—arguably the most natural way to learn important math concepts.

And the math needed for college? While advanced math may be needed for *admission to college*, it is not the math required for students to *succeed in college*. A 2013 study by the National Center on Education and the Economy found that "the mathematics that most enables students to be successful in college courses is not high school mathematics, but middle school mathematics, especially arithmetic, ratio, proportion, expressions and simple equations."[5]

With the 1950s advent of the electronic computer, the world of computation changed. Computers could instantly perform low-level tasks better than a person could ever do by hand. Initially confined to windowless rooms in basements, computation soon found its way to our pockets. In 1972, Hewlett-Packard capitalized on the semiconductor to develop the HP-35 pocket calculator, a vast improvement over the slide rule. These calculators sold like hotcakes, despite their price ($395 in 1972, corresponding to $2,250 today), and within just a few years, slide rules were destined for science museums.

But electronics didn't stop there—personal computers became widely available in the 1980s. Today's smartphone has ten thousand times more computational power than a 1970 multimillion-dollar supercomputer. In the near future, we'll all have access to computational power beyond the wildest imagination of twentieth-century science fiction writers . . . and curriculum designers.

Software advanced along with hardware, and math application packages first reached the market in the 1980s. Now, resources like WolframAlpha, MATLAB, Calca, and PhotoMath are ubiquitous and powerful. Download one of these apps to your phone and you'll be blown away by how readily you can perform math operations—often with visual context that helps understanding.

So any kid, whether labeled as gifted or remedial in math, no longer needs to excel at low-level, tedious procedures. Students can focus on challenging problems requiring creativity and imagination. Surely, this must be great news for everyone.

No? Wait! Why not?

Because standardized tests can't measure creative problem-solving. If math students didn't need to master the quadratic equation, all hell would break loose in the education industry. Existing texts, lesson plans, and finely honed standardized tests would be as obsolete as the low-level tasks they teach and test. While resources like WolframAlpha are amazing, students can't use them when taking standardized tests. Consequently, schools don't let kids use them on in-school tests or even homework assignments, for fear of impairing high-stakes test performance. The only devices a student can use on an SAT or ACT test are clunkers like the TI-Nspire Calculator—an albatross in the field of electronics, costing $150 (more than many smartphones) and requiring extensive practice and tutoring to yield any advantage.

By allowing these single-purpose calculators, test organizations give lip service to keeping pace with technology, while claiming that their "calculator policy is designed to ensure fairness for all examinees."[6] But kids from low- and middle-income families can't afford the approved calculator. Test companies present kids with a Hobbesian choice: purchase and master a bizarre device or drill away on low-level procedures by hand. Neither skill is of any use the minute after they've finished their last standardized test.

We interviewed Conrad Wolfram, one of the world's foremost mathematicians and founder of computerbasedmath.org. He described how standardized math tests focus entirely on students' ability to do repetitive computations by hand, quickly and error free, saying, "These tests have nothing to do with creative problem-solving." He added, "They don't assess what people actually do in real life with math—solve hard problems using the power of math leveraging the best of modern computing. No one finds integrals or inverts matrices today outside education. They use a computer, tablet, or phone." At a 2013 forum hosted by UNICEF on the future of high school math education, Wolfram delivered the keynote address, leading off by dictating some AP calculus questions into his smartphone and getting the perfect answer back seconds later. He noted, "I like to ask Siri on my iPhone questions like 'solve x cubed plus two x plus one equals zero' and back an answer comes from WolframAlpha way faster than I could do it; indeed, many students after years of math study could not find that solution at all. It's sheer lunacy to make students compete with computers. Let them go further with the computing power in their pocket. Get them to take on harder and harder real-life problems— messy ones with hair—and use computer-based math to work out the answer." Wolfram's TED Talk "Teaching Kids Real Math with Computers" now has over a million views, but apparently few or none from U.S. curriculum and test designers.

So we ask this not entirely rhetorical question: Should our students still be required to learn to use a slide rule? Grizzled slide-rule experts can provide great reasons for why it should still be part of mainstream math education: Using the device requires understanding math fundamentals. It teaches kids how to think. Mastering it requires grit. And, without a doubt, slide-rule proficiency is highly correlated to college GPA, career prospects, and lifetime earnings.

With logic eerily similar to our slide-rule experts', math educators steadfastly defend the value of drilling endlessly on low-level rote procedures. They argue that kids really, really need to master these mechanics and that it's essential to deeper conceptual understanding. Yet students tell us all the time how de-motivating it is to ask a math teacher, "When will we ever use this?" and get a response that doesn't ring true. Once students realize that the teacher can't give a satisfying answer to this question, they question the point of the class.

And so do we. Drilling on factoring polynomials gets you good at one thing, factoring polynomials. Learning how to compute integrals by hand is of no use whatsoever without learning how or when to apply them. Low-level procedures are a means to an end that the curriculum never manages to reach: gaining insight into meaningful problems. If all math is about is symbolic manipulation and low-level procedures, we might as well let kids play Sudoku.

In the last century, teenagers practicing to get a first driver's license spent many hours drilling on shifting gears manually and parallel parking. These low-level skills used to be essential to driving a car. But as technology brought us automatic transmissions, our DMVs eliminated the requirement to master a stick shift. And, as new cars begin to incorporate automatic parallel parking technology, some DMVs have *already* eliminated parallel parking from the driver's test. If our math educators designed our driving tests, teenagers would still be required to memorize definitions about how to crank-start a Model T. Is it too much to ask that our math curriculum keep up with the pace of innovation coming from our DMVs?

Don't get us wrong about the need to drill on lower-level math operations. Any young adult needs to be facile with core operations (+, -, ×, ÷, %, fractions, and decimals). Adults need to deal with quantitative information confidently. But just as we know adults will deal with basic operations daily, we know they will never have to solve the quadratic equation by hand. There's a world of difference between daily and never.

There's an inherent conflict between what's best for our kids and what's best for the organizations selling tests, textbooks, and test prep materials. The endless stream of tests, and our ravenous appetite for improving scores, crowd out time for creative, collaborative math challenges. Deborah Stipek, dean of Stanford's School of Education, commented, "The people who sell test, textbooks and test prep materials are following, not leading. They create their materials to conform to what states and districts are asking for. The problem is that teachers don't know how to teach any differently."

The status quo for our math curriculum has a powerful ally: college admissions. Colleges put high priority on standardized test scores, and math counts for half. In the next chapter we will discuss the importance of SATs in the *U.S. News and World Report* rankings for colleges. Since colleges seek higher test scores, high schools are pressured to maintain a math track that readies students for these tests. And college admissions officers salivate over AP calculus, saying, "Calculus is a must for anyone planning to major in STEM. But, really, we'd like to see it from all of our applicants."

What admissions officers care about is a way to compare all applicants on the same metric, not for applicants to take things that are important, or to make creative choices. Calculus is not needed for most college courses, as we've seen. In fact, the NCEE 2013 study cited earlier reports that only 5 percent of all Americans ever use calculus on a regular basis—and we'd guess that most of them are actually calculus teachers![7]

After one of our recent talks, a parent related that his daughter had done well at a top private boarding school. She applied to colleges with strong programs in dance, her passion, but was rejected everywhere. She took a gap year, reapplied, and again got no acceptances. The family hired a consultant with a direct pipeline to college admissions officers, and he learned that they had all turned her down for the same reason. She hadn't taken calculus, "the most rigorous course available." Well, eventually, she got into one of her choices and went on to have a great college experience. But you have to ask, how is calculus relevant to a dance major?

The concepts of calculus may be of use, but the mechanics—fortunately—belong to smartphones. Yet students remain buried in a mound of obscure "tricks" of the trade (integration by parts, hyperbolic cosine substitutions, the chain rule), and even the best students struggle to explain what an integral or derivative really means. If we just took kids to an amusement park instead of spending months working on integration techniques, they'd develop a better understanding of the essence of integrals and derivatives.

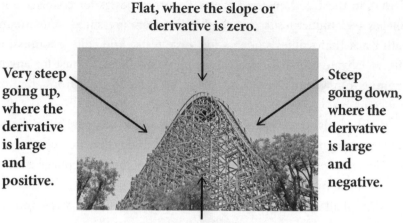

Flat, where the slope or derivative is zero.

Very steep going up, where the derivative is large and positive.

Steep going down, where the derivative is large and negative.

The area under the track is the integral.

If college admissions officers are going to encourage kids to take the same AP math class, why not statistics? Almost every career (whether in business, nonprofits, academics, law, or medicine) benefits from proficiency in statistics. Being an informed, responsible citizen requires a sound knowledge of statistics, as politicians, reporters, and bloggers all rely on "data" to justify positions or encourage followers to support their positions. Being an effective scientist, able to test hypotheses, requires statistics expertise. But the number of high school students taking the AP statistics exam is an order of magnitude lower than the number taking AP calculus. In fact, several high school students have told us they had to fight to take statistics instead of calculus, since their guidance counselor warned them that they were hurting their college prospects.

While it's obvious that statistics warrants higher priority than calculus, the changes needed in the math curriculum are far more extensive. Imagine if we discarded the entirety of the current math curriculum, textbooks, tests, lesson plans, and homework problems. Imagine that all students have access to the same resources they'll have as adults—laptops, Khan Academy, WolframAlpha. What would a reimagined high school math experience look like?

Beginning of Year One: Teach students to use resources accessible through their smartphone to perform math operations. Teach the mechanics of how you represent things like exponents and equations. Make sure all students understand basic math operations and use visual representations to make these operations intuitive.

Rest of Year One: The concepts of algebra, geometry, trig, and calculus, with students spending lots of time working collaboratively to come up with creative ways to apply them to engaging problems.

Year Two: Probability, statistics, decision-making, and ethics/values.

Year Three: Estimation techniques, math modeling, algorithm development, and data analytics.

Year Four: Independent study, interdisciplinary applications, and a capstone project using some aspect of math. Learning how to find and learn the right math concepts needed to solve problems.

Here are examples of challenges students would work on in a reimagined math curriculum:

Students, individually or in small groups, pick an organization they care about, set up a website and a Facebook page on behalf of the group, and create their own way to support the organization. They develop a plan to use social media cost-effectively to drive traffic to the site and translate it into support. They learn the math underlying optimal use of a social media budget. They create and assess a statistic reflecting campaign effectiveness.

Students, working individually or in small groups, use any available resource to come up with one or more ways to predict the world's population in the year 2100. They prepare and deliver a presentation describing their approach and engage in constructive dialogue with classmates about the merits of each approach. They learn what so few math students realize: Real math usually doesn't have one "right answer." Students discuss and debate the implications of various predictions for the world the students will live in as adults.

Each student identifies a few different places where he or she might live as an adult. Students estimate how much it will cost them to live in these locations when they are thirty years old. They estimate what minimum salary they need to earn to meet all expenses. Now, they layer in amounts of debt in increments of $10,000, up to $250,000, and estimate what annual salary they would need to meet living and debt servicing expenses, paying down the debt over a certain period of time.

Students, individually or in small groups, identify a sport or a hobby they enjoy, and create one or more new statistics that would be useful in predicting outcomes in that activity. They create ways to assess the value of their newly created statistic. Then they make a presentation to the rest of the class on the approach and respond to questions.

Challenges like these require thought and creativity, encourage multiple innovative approaches, and help kids understand the power of math. Kids who think they aren't good at math are given the conditions to view their math potential in a whole new light. Creative kids, or kids who lack attention to detail, might find math engaging, and might learn that their strengths are exactly what's required of top mathematicians. High school math class would inspire kids who dream of being scientists and engineers, instead of weeding them out based on extraneous criteria.

In this curriculum, computer programming wouldn't be a stand-alone course, but would be integrated (pun intended) into other courses. If the teacher can't lead the computer programming effort, students would take the lead. Even better, math would be integrated broadly across other disciplines. There's no better setting for calculus than physics. Algebra and chemistry come to life when combined. Introduce dynamic systems to a biology class and you begin to elevate it above memorizing definitions and dissecting frogs. Social studies and statistics go hand in hand.

And what stands between our current math education model and the world we just described? High-stakes tests. If a team comes up with an ingenious way to predict the world's population, we can evaluate it. Gauge its originality. Check for logical or computational flaws. Give feedback on their ability to present and defend their work. We just can't rank their work on a bell curve against that of millions of peers.

21st-Century Model
Math Skills Needed to Succeed

Deeply understanding the problem

Structuring the problem and representing it symbolically

Creative problem-solving

Pattern recognition to understand which math "tools" are relevant

Adept use of available computational resources

Critical evaluation of first-pass results

Estimation, statistics, and decision-making

Taking chances, risking failure, and iterating to refine and perfect

Synthesizing results

Presenting/communicating complex quantitative information

Collaboration

Asking questions about complex quantitative information

Our math priorities affect the futures of millions. Our world is awash in data. Today, organizations are overwhelmed with the opportunities and challenges presented by this flood of information. Young adults with skills in statistics, data analytics, math modeling, estimation techniques, algorithm development, and Internet infrastructure can create ways to contribute to an organization and their community, and will be off and running in life.

Math can be as much fun as driving a sports car on a country road on a gorgeous spring day. But if all we do is have our kids drilling on shifting gears and parallel parking, they'll never experience the joy of driving. We can't say it better than Paul Lockhart did in his moving book *A Mathematician's Lament*:

If I had to design a mechanism for the express purpose of *destroying* a child's natural curiosity and love of pattern-making, I couldn't possibly do as good a job as is currently being done—I simply wouldn't have the imagination to come up with the kind of senseless, soul-crushing ideas that constitute contemporary mathematics education.[8]

English

The 1893 charter of the English class was to prepare students for the industrial economy. Jobs required basic reading and writing skills. Informed citizenry required comprehending news sources, which were limited and superficial. English class exposed many pulled-up-by-their-bootstraps Americans to great literature and an appreciation for the arts. In an era where the purpose of school was the three R's, English class was responsible for two of them . . . and it delivered.

A century ago, books were expensive, so schools and districts standardized judiciously. The teacher was a student's only source of instruction, so students in a class worked on identical assignments. Assignments were handwritten, so clear penmanship was a must. Copy machines and computers didn't exist, so the only person who reviewed student work was the teacher. The handful of graduates who went on to write for a broader audience tended to publish in scholarly journals requiring rigorous research and footnoting.

20th-Century Model
Language Arts Skills Needed to Succeed

Clear penmanship
Proper spelling and grammar
Sound vocabulary

> Ability to read written materials (novels, poems, and plays)
> Ability to write in complete sentences

Over time, the value of some of these skills has diminished in importance—in part due to technology. While some adults decry the fading role of penmanship in school, today's students do little handwriting other than signatures. The days of the Palmer method and grades for penmanship are behind us.

So much for the rearview mirror. What literacy skills does the world require of our students today, how are our schools doing, and how do we know?

The answer to the first two questions is simple: The world demands that our students write, speak, and present with precision, skill, and persuasiveness, as we'll see. To the second question: We're doing a horrible job of teaching these most essential skills.

Tony interviewed a wide range of business and military leaders on the skills that matter most in today's world for his book *The Global Achievement Gap*, first published in 2008. High school and college graduates' lack of communication skills emerged at the very top of their list of concerns.

He talked to Rob Gordon, a retired U.S. army colonel who had done postgraduate work at Princeton and whose last assignment was as director of the American Politics Program at West Point. He asked Rob what advice he had for teachers today. His answer was emphatic:

Teach them to write! Effective communication is key in everything we did in the military—people need to learn to communicate effectively with each other and with external communities. Even enlisted men need to communicate effectively via email. . . . I saw the importance of this in Iraq when I went back in January of 2004. When we asked a brigade commander what he'd learned, he talked about the importance of relying on soldiers who understood not only what they were seeing on screens that showed near real-time combatant movements but also how to interpret and communicate what they saw.

Mike Summers, who was then vice president for Global Talent Management at Dell Computers, also spoke forcefully on this issue: "We are routinely surprised at the difficulty some young people have in communicating: verbal skills, written skills, presentation skills. They have difficulty being clear and concise; it's hard for them to create focus, energy, and passion around the points they want to make. They are unable to communicate their thoughts effectively. You're talking to an exec, and the first thing you'll get asked if you haven't made it perfectly clear in the first sixty seconds of your presentation is, 'What do you want me to take away from this meeting?' They don't know how to answer that question."

When Tony first interviewed Annmarie Neal, the former Cisco executive and author, she told him that poor communication skills were a "huge issue" for her company. In December 2014, Tony asked Annmarie whether or not she'd seen any improvements in these skills among the young executives with whom she worked. She responded:

Their communication skills are, if anything, even worse than when we first spoke seven years ago. The gap in this capability increases (a) as the education system deemphasizes the importance of critical thinking and expressive writing in order to prepare students for standardized tests; and (b) as social technologies encourage the expression of thoughts without any expectation of rigor of these thoughts. I continue to believe that two of the most important skills in the innovation economy are in thinking critically (about problems, situations, markets, ideas) and then the ability to communicate (an idea, a recommendation, a plan forward) in a way that is not only thoughtful and compelling but also in a way that influences others to take action.

Writing

The ability to write and speak persuasively go hand in hand. Rarely can someone learn to present a coherent argument to an audience without having honed the skill through writing. Having spent more than fifteen years teaching writing to a wide range of high school students, as well as to college and graduate students, Tony came to discover the hard way what are, in fact, the key ingredients for learning to write.

First, students need to be writing constantly. Learning to write well, like any other skill, takes many, many hours of practice. Second, students need to write for a real audience and to receive regular, structured feedback from their audiences. Other than looking at the grade on the front of the paper, students are usually totally indifferent to the teacher's opinions of their work. But when they are writing for or presenting to an authentic audience, which has been asked to assess the work being presented—whether it is their peers or someone outside of school—they work much harder to polish their work, and they seek and pay attention to feedback. Writing for a real audience, and writing about things they know and care about, are central to students' development of an authentic *voice* in their work. This is what Summers meant when he talked about the importance of "focus, energy, and passion" in communication.

Such education greats as James Moffett, who began his teaching career at Phillips Exeter Academy in the 1950s, and UC Berkeley's James Gray, who founded the Bay Area Writing Project in 1974, were pioneers in developing the new, more student-centered approaches to teaching writing described above. More recently, Nancie Atwell, who continues to teach writing at a K-8 school she founded, the Center for Teaching and Learning in Edgecomb, Maine, and Lucy Calkins, who currently teaches at Columbia University, have espoused what has come to be known as the "writers' workshop" approach to teaching writing. In fact, there is a vast wealth of research that proves the value of this approach. And extensive resources are available online for educators at the website of the National Writing Project and elsewhere.[9]

Given the importance of writing, the long history of excellent R&D to develop better approaches to teaching writing, and extensive available resources, you would think that, first of all, there would be lots and lots of writing going on in schools today. And you'd think that you would see frequent examples of the approaches we've just described being widely used in classrooms.

Nothing could be further from the truth.

The National Assessment of Educational Progress (NAEP)—more commonly known as The Nation's Report Card—is currently the most difficult battery of tests given to American students, other than PISA. Because it is given only every few years to representative sample populations of students, researchers can afford to spend far more money on the development and assessment of these tests. It's not a great test—as you'll see—it's just the best one we've got at the moment.

As part of the 2011 Writing Assessment, twelfth graders were asked how much writing they did in their English classes in a week. Here are the results.[10]

Percentages for writing, grade 12, by pages written for English/language arts homework: 2011 – 2011, National

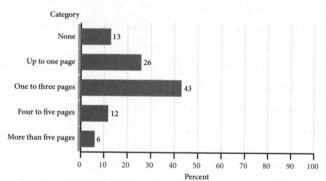

Note: Detail may not sum to totals because of rounding. Some apparent differences between estimates may not be statistically significant.

Source: U.S. Department of Education, Institute of Education Sciences, National Center for Education Statistics, National Assessment of Educational Progress (NAEP), 2011 Writing Assessment.

Given how little time students actually spend writing, it should come as no surprise that the scores on the Nation's Report Card Writing Test for twelfth graders have remained essentially flat since 1998, when the test was first given.[11]

Average scale scores for writing, grade 12 by all students [TOTAL] for year and jurisdiction: 1998, 2002, and 2007 — National

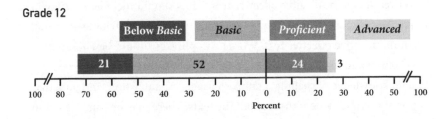

Note: The NAEP Writing scale ranges from 0 to 300. Some apparent differences between estimates may not be statistically significant.

Source: U.S. Department of Education, Institute of Education Sciences, National Center for Education Statistics, National Assessment of Educational Progress (NAEP), 1998, 2002 and 2007 Writing Assessments.

The 2011 Nation's Report Card Writing Test used a very different, computer-based format for assessment than earlier versions, and so the results are not directly comparable to those above. Nevertheless, this summary chart of the results for twelfth graders tells us what we need to know.[12]

Grade 12

And here are NAEP's definitions of the performance categories used above: [13]

Basic

Twelfth-grade students writing at the *Basic* level should be able to respond effectively to the tasks and accomplish their communicative purposes. Their texts should be coherent and well structured. Most of the ideas in their texts should be developed effectively. Relevant details and examples should be used to support and extend the main ideas in the texts. Voice should support the communicative purposes of the texts. Texts should include appropriately varied simple, compound, and complex sentence types. Words and phrases should be suitable for the topics, purposes, and audiences. Substantial knowledge of spelling, grammar, usage, capitalization, and punctuation should be clearly evident. There may be some errors in the texts, but these errors should not generally impede meaning.

Proficient

Twelfth-grade students writing at the *Proficient* level should address the tasks effectively and fully accomplish their communicative purposes. Their texts should be coherent and well structured with respect to these purposes, and they should include well-crafted and effective connections and transitions. Their ideas should be developed in a logical, clear, and effective manner. Relevant details and examples should support and extend the main ideas of the texts and contribute to their overall communicative effectiveness. Voice should be relevant to the tasks and contribute to overall communicative effectiveness. Texts should include a variety of simple, compound, and complex sentence types that contribute to overall communicative effectiveness. Words and phrases should be chosen purposefully and used skillfully to enhance the effectiveness of the texts. A solid knowledge of spelling, grammar, usage, capitalization, and punctuation should be evident throughout the texts. There may be some errors in the texts, but they should not impede meaning.

Advanced

Twelfth-grade students writing at the *Advanced* level should be able to address the tasks strategically, fully accomplish their communicative purposes, and demonstrate a skillful and creative approach to constructing and delivering their messages. Their texts should be coherent and well structured; they should include skillfully constructed and effective connections and transitions; and they should be rhetorically powerful. All of the ideas in their texts should be developed clearly, logically, effectively, and in focused and sophisticated ways. Supporting details and examples should be well crafted; they should skillfully support and extend the main ideas; and they should strengthen both communicative effectiveness and rhetorical power of the texts. A distinct voice that enhances the communicative effectiveness and rhetorical power of the texts should be evident. Texts should include a variety of sentence structures and types that are skillfully crafted and enhance communicative effectiveness and rhetorical power. Words and phrases should be chosen purposefully, with precision, and in ways that enhance communicative effectiveness and rhetorical power. A highly developed knowledge of spelling, grammar, usage, capitalization, and punctuation should be evident throughout the texts and function in ways that enhance communicative effectiveness and rhetorical power. There may be a few errors in the texts, but they should not impede meaning.

Quite decent criteria, we'd say. We especially like the references to demonstrating a "creative approach" and having a "distinctive voice" in the Advanced criteria. They are essential elements for communicating effectively in the innovation era, as we've learned. Too bad only 3 percent of our kids made the cut.

So what explains the miserable results from this test? Let's first look at what the twelfth-grade writing test prompts were in 2011. Students had thirty minutes to write on each of the following two topics.[14]

1. Write an essay for a college admissions committee about one kind of information or communication technology you use. Describe what it is and explain why the technology is important to you. Develop your essay with details so the admissions committee can understand the value of this technology. You may use information from the presentation in your essay.
2. Write a letter to the local council members arguing for or against the building of Big Discount (store) in your area. Support your argument and defend it against the arguments the opposing side might make.

Hardly what we'd call inspiring topics. If you were asked to write on these for a test that you weren't being graded on, how likely would you be to use a creative approach that showed your authentic writer's voice—especially given that you hadn't learned or practiced these skills in your classes and you had no interest in the required essay topics? Of course you don't always get to write about what you care about. But infants don't learn to speak by saying essentially meaningless paragraphs that have no purpose to a blank wall. They learn to speak because they have something to say, something to communicate to someone who cares to hear them speak. Writing is exactly the same! This is the premise behind "the writers' workshop" approach to writing instruction, and it is the reason why it is so successful.

The problem with the way writing is currently taught, then, is the same problem that we have described throughout this book. Teachers spend an inordinate amount of time teaching the *mechanics* of writing—parts of speech, grammar, spelling, punctuation—without giving students any reason whatsoever to *want* to write, because that's the way we have done it since 1893. And in the last ten years teachers have spent less and less time assigning and grading students' writing because they must prepare students for meaningless tests that tell us absolutely nothing about the competencies that matter most. What little writing that gets done in high schools today is almost always practicing short answers to test prompts and memorizing the mechanics of the standard five-paragraph essay, and nothing else. We are told that the new Common Core tests will require more writing, but it will only be more of the same kind of writing.

For the first few years of his high school English teaching career, Tony dutifully spent considerable class time teaching his students the parts of speech from the legendary *Warriner's Handbook*. But he saw no improvement in his students' writing and, to be honest, he had the hardest time remembering all of the parts of speech and had to review them every night before his lesson. After a few frustrating years, it occurred to him that requiring students to memorize all of the parts of speech in order to write well was like requiring drivers to memorize the parts of the internal combustion engine in order to drive safely. He later discovered extensive research that proved the futility of teaching the parts of speech as a way to improve writing. So he began to spend far more class time having students actually write—instead of memorizing the meaning of a gerund—and got much better results! To this day, he has a little trouble remembering that one. However, not remembering the definition of a gerund hasn't seriously impeded his writing career so far. Besides, he can Google it now!

The Problem of Time

Finally, there is the larger issue of time, the scarcest resource in an English class, not including all of the hours wasted on test prep. Suppose you are a conscientious high school English teacher today who completely agrees with everything that we have just written—and we know plenty of you! You have class sizes that are among the largest of any in developed countries. (Five or sometimes six classes of twenty-seven students is the average load of secondary teachers in America, with teachers in schools serving disadvantaged students often having far more.) You also spend more time in the classroom than teachers from almost any other developed country:

1,100 hours versus the 800-hour OECD average and only 600 hours in Finland.[15]

Suppose that, because you are so conscientious, you assign each one of your five classes the equivalent of five pages of writing a week. And you teach in a good suburban public school and so only have to take home 135 papers. Let's assume you're a pro, and you can read and assess one paper every ten minutes. That's 22.5 hours a week spent just grading one batch of papers, without a break, and you have yet to spend even one minute planning any of the twenty-five classes you will teach in the coming week.

So how many weekends would you be willing to spend doing this in a month, or even in a year? And why would you bother spending so much time on teaching writing when your job depends upon improving students' state test scores that have very little or no writing in them? And let's not forget that you've had absolutely no training in how to draw students out to discover what they truly care to write about, and to connect the importance of writing to the lives of your kids.

There's plenty of blame to go around, but the last people we should be blaming are the teachers! In chapter 7, you'll learn about schools where students write in every single class, not just in their English classes. You'll also learn about much more valuable and motivating approaches to assessing writing through juried digital portfolios where students present and defend a body of work, which is then assessed by teams of adults using clear, objective performance standards.

Speaking and Presenting

So now let's talk about oral presentations in high school classes. We will be very brief because, essentially, there aren't any. Most students get through high school without ever having to practice and perform a single speech before a real audience. And one of the commonalities of nearly every class that we've observed is students' stunning inability to clearly articulate a thought. We can barely make out anything students are saying when they answer a teacher's question. Their responses are often half sentences, spoken in half whispers that cannot be heard by half the people in the room. Students are sometimes required to give PowerPoint presentations to their inattentive classmates in a few classes, but the ones we've seen are almost always incoherent.

So what happens when these kids become adults and are asked to present? Unfortunately, far too many adults have become so dependent upon PowerPoint to try to communicate that they are often lost without it. When General Dempsey was head of the U.S. army's Training and Doctrine Command, he found this problem to be so prevalent that he banned the use of slide presentations by his command staff and told them to dramatically reduce or eliminate altogether their use in courses taught throughout the army.[16]

This dependency on a blizzard of PowerPoint bullet points to make a coherent argument can have disastrous results. Consider the story that Annmarie Neal recently told us:

A few years ago, I was leading an executive development session in Bangalore for Cisco's Center for Collaborative Leadership [a program to develop the innovation skills of the most promising young Cisco executives, described in *Creating Innovators*] where project teams were reporting out on the progress of their ideas. They were using PowerPoint to help them communicate their story. The electricity went out, and the team lost the ability to follow their slides. It was shocking to see how many of the leaders could not carry on with their presentation. The one team that did could because they really understood and could clearly communicate the message they were intending to deliver. They had done the necessary critical thinking such that their presentation held without the benefit of props. The team went on to propose a brilliant solution, and the fact the power went out mattered not at all!

What about the debate classes that some remember so fondly? Both of us were strong believers in the value of debate classes. We believed—naively, it turns out—that it is in these classes, if nowhere else, that at least a few students still learn how to make an effective presentation, how to speak clearly and coherently, and how to use evidence effectively to make a point.

We've recently learned that most of the debate classes and competitions today bear absolutely no resemblance to the ones we remember from many years ago. Greg Whiteley, the filmmaker who recently completed the documentary we've worked on, *Most Likely to Succeed*, opened our eyes with his 2007 film, *Resolved*.[17] Today, to compete as a debater, you are trained to speak at 200 percent or more of your normal speaking cadence in order to make more points in the allotted time. You speak so quickly that ordinary mortals cannot understand you. And what you talk about has come from the bins of research that you have dug up on often arcane topics that no one really cares about. Sadly, watching high school debate is like listening to two different podcasts being played at three times the normal speed and then having someone tell you in the end which podcast contained more sentences.

Spelling, Vocabulary, and Reading

Computational resources are now affecting aspects of English classes in significant ways. Students type or dictate essays and benefit from embedded spelling and grammar tools. Granted, autocorrect software has a mind of its own. But when it's almost impossible to write a word like *receive*, the days of memorizing rhymes like "*i* before *e*, except after *c*, or when sounded like *a*, as in *neighbor* and *weigh*" are over.

To appreciate the importance of these advances, consider the plight of dyslexics. Because of learning differences, dyslexics get hammered in school. In the context of English, they struggle to read and spell, and standardized tests are torture for them. Since our measurements of aptitude revolve around these tests, dyslexics sense from early childhood that they fall short in aptitude. But the data on how dyslexics perform in life is stunning, with amazing careers following dismal school experiences.

In many ways, the story of dyslexics—in school and life—is the story of U.S. education. Driven by standardized tests, schools focus on low-level capabilities (e.g., memorizing the proper spelling of words). High-potential kids (e.g., dyslexics, smart creative types, rebels) get "down-graded" and left behind. Advances in automation shine light on the fact that these low-level tasks (e.g., spelling *receive* correctly) are incidental to, not essential to, a person's life prospects. But as long as our education model insists on placing outsized importance on menial skills, any child or family faces an ugly choice: drill endlessly to improve on rote exercises or score lower on high-stakes tests. Heads, you lose; tails, you lose. It's heartbreaking.

Many statisticians have been fascinated by the relationship between a child's vocabulary and his or her prospects later in life. One study found that children in professional families hear approximately eleven million words per year, children in working-class families about half that number, and children in families receiving public assistance hear just three million words annually.[18] It's easy to show that children hearing more words do better later in life; those variables are strongly correlated. But many jump to the erroneous conclusion that the key to helping kids in public housing is to have them hear more words when they're three years old. Fortunately, some education experts clarify this confusion. David Dickinson, education professor at Vanderbilt University, calls attention to the confusion between correlation and causality in preschooler vocabulary. He cautions, "The worst thing that could come out of all this interest in vocabulary is flash cards with pictures making kids memorize a thousand words." The key point is that toddlers with exposure to more vocabulary are generally the beneficiaries of a whole host of life advantages: educated parents, adequate financial resources, strong parental support, plenty of food and a nice home. These broader factors are what drives life outcomes for the more advantaged youth—not insisting that a five-year-old memorize more vocabulary words."[19]

Like low-level math procedures, vocabulary is a test-designer's dream. Obscure words lend themselves readily to a range of quick questions in the language arts sections of high-stakes exams and, if chosen correctly, can produce the desired bell curve distribution. (More on this in chapter 6.) Students need a broad vocabulary to score well. And you can count on a test at any level to include its share of words no one ever uses, just to get the right distribution at the upper end of the statistical tail.

So when we turn to middle/high school, we find that Dickinson's worst fear is realized. Parents obsess over their child's SAT prospects. Kids as early as fourth grade spend an hour a day on vocabulary test preparation for the SAT—a test they'll take seven years later. Kids dedicate an entire summer to SAT test prep, even going to sleep-away SAT test prep camps. Parents force their child to take Latin, for the sole reason of increasing their verbal test scores.

In economics, there's an important concept called diminishing marginal returns. The more you have of something, the less you value the next increment. Having one comfortable pair of shoes is way better than having none. But having fifty-one pairs isn't a whole lot better than fifty. And so it goes with vocabulary. Adults need, and benefit from, a broader vocabulary. But at a certain point, the benefits diminish. Every adult should know what *stubborn* means. Knowing one or two synonyms (e.g., *intransigent*, *recalcitrant*) is even better. But will an adult fail in life because he doesn't know the word *obdurate*?

Suppose you meet someone in the context of a business meeting or a volunteer committee. This person starts the conversation with, "Salutations. Numinously resplendent to garner a new comate. The elements have been assuredly effulgent during this most proximate interregnum. Can I surmise you concur, given the canton in which you abide?"

Is this someone you'd want to spend time with? Or someone you'd dump as soon as possible . . . or sooner? It's quite possible for the marginal returns of an extensive vocabulary to turn negative, even odious (a favorite SAT word!).

Our hypothetical "Salutations" fellow uses words straight from an SAT prep list. Clearly someone who speaks this way is not more likely to succeed in life than someone who doesn't pepper his speech with obscure words. Yet a kid who has memorized more words will score higher on the SAT. And the prospect of better test performance drives our schools and parents to push, and push, our K-12 kids to expand their vocabularies well past the point of diminishing marginal returns.

This regime of high-stakes testing creates challenges for English teachers and beleaguered students across our country. These tests often undermine the goal of having kids develop a love of the written word. And, in this death march of memorizing, many kids conclude—with reason—that vocabulary is just one more event in the college admissions equivalent of the Olympic decathlon.

Another by-product of the standardized curriculum on our English students is the push for all students to read the same books, making it possible to test kids nationally on particular works. Today, when kids have ready access to an enormous range of written material, we should encourage them to become great readers by devouring everything they can that's aligned with their passion—whether it's nature, sports, or Harry Potter. But if you're designing tests, there's no way to standardize based on students reading mostly what interests them. Once again, the education model revolves around what makes life easy for test designers, not what's best for kids.

Even programs designed to foster readership end up focused on the wrong things. A program used extensively in schools assigns points to books, and students are required to amass a certain number of points during the school year. To earn points, students read a book and then take multiple-choice quizzes of factual recall. Some schools display point totals publicly and kids compete to "win" the reading contest. Of course, savvy kids figure out that their best strategy is to read lots of simple books and watch the points soar. And more deliberate readers, or kids with learning challenges, plunge publicly to the bottom of the reading contest. Daniel Pink, author of *Drive*, says that fifty years of behavioral science calls into question the validity of this approach: "These sorts of 'if-then' motivators— as in 'If you do this, then you get that' can be effective for simple, routine, short-term tasks. But for longer-term behavior that requires creativity and conceptual thinking, there's practically no evidence that they're effective." Indeed, he says, there's evidence that layering an "if-then" reward on top of something children already enjoy can actually make them *less* interested in that activity.[20]

The AP English exam has an outsized impact on our English track. Our affluent high schools live and breathe the currency of scoring 5's and 4's; our less affluent schools aspire to have their strong students perform well. So let's look at the kind of written materials kids need to read and analyze in order to do well on an AP English exam. The following sample exam question comes directly from the College Board website. [21]

Questions 1–11. **Read the following passage carefully before you choose your answers.** *This passage is excerpted from an essay written in nineteenth-century England.*

It has been well said that the highest aim in
education is analogous to the highest aim in
mathematics, namely, to obtain not *results* but
Line   *powers*, not particular solutions, but the means by
5   which endless solutions may be wrought. He is the
most effective educator who aims less at perfecting
specific acquirements than at producing that mental
condition which renders acquirements easy, and leads
to their useful application; who does not seek to make
10   his pupils moral by enjoining particular courses of
action, but by bringing into activity the feelings and
sympathies that must issue in noble action. On the
same ground it may be said that the most effective
writer is not he who announces a particular discovery,
15   who convinces men of a particular conclusion, who
demonstrates that this measure is right and that
measure wrong; but he who rouses in others
the activities that must issue in discovery, who awakes
men from their indifference to the right and the
20   wrong, who nerves their energies to seek for the truth
and live up to it at whatever cost. The influence of
such a writer is dynamic. He does not teach men how
to use sword and musket, but he inspires their souls
with courage and sends a strong will into their
25   muscles. He does not, perhaps, enrich your stock of
data, but he clears away the film from your eyes that
you may search for data to some purpose. He does
not, perhaps, convince you, but he strikes you,
undeceives you, animates you. You are not directly
30   fed by his books, but you are braced as by a walk up
to an alpine summit, and yet subdued to calm and
reverence as by the sublime things to be seen from
that summit.

The complete sample goes on for many more paragraphs, all equally murky. While the length of these sentences (one is eighty-one words long) isn't quite as challenging as the last chapter of James Joyce's *Ulysses*, you'd hardly call this writing representative of what we encounter in normal life. You can see the influence of literature PhDs in shaping this exam. For the 0.01 percent of the population that goes on to pursue a doctorate in English, dissecting archaic writing is an important skill. But for the other 99.99 percent of us, being good at comprehending clunky prose under time pressure is of little value. Yet, to prepare their students for an AP exam, schools assign students reading of this nature—eroding student interest in literature.

This focus on preparing for tests over fostering real-life skills is especially troubling given the fact that over the past twenty years information sources, many with distinct biases and questionable credibility, have proliferated. Last century, adults needed to comprehend written information but seldom needed to verify it. Almost anything published had passed through a careful editing and fact-checking process. Today, though, we need to critically analyze any information we read. That means that schools need to help kids learn how to ask probing questions, critique validity, and scrutinize credibility. Simply being able to understand content is no longer adequate.

21st-Century Model
Language Arts Skills Needed to Succeed

Use sound vocabulary

Read a wide variety of written materials (novels, poems, plays, essays, news) critically

Communicate clearly across multiple media forms, with a range of styles

Form and justify independent bold perspectives

Ask thoughtful questions

Engage in constructive debate

The Common Core

The Common Core is an attempt to standardize what is taught in English and math classes across the country and to raise the level of rigor in these classes. As we write this, it is the subject of heated debates and will likely be a significant issue in the primaries and elections to come. Many on the right claim that the Common Core represents an effort by the federal government to "nationalize" the curriculum. Some on the left worry about the increasing number of hours that will be spent on testing. Educators justifiably bemoan the lack of good curriculum materials and lack of teacher preparation. In our view, very few people are asking the right questions.

Should Massachusetts, Minnesota, and Mississippi have common academic standards? Of course! Most developed countries have some form of a national curriculum framework. But the first question to ask is: Are these the right standards?

In an effort to implement the policy mandate of "all students college ready," the Common Core state standards have been designed to align quite specifically with college admissions requirements that have gone unquestioned. Because colleges require all applicants to take advanced math—at least *Algebra II*—this is the math standard that all students in the country will now have to meet. As we've seen, this requires mastering mathematics that adults never use. In English, high school student writing will be limited to essays because it is assumed that's what is most needed for college. The ability to tell stories, which is an essential narrative device for making one's point in the adult world, is not in the curriculum.

Are there too many standards? Absolutely! The opening few pages of the Literacy and Math Standards express broad outcomes. If only the authors had stopped there—as the countries with the best educational systems, like Finland, do. Instead, the authors go on to prescribe what should be taught and at what grade levels for literacy and math for nearly another two hundred pages combined. Covering every single topic that the standards prescribe is simply an impossible task.

Will the Common Core tests be significantly better than the ones currently used? When the program was first being pushed by education leaders, promises were made about the creation of significantly improved standardized tests to accompany the higher academic standards. Supporters argued more critical thinking would be required, and that there would be more writing.

However, the two consortia developing the new tests have had to eliminate many performance tasks—where students apply what they've learned—in favor of the cheaper-to-grade multiple-choice test items. Even so, state education leaders continue to worry that they will not be able to afford the new tests. So long as we insist on testing every student every year, instead of testing only a sample of students every few years, we will be unable to afford the kinds of assessments, like the College and Work Readiness Assessment, that measure the skills that matter most.

Then there is the question of what won't be tested. Even at its best, the new Common Core tests will not assess any of the so-called soft skills that matter most and, in fact, are the hardest to teach and learn. Also, because there are Common Core standards for only language arts and mathematics, the time given to teaching other subjects such as science, history, and the arts will continue to decline. New York City schools saw an 84 percent decline in spending for arts supplies and equipment between 2006 and 2013, and 20 percent of the schools do not have an arts teacher of any kind—even though arts instruction is required by law.[22] As we've seen, in our current high-stakes testing environment, teachers are pressured to spend ever-increasing amounts of class time on the subjects that will be tested.

Finally, there is the question of whether the Common Core curriculum will result in students working on material that is merely more difficult (and more frequently tested) rather than spending time on content that actually interests them. Will students be more actively engaged as learners with the new curriculum? In one popular video about recommended approaches to teaching the Common Core, teachers are encouraged to spend eight days teaching Martin Luther King's famous "Letter from Birmingham Jail."[23] In all of this time spent discussing the text, there is no suggestion that the teacher might want to explore students' experiences with racism or other topical issues. Teachers are supposed to require students to "just stick to the text" in the discussions. Outstanding urban teachers who have seen this video laugh at it. One told us, "This guy wouldn't last a day in our classrooms."

While we agree that far too many high school discussions lack rigor, a consideration of literature that eliminates any questions about students' emotional responses, prior experience, or current events is an exercise in pedantry. One of the most important tasks teachers have today is helping students to understand why learning something should matter. Why should they care? "Because it will be on the test" or "Because you might need it someday for college" simply don't suffice as answers for a growing number of today's students.

Student motivation remains a critical—and largely ignored—issue in education. Our friends at Expeditionary Learning—a network of schools around the country that has now surpassed the KIPP network in total number of students—focus on giving students "work worth doing." Expeditionary Learning teachers strive to design inquiry lessons and projects that build on students' interests, knowing that this approach will result in higher-quality work. They believe that the first few pages of the Common Core standards are very helpful reminders of the most important goals of literacy and math, but they worry that districts and schools may be intimidated by the pressure of the new standards and create a constrained and simplistic formula to address them.

For Expeditionary Learning teachers, the Common Core standards are not the end goal but the beginning point, and they can be woven into complex, relevant, and engaging tasks and curriculum. The standards should not constrain and deaden classrooms; they should be a provocation to create work for students that brings classrooms to life.

The Other "Majors"

The previous discussions on math and English apply here: The focus on minutiae, mechanics, and testing comes at the expense of opportunities to explore key issues, think about the topics, or apply what's being learned to the real world. In the following sections on history, science, and foreign languages, we focus on highlighting aspects that are specific to each discipline.

HISTORY

When we observe history classes, a variant of the noted line from Dickens's *A Tale of Two Cities* comes to mind. We see the best of classes. We see the worst of classes.

An 1893 history class had big advantages over today's equivalent. There was a lot less history to cover, and far less was known about it. By and large, the goal of a history class was simple: teach students what to think, not how to think.

The imperative for today's history class goes far beyond recalling facts. Today we're bombarded with news from a wide range of sources. Some of the information is credible; much isn't. Our kids will be required to analyze chaotic reports and opinions, and synthesize and form their own views. In dealing with immense societal challenges, they'll need to draw on history to inform their opinion and fulfill citizenship responsibilities.

20th-Century Model
History Skills Needed to Succeed

Coverage of important events and figures

Ability to recall important historical facts

Write short essays clearly recounting historical information

21st-Century Model
History Skills Needed to Succeed

Critically analyze historical events and sources

Form independent views on dynamics and implications

Write clear and thought-provoking theses

Ask questions and engage in constructive debate
Relate historical developments to current issues shaping the world
we live in

For the better part of the century after the Committee of Ten's 1893 edict, the primary source of information for a student was the teacher. Costly textbooks were few and far between, and every grade in a school would use the same history text, limiting its utility. The *World Book Encyclopedia* wasn't published until 1917, more than two decades after the Committee of Ten was formed. Libraries were hardly on the map, although 1893 marked the start of a thirty-year, $1.2 billion initiative funded by Andrew Carnegie to build libraries throughout the country.[24] Carnegie, a member of the Committee of Ten, funded the construction of some 1,700 libraries, many in small towns, in what ranks as one of history's most transformational philanthropic initiatives.

History curriculum today remains organized by era and geography. Lower and middle schools cover a year or two of U.S. history, including the fifty states, and a year or two on the school's home state. Before graduating from high school, students take a course on U.S. history, a course on world history, and maybe a course on ancient civilizations. At more advanced levels, students may take various AP history courses. The curriculum design is structured to ensure that students don't miss any important development in history—the mindset is "No Event Left Behind."

In schools we visit, the majority of history classes are as they were at the turn of the last century. The history teacher, from the front of the room, lectures students, who take notes or follow along in the textbook or a handout. The course is peppered with quizzes on factual recall. Exams cover broader sweeps of time and, accordingly, more kilograms of historic facts. And as the decades roll forward, new historical periods/events get added to the curriculum, reducing the amount of time spent on everything else.

To this day, the debate rages on over whether history classes should teach students "what to think" or "how to think." The Republican Party in the state of Texas, in forming its 2012 platform on education, included this enlightened plank: "*We oppose the teaching of Higher Order Thinking Skills (HOTS) (values clarification), critical thinking skills, and other similar programs . . . [that] have the purpose of challenging the student's fixed beliefs and undermining parental authority.*"[25] We think Stephen Colbert's report on this position had it right.[26]

While we've observed many clunker history classes, we've also seen some classes that change students' lives. History at its best inspires kids, helps them develop essential skills, and shapes their worldview. The most compelling classes share similar design principles. They are student-centered. They assume the facts are a given and immerse students in thought-provoking challenges. Students learn to critically analyze historical documents, form independent opinions, and engage in constructive debate. They connect aspects of history to their world today and can draw on other disciplines such as math, science, the arts, and literature to fully understand and communicate what they learn. And, even though the facts of the period aren't the focus of the class, they retain far more information about that period than they would in a conventional lecture-based class.

Let's contrast a couple of history experiences we've observed to illustrate ineffective and inspiring history classes.

Case Study #1.

In one middle-school class, students spend a week memorizing the capitals of the fifty U.S. states. (Note: In elite schools, they might memorize African countries and capitals.) Students cram for test questions like "What is the capital of North Dakota?" Some get it right, others get it wrong, few remember it, and those that do derive no benefit as an adult from this retained trivia (sorry, North Dakota!).

A second class goes back in time and reads newspapers, journals, and diaries from the year 1850, when the seat for the first Legislature of California was, believe it or not, Monterey. Students—at first alone, then in groups—are asked to take a position on where they would locate the capital of California, explain why, present their conclusions to classmates, and debate with peers. Then they analyze whether the choice California made in 1854 (Sacramento, for you laggards who forget capitals) was a good one.

Case Study #2.

In this conventional high school class, the teacher lectures for two class periods on the history of the Vietnam War. Students take notes, cram on material (e.g., the year the first U.S. troops went to Vietnam), and are tested on factual (or near factual) recall. Kids develop some familiarity with the historical timeline around the Vietnam War, its outcome, and its consequences.

In a second high school class, students read a manageable number of primary documents (newspaper articles, essays, op-eds, excerpts from history texts) from 1964. They are presented with the fact that when the Gulf of Tonkin Resolution came to a vote in the U.S. Senate, only two senators opposed it. They work in teams on the following question: "Why do you think the Gulf of Tonkin Resolution gained overwhelming support?" Each team presents its views to classmates and responds to questions. Students can use any available resource to support their work (we observe kids doing these types of challenges who resourcefully find people or classes all over the world and interview subjects via Skype as part of their research). They then explore whether the Gulf of Tonkin vote should have imparted lessons to our legislators in 2002 when the overwhelming majority of U.S. senators voted to authorize the invasion of Iraq.

In these case studies, the first class spends a week largely memorizing facts—any of which can be readily looked up. The second class spends a comparable amount of time on engaging issues that help them develop critical skills. The first class is characterized by boredom, irrelevance, and a lack of retention. With the second model (and Stanford's Reading Like a Historian program has 150 challenges like these),[27] classrooms are bursting with energy, and the student learning is consequential. Teachers and peers give excellent feedback. Students assess their own work in a way that's reflective. Achievements can be captured on digital portfolios.

But you can't assign a student a precise score, or rank students on a national basis, on a nuanced argument about support for the Gulf of Tonkin Resolution. And that's why our history classes are, in Joe Friday's words, "Just the facts, ma'am."

SCIENCE

In 1893, the concept of genetics had yet to emerge. The basic structure of an atom remained a mystery. A model of chemical bonding had yet to be formulated. Interdisciplinary research was almost nonexistent. Fields like ecology, geology, economics, neuroscience, materials science, engineering, and psychology were nascent. In short, science was still a toddler at the time of the Committee of Ten.

When the Committee of Ten made science a priority, they partitioned it into three subjects: physics, chemistry, and biology. The goal of these courses was straightforward: to cover the important definitions, formulas, and concepts, and the basics of lab work. Given that each field was early in its development, classes could spend a fair amount of time on a small number of concepts. And since so little was done at the boundary of disciplines or in emerging fields, organizing science into these three silos reflected the reality of the academic and professional worlds.

High school science classes today have much in common with their century-old ancestors. Most students take physics, chemistry, and biology courses. They learn definitions, formulas, and concepts and do lab experiments. On a superficial basis, any observer of a high school science class would conclude that the students are learning important material. They spend time on difficult content and weighty scientific nomenclature. They study what's tested by the College Board's AP exams and what's valued in the college admissions process.

But looks can be deceiving. Students learn very little, if anything, about important recent discoveries, or even neglect entire sciences, such as ecology, which have more importance for our future survival as a species than any of the required sciences. Secondly, students aren't learning what should be at the heart of science classes: how to think like a scientist and apply the scientific method.

William Wallace has a PhD in Biochemistry and ran his own lab in neuroscience research for twelve years. When he came to teach at Georgetown Day School in Washington, DC, he had taught AP biology for fourteen years, but he was very disappointed by how little real science students were learning. So he was encouraged by the school to create his own course, which requires students to develop a hypothesis, conduct an experiment, and analyze the results. He lectures for the first couple of weeks of the course, giving students sources and skills they need, and then he gets out of their way. You walk into his class, and you might think you were in a real science lab. You see students—some in teams, some working alone—hard at work on their experiments.

We talked to Bill after class one day, and he explained his approach: "Science really must be taught experientially. No scientist I know takes multiple-choice exams or conducts experiments with expected outcomes. The most important skills we need to teach our science students should be to make them better scientific thinkers. Experiential learning has the added advantage of making science an engaging activity. As a science educator, I want to emphasize that science is much more than a body of knowledge; it is a way of discovery. My students find that exciting and empowering."

20th-Century Model

Science Skills Needed to Succeed

Cover core disciplines—physics, chemistry, biology
Cover key definitions, formulas, and concepts
Gain familiarity with basic lab procedures

21st-Century Model

Science Skills Needed to Succeed

Understand how the world works

Be able to form and test scientific hypotheses

Be able to ask insightful questions and design experiments

Build things based on scientific principles

Apply principles across disciplines

Develop scientific creativity

There is an enormous gap between what we assume is learned in high school science and what is actually learned. To make that gap tangible, we'll start at the pinnacle: Harvard physics students. While far from representative, students who excelled at high school physics, the AP exam, and freshman physics at Harvard must have learned an enormous amount in these courses. We can only hope that our high school students studying physics might come close to learning as much as these Harvard kids have learned. Right?

Eric Mazur is the area dean of Applied Physics at Harvard and one of the world's most respected scientists. He's also keenly interested in education, having taught at Harvard for over thirty years. For his first decade there, he taught physics the way he had been taught. He lectured his students, covering definitions, formulas, and concepts. His students did some experiments to ensure lecture material was connected to the real world. These students did well on tests and gave him glowing evaluations. Science education can't get much better than this, or so it would seem.

Twenty-four years ago, a funny thing happened to Eric's outlook on teaching. He read about a study involving science students in Arizona who were tested on the simple concepts about the way the world works.[28] Students were asked, at the beginning and then again at the end of their college-level science courses, questions like the following:

---

1. Two ice cubes are floating in water. After the ice melts, will the water level be
   a. higher?
   b. lower?
   c. the same?

---

or,

---

2. Two metal balls are the same size but one weighs twice as much as the other. The balls are dropped from the roof of a single-story building at the same instant. The time it takes the balls to reach the ground below will be
   a. about half as long for the heavier ball as for the lighter one.
   b. about half as long for the lighter ball as for the heavier one.
   c. about the same for both balls.
   d. considerably less for the heavier ball, but not necessarily half as long.
   e. considerably less for the lighter ball, but not necessarily half as long.

The Arizona researchers, Halloun and Hestenes, were shocked at what they learned from these seemingly easy conceptual questions. Students at the beginning of their physics course scored not much better than random. Most tellingly, even the best students showed little improvement in conceptual understanding at the end of the course. The researchers concluded that students were great at memorizing formulas and doing arithmetic, but hadn't learned anything about how the world works.

Mazur isn't a complacent man. After hearing about these results, he decided to see how his students would do on these conceptual questions, which he calls ConcepTests. He reported that "the results of the test came as a shock: The students fared hardly better on the Halloun and Hestenes test than on their midterm examination. Yet, the Halloun and Hestenes test is simple, whereas the material covered by the examination (rotational dynamics, moments of inertia) is of far greater difficulty or so I thought."[29]

At the end of the course, his students retook this simple test. His students—even his superstars—made relatively little improvement after completing their full-year course on physics at Harvard. Mazur commented, "Clearly, many students in my class were concentrating on learning 'recipes,' or 'problem-solving strategies' as they are called in my textbooks, without considering the underlying concepts. Plug and chug!" He noted that the experience helped him understand why students often made "inexplicable blunders" on basic physics concepts, and why students often expressed frustration and boredom with physics.[30]

Mazur's experience connects the dots of our previous chapters. We live in a world that values procedural and symbolic (equated to aristocratic) content over hands-on (equated to working-class) learning. Colleges live and breathe the symbolic, which in turn dictates the high school agenda. We hold out the myth that real learning is taking place, comforted by the makeup of our high-stakes tests. And test designers love the procedural, since it's easy to evaluate. Yet when students take tests of real skills—the College and Work Readiness Assessment used in the research of Arum and Roksa, or the science test pioneered by Hestenes and Mazur—we find students are learning little or nothing.

Consider how students study electricity in a high school or college physics class. They memorize Coulomb's law:

$$F = \frac{kq_1q_2}{r^2}$$

They dutifully practice taking three parameters as input and computing the fourth, precisely and with the correct units. If a student can do several without error, he or she surely understands electrical forces. If a student struggles, he or she just isn't a "science kid." Most kids—irrespective of science aptitude—find the work boring. But those that are facile at manipulating the formulas (generally the same kids who thrive on high school math) excel at physics.

When they finish covering electricity, students haven't learned any-thing about the home electrical system. The purpose of a fuse box and what causes it to fail. How a city or national electrical grid works. What causes a blackout. The impact of radiation on electrical systems. How solar, fossil fuel, and nuclear power are generated.

And why isn't science more hands-on, with students building things and taking things apart, or studying everyday phenomena? Well, put yourselves in the shoes of someone designing an AP physics exam. To test a student's "understanding" of electricity, Coulomb's law is a gift from heaven. It's easy to frame questions around it. There's one unambiguously correct answer. It takes thirty to sixty seconds to answer a question, so we can fill the exam with these questions and refine the mix to get the right distribution. So you design questions like the one below from the College Board's guide to AP physics:

17. Two massive, positively charged particles are initially held a fixed distance apart. When they are moved farther apart, the magnitude of their mutual gravitational force changes by a factor of n. Which of the following indicates the factor by which the magnitude of their mutual electrostatic force changes?
    a. $1/n^2$
    b. $1/n$
    c. n
    d. n^2

While ideal for a standardized test, all this question tests is a student's ability to memorize and recall formulas and perform symbolic manipulation. Being able to answer this question has nothing—*nothing*—to do with understand-ing gravitational or electrical force, as Mazur and others have demonstrated.

We've chosen examples from physics, but could easily do the same for chemistry and biology. The tragedy is that the focus on procedural formal-ism isn't serving the best long-term interests of even those students who go on to become PhD scientists. They aren't developing the instincts and insights they need to bring conceptual insights to advanced science fields.

Suppose that our goal in science classes was to excite kids about their world. Suppose the high school curriculum started with ecology—a topic almost all kids find interesting, and one of immense importance to their futures on our fragile planet. Then suppose we went to the science of stuff, where we covered everything from subatomic particles to cells, to molecules, to materials, to geology, to planets, to galaxies. Then suppose we covered building things—structures, computer programs, electronic circuits, materials. And then suppose students did a yearlong independent research project, where they used science to make their world better in a way of their choosing.

Just suppose. Do you think more of our students would leave high school interested in careers in science? Do you think they'd be far more engaged? Do you think they'd learn and retain more? Of course they would.

FOREIGN LANGUAGES

Proficiency in a foreign language is a lifetime gift that expands horizons and provides life and career advantages. Whether for cultural exploration, touring, professional growth, or advanced research, language proficiency means you can engage with a foreign culture in a way otherwise not possible.

When foreign language was first incorporated into our high school curriculum, few Americans traveled abroad. Electronic communication didn't exist. Priority on conversation was low compared to translating written material—academic research, historic works, letters, literature. The focus, appropriately, was reading and writing. And the languages emphasized were Latin, Greek, German, and French—the languages of Western culture and science.

As the decades rolled by, our education model phased out certain languages and added new ones. Few schools still offer German, as Germany's leadership in science has faded from the days of Einstein, Bohr, and Heisenberg. Greek is pretty much ancient history. Schools have added Spanish and occasionally Mandarin to their offerings. But the emphasis on reading and writing—not speaking—remains.

Today, adults need to work across national boundaries, understanding other cultures and how to collaborate on important problems and achieve results. Our global innovation economy spans cultures and languages. Imagine a customer service leadership team of a global company having a regular meeting—one based in the United States, one in Singapore, one in India—all on Skype or GoToMeeting. It is scheduled for 9 p.m. to best span the time zones. How do these teams work together, given their differences in cultures? Who speaks first? When is it okay to disagree? How do you disagree? Managers and team members must pay attention to these cultural differences to ensure they achieve the desired goals. In addition to having some spoken language proficiency, students will need to master what is now called "global competence." The Asia Society has done extensive research and developed many outstanding resources for K-12 teachers on this subject.[31]

20th-Century Model
Foreign Language Skills Needed to Succeed

Sound vocabulary and knowledge of verbs and tenses
Ability to read and comprehend written materials
Ability to write basic compositions in the language
Focus on languages for science or ancient cultures

21st-Century Model
Foreign Language Skills Needed to Succeed

True proficiency in speaking
Understanding cultures and the ability to navigate them
Ability to collaborate across cultures
Technology-leveraged polylinguality

If you studied a foreign language in school, you probably went through this sequence: Start with basic vocabulary words, and add several new words each week. Start with core verbs in the present tense. Over time, add more verbs and tenses. Repeat elementary sentences spoken by the teacher. Read works in the language, and write short essays. Put on an occasional skit, reciting memorized sentences. Occasionally field questions from the teacher, usually with a short response or a simple inversion of the question. At advanced levels, take AP courses or courses about the history of ancient civilizations that speak the target language.

Over time, foreign language study has been baked into our high school curriculum, and two to three years of completed coursework is now a mandatory requirement to graduate from most schools. When we observe students near the finish line in meeting their graduation requirement, most aren't conversationally fluent. We recently polled adults, asking, "How many of you use the foreign language you were required to study to graduate from high school?" Less than 15 percent. It reminds us of Father Guido Sarducci's Five Minute University, which promises to teach people in five minutes exactly what graduates remember five years after earning a college degree.[32] For his foreign language offering, students learn to say, "*Como está usted*?" and respond, "*Muy bien*," because "that's all you'll remember five years after studying Spanish in college."

Helene Rassias-Miles is the executive director of Dartmouth College's Rassias Center for World Languages and Cultures (RC), http://rassias. dartmouth.edu/ . The RC is a language instruction and teacher development resource for the Peace Corps, other strategic branches of the U.S. government, as well as a wide range of organizations around the globe. Rassias-Miles's father, John A. Rassias, founding president of the RC (and creator of the Rassias Method®), states that the key to second (third, etc.) language study is to "speak to learn, not learn to speak." Rassias-Miles goes on to note, "The key to our philosophy is to speak, and speak, and speak some more. Programs and curricula that emphasize speaking and 'living' the culture from the get go can create a genuine learning atmosphere (using a variety of techniques) that will acclimate students and generate a feeling of 'being there.' Our goal is for every classroom to have comfortable and engaged students who are willing to take linguistic risks; progress comes when one is not restricted by the fear of making mistakes. And, of course, the younger one is when one begins the language acquisition journey, the better."

College admissions generally value an applicant who completed four full years of foreign language study in high school. They review grades and AP test scores—none of which indicate whether the student has gained speaking proficiency. And since AP exams represent the high-water mark of high school foreign language accomplishment, teachers focus on an approach that will lead to high AP exam scores. These exams consist almost entirely of reading, writing, vocabulary, and grammar, with less than two minutes of canned speaking into a microphone. We'd love to see a study of how many students with scores of 4 or 5 on an AP exam could carry on a twenty-minute discussion with a native speaker.

What would we do with foreign language instruction if we looked to the future and not the past? It's safe to say that almost no student today needs to translate written material from a foreign language into English. Automated translation software is good and improving exponentially. Ditto for the writing. Many high school students tell us that they complete their writing assignments by (a) writing the essay in English, (b) running it through a software translator, and (c) purposely introducing a few errors into the essay so it won't be obvious they used automated tools. Given the realities of the world we live in, we question the value of spending years developing rudimentary skills to read and write in another language.

We hear the most amazing stories of young kids who develop online connections with other kids in countries around the world—often through video game forums. These kids, without the benefit of being taught the language, figure out how to communicate by resourcefully tapping into language translation software. In the process, they learn to reach across country boundaries, establish connections with non–English speakers, and learn about life in obscure places all around the globe. These kids are hacking a "foreign language" skill with lifetime value.

In the future, we'll see spectacular advances in real-time spoken translation software. If you encounter someone who doesn't speak English (whether from Spain, China, or Zimbabwe), you will be able to talk to each other, using a smartphone as your translator. Microsoft just announced Skype Translator, which enables real-time video and audio communication between people speaking different languages. Granted, this automated intermediary is no substitute for being fluent in another language. If you're fluent in someone's native tongue, the interaction is qualitatively different. And that's the point. True proficiency in speaking a foreign language can be invaluable to an adult. Anything less, and the time spent studying a foreign language is wasted.

When we ask school heads about their foreign language departments, they say, "In this global world, it's important for students to speak another language." But their students aren't learning to speak. They'll add, "It's important to understand foreign cultures." But the students don't interact with students abroad. And priority is placed on learning about life in that country centuries ago instead of today. Oh, and for good measure, educators will say, a bit halfheartedly, "It exercises a different part of their brain," but fumble when asked for the evidence.

No child in America will struggle as an adult because he or she didn't put in three years of foreign language seat time. If our education system wants to equip kids with a definitive lifetime advantage through foreign language mastery and global competence, we need to do it right. Immerse a child in the early grades. Help the student attain true conversational fluency. Look for opportunities to speak frequently in the language through travel if possible, Skype sessions with students in foreign countries, or field trips to immigrant communities in surrounding areas to learn about their culture and speak with them. And, above all, make it fun. Read books the students care about. Have entertaining discussions in class in the language. Watch movies in the language. Find a partner class or student in a foreign country and use tools like Skype to really learn about life there. But don't require our kids to spend several years on something of no long-term value just to check off a thoughtless graduation requirement.

A New Kind of Course

In the preceding pages, we have tried to suggest the sweeping changes needed in the teaching of traditional subject content areas. We have not talked about the importance of interdisciplinary approaches to learning. In fact, the best high school classes we've observed are organized around a complex question or problem that must be considered in light of several disciplines.

We also have not mentioned the arts. We think exposing students to the arts as tools for understanding and problem-solving, and as a means of self-expression, is essential. But we are often disappointed to see the arts relegated to the distant corners of the building where only those students who think they have a talent dare to go. We'd like to see the arts integrated into all humanities courses, as well as in engineering and design classes.

Imagine, for a moment, a new required high school class called "What Does It Mean to Be an American?" Imagine that the course begins with posing big questions that have no easy or right or wrong answers, such as, "Who are we as Americans?" "What are the forces that have shaped us as a people and as a country?" and "What are the challenges that our country faces in the future?"

Now imagine that students are challenged to consider these questions over the course of a year, using multiple disciplines. They would come to understand who we are as Americans from history, of course, but also from literature and the arts. They would learn what immigrants from other countries have contributed to our country's culture. They would learn about important new technologies that have shaped our history, mathematical and scientific discoveries that have brought us both enormous wealth and prosperity, as well as life-threatening challenges for the future.

Now further imagine that teams of students would have responsibility for researching specific eras in depth and then teaching their peers the highlights of what they have learned. Perhaps they'd make a movie or write a play to illustrate a particularly important point. Some might compose a song or write a poem or a short story.

So what would the "final exam" look like for this course? Students would be asked to write an extended, take-home essay addressing the question of what it means to be an American. They would know from the first day of class that this was the final exam question. They would have been considering the topic in ongoing discussions and debates throughout the year, and they'd be encouraged to draw on all the resources they'd used for learning throughout the year—especially the Internet.

The second part of students' final exam would require them to present and defend their papers in a public exhibition of mastery—much like a dissertation defense—where parents and guests would have a chance to observe and ask questions. Students' oral and written work would be assessed on their ability to marshal a range of evidence to make their points. They would not be compared to one another; they would not be time-tested. But they would have to meet a specified performance standard in order to get a credit for the course—a Merit Badge in American Studies.

Do you think that if every high school student in America took a course like this, our students might better understand our past, our present, and our future? Do you suppose they'd be better collaborators, critical thinkers, communicators, and citizens? We think so.

Great idea for kids in our elite schools, you may be thinking, but what about kids in poor communities? Could they succeed with these kinds of challenges? The answer is a resounding YES! In the 1980s, Deborah Meier, the originator of the "Five Habits of Mind" we mentioned earlier, was principal of Central Park East Secondary School in Harlem. To graduate from this school, students had to submit portfolios that met clear performance standards, and they were required to present and defend major elements of their portfolios.[33] Today, hundreds of schools continue to develop variations of this approach first pioneered by Deborah and others associated with the Coalition of Essential Schools, and many of them serve our most disadvantaged communities. We'll learn more about some of these schools in chapter 7.

The Opportunity Cost

Suppose you were president of the United States, and responsible for ensuring that our nation had a healthy, growing, competitive economy. Now suppose, in touring the country, you encountered a transportation system consisting of covered wagons. A communication system relying on the telegraph, using Morse code. Factories based entirely on manual labor. If someone in a press conference asked you whether the United States could compete against China, India, or other aggressive economic powers, you'd say, "Well, we don't stand a chance of beating them. But I think we can hold our own against Bhutan and Chad."

Our education model dates back to the dawn of the industrial era. We're fortunate that most other countries also educate with this obsolete model. Our failure to innovate and our lack of commitment to real research and development in education has put us at a competitive disadvantage against those countries that have invested in moving their citizens forward.

Educrats love to tie our system up in knots by adding new requirements, imposing new regulations, and dangling carrots for compliance. But they have completely failed to create the conditions for real innovation, or to make it possible to eliminate obsolete content. We demand that our teachers cover more content, do more test prep, and keep feeding the high-stakes test beast—a beast with an insatiable appetite. So there's just not enough time in schedules or budgets to reimagine education.

If we fill up the school year with second-order priorities, our kids won't have time to learn the skills, or develop the characteristics, that they'll need as adults. Our best teachers will leave the field. Accountability tied to a standardized-test regimen will absorb every hour in the school year. And when we stuff our classroom schedules with preparation for tests of low-level skills, what won't we have time to do? What aren't we teaching our kids?

Our choice is stark. We can continue training kids to be proficient at low-level routine tasks and to memorize content they won't remember on topics they'll never use. Or we can embrace the reality that much of what school is about today can be "outsourced" to a smartphone, freeing up time for kids to immerse themselves in challenges like the following:

Learning how to learn. This is arguably the single most important skill a student can develop, yet most schools accomplish the exact opposite. The teacher structures the content around a textbook, assigns the homework, designs the test, and grades the student on ability to jump through the hoops laid out by the teacher. Given an almost dizzying array of resources, we should be teaching young adults how to be effective in "learning how to learn."

Communicating effectively. This life skill will be important almost every day of an adult's life, unless he or she ends up in solitary confinement (this may sound flip, but it's one of the real risks we face with so many kids). Schools teaching grades seven through twelve do a miserable job of teaching kids to write—for lack of time and teacher preparation, as we've seen. Kids will also need to be good at public speaking, making a video, writing a blog and cultivating a following, and using communication to achieve a range of objectives.

Collaborating productively and effectively with others. These are essential skills that don't just come down from the heavens the day students get their diploma. Over and over, educators tell us, "We tried having kids work together on projects, but it never seems to work. One kid ends up doing all the work and the others just tag along." School networks like New Tech High have learned how to teach students team accountability through 360 peer reviews, so that there is genuine collaboration with every project.

Creative problem-solving. Over and over, employers tell us that the ideal characteristic they'd like to find in new hires is being a creative problem-solver. And, over and over, it seems to have been "schooled" out of fresh graduates, irrespective of their academic pedigree. For almost all schools we visit, the prevailing attitude among students is, "Just tell me what I need to know to get the right answer." And too many faculty members unconsciously seek a specific answer. We need to teach kids to be innovative and creative problem-solvers.

Managing failure. School today is all about risk aversion. Both kids and teachers are discouraged, almost hourly, from trying anything that might not work. Understanding how and when to take risks, how to deal with setbacks, and how to handle the expectations and criticisms of others are all skills that need to be taught and learned. Innovative progress necessarily requires a healthy degree of risk-taking and "failure." The motto in most innovative companies is "fail early, fail often." There is no innovation without trial and error. We argue that there is also no real learning without trial and error. So not only do our schools not teach our kids the skills and perspective required to deal with risk, we actively dissuade kids from taking considered risks.

Effecting change in organizations and society. One of the most important contributions any adult can make is to effect positive change in existing organizations or communities. As we know all too well from our work in education, changing things is *hard.* Schools are the most natural of microcosms for helping kids learn how they can work hard to effect positive change. But when we ask schools to describe opportunities for students to take leadership in moving the school ahead, we're generally met with blank stares. Strategic planning processes are led by consultants, board members (who went to school decades ago), and school officials. Department reviews are driven by faculty. Even most clubs and after-school programs are defined and led by adults, with modest student input. Wouldn't it make sense to give students as many opportunities as possible to improve their school? Their community? And provide students with guidance and resources to help them learn how to effect change productively and develop leadership skills?

Making sound decisions. As we overschedule our kids, they have fewer opportunities to make their own decisions and experience the consequences. We take it for granted that they're learning how to make decisions, but how do they get good at something they never do? Effective decision-making can be taught using powerful and important math and emphasizing clarity on values and ethics.

Managing projects and achieving goals. In order to be successful, it's important to understand how to set goals and manage projects. It's curious that this course can be found at the college level, but it's something every high school student needs to be good at.

Building perseverance and determination. Paul Tough, in his groundbreaking book *How Children Succeed*, cites the research of MacArthur Award winner Angela Duckworth and others on the importance of a set of character attributes that are more important than IQ in determining adult success and well-being. These traits can be summed up with one word: grit. Much has been written about the importance of putting in ten thousand hours in order to master something difficult. But both in Duckworth's work and in our friend Dan Pink's excellent 2011 book, *Drive*, there has been little discussion of where the motivation to persevere comes from. Do all students need to have a Tiger Mom sitting on their shoulders? No! What Tony learned in student, teacher, and parent interviews for his book *Creating Innovators* is that play, passion, and purpose are essential ingredients for helping students to *want* to put in the time required to achieve or learn something of value.

Leveraging your passions and talents to make your world better. Most parents and educators would agree, at least in theory, that the single most important lesson we can impart to our youth is that they can, through their passions and talents, make their world a better place, in a way they define. Learning how to identify your passions and use them to make an impact doesn't just emerge from passively sitting through a school day. It requires practice in the real world.

Compare this list of skills with a typical night of homework for a high school student. Does anyone, besides high-stakes test designers, really think our kids should be spending all of their time memorizing the placement of accent marks in French vocabulary? Memorizing the definition of an isosceles triangle? Studying the definition of covalent bonds? And on and on. But when you fill up every waking hour of a teenager's life with these drills, you don't have time for what really counts. And you produce disengaged kids doing the most mind-numbing of tasks, rather than developing the skills they'll need to take on life's biggest challenges.

CHAPTER 5

The Gold Ring:
The College Degree

Bill Clinton: "*We have made education a high priority, focusing on standards, accountability and choice in public schools, and on making a college education available to every American—with increased Pell Grant scholarships, better student loan and work-study programs, and the HOPE scholarship and other tax credits to help families pay for college tuition. Because of these efforts, more young people have the chance to make the most of their God-given abilities, and take their place in the high-tech world.*"

George W. Bush: "*I've got more to do to continue to raise standards, to continue to reward teachers in school districts that are working, to emphasize math and science in the classrooms, to continue to expand Pell Grants, to make sure that people have an opportunity to start their career with a college diploma.*"

Barack Obama: "*You know, sometimes I'll go to an eighth-grade graduation and there's all that pomp and circumstance and gowns and flowers. And I think to myself, it's just eighth grade. To really compete, they need to graduate high school, and then they need to graduate college, and they probably need a graduate degree too.*"

Bill Gates (college dropout): "The data on the value of a college degree is pretty clear. Today, 97 million U.S. jobs require high-level skills. Yet only 45 million Americans currently qualify for these positions. By the year 2018, 63 percent of all jobs in the U.S. will require some form of postsecondary education. Over an adult's career, on average, college graduates will earn almost $1 million more than high school graduates. In addition, the unemployment rate for college graduates is about half that of those with a high school diploma." (Source: March 13, 2013 interview with the Daily Texan.*)*

As underscored by our nation's leaders, a college degree is *the* essential credential for a young adult seeking a productive, respected career. This premise is baked into our society's DNA. It's a given. No matter how much it costs to get that credential, and no matter how effective it is in preparing you for a career or citizenship, this credential is the gold standard.

There's only one problem. This premise is completely out of date.

College was, for many adults, a magical time. A time of personal development and discovery. Exposure to new ideas. Transformation and growth. For many who left home to study on a college campus, it was their first experience being truly independent. At its best, college is an immersion in great ideas, surrounded by engaged classmates and faculty, turning aimless teenagers into focused adults. And college is a time when people form defining lifetime bonds—with fellow alumni, with faculty, and with the entire ecosystem of their college (alumni chapters, passionate allegiance to sports teams, college swag, and—in a very real sense—personal identity). Naturally, parents—whether they attended college themselves or missed out on the opportunity—want this magical experience for their children.

We understand the nostalgic view adults have about college, and we know that many will squirm at what we have to say in this chapter. It goes against entrenched beliefs. But we encourage you to have an open mind. You can probably remember the first music-playing device you or your family owned: an LP record player, a stereo console, an eight-track tape player in your car, a CD player, or maybe a Sony Walkman. This cherished device likely brought many hours of enjoyment, exploration, and learning as you formed lifelong affection for the music you love to this day. But if someone offered to sell your child a beat-up eight-track tape player for $25,000, you might raise a red flag. And you should, no matter how much importance you place on music appreciation for your child.

The Direct Cost of a College Credential

How have college costs done relative to the cost-of-living index? Well, compared to the aggregate Consumer Price Index, college tuition levels have soared. Over the past three decades, college costs have risen *three times* faster than the cost of living, increasing almost 8 percent per year, for thirty years! If you're like a lot of people, you might say, "Yes, I know college has gotten really expensive. But it could be worse. Just look at what's happened to the cost of healthcare." Yet the data shows that education costs make our healthcare system look like a shining example of cost control.[1]

Inflation of Tuition and Fees (Private Four-Year Colleges), Medical Costs, and Cost of Living, 1978–2008

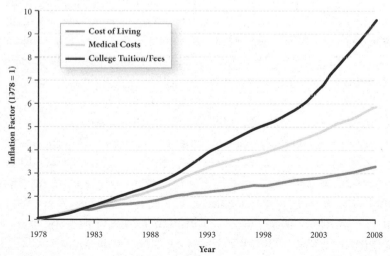

College has gotten expensive far faster than wages have gone up.

Consider how the cost of college has escalated relative to everything else we spend money on. We live in a world where productivity advances have made almost everything in our lives better, cheaper, or both. Everything except college.

When we visit college campuses, we see construction cranes everywhere. Large investments are being made in fitness centers, cushy dorms, plush student centers, and luxurious sports facilities. We recently sat down with Richard Hersh, former president of Hobart & William Smith College and Trinity College, co-author of *We're Losing Our Minds: Rethinking American Higher Education* and creator of the groundbreaking Collegiate Learning Assessment, described later in this chapter. He explained what's going on in colleges today:

> There is an arms race playing out among U.S. colleges and universities based on and reinforcing, unfortunately, the well-founded belief that the physical plant is the key to attracting more applicants. This is the corporate and business paradigm in full force whose metric of success depends on filling those seats and beds with students who can pay optimal tuition, skewing campus priorities to move up the spurious *U.S. News and World Report* rankings, generating more applications and getting more accepted applicants to matriculate, marketing the college "brand," and making the college experience more "fun." Little is said about increasing and improving student learning.

As colleges are run more like bad businesses and are driven by the inane *U.S. News and World Report* metrics (more in a bit on that topic), they add layers of administrative staff and bureaucracy. Gary Rhoades, a respected education economist, finds that over the past three decades, nonfaculty support professionals have "become the fastest growing category of professional employment in higher education."[2] As head count expands, it's going to the business side of colleges, not the learning side. Derek Bok, longtime and revered former president of Harvard University, notes:

While (academic) leaders have considerable leverage and influence of their own, they are often reluctant to employ these assets for fear of arousing opposition from the faculty that could attract unfavorable publicity, worry potential donors, and even threaten their jobs. After all, success in increasing student learning is seldom rewarded, and its benefits are usually hard to demonstrate, far more so than success in lifting the SAT scores of the entering class or in raising the money to build new laboratories or libraries.[3]

Richard Keeling and Richard Hersh, in *We're Losing Our Minds*, add:

Intoxicated by magazine and college-guide rankings, most colleges and universities have lost track of learning as the only educational outcome that really matters. Other priorities—higher rankings, growing enrollment, winning teams, bigger and better facilities, more revenue from sideline businesses, more research grants—have replaced learning as the primary touchstone for decision making.[4]

Meanwhile, the college "market" is being profoundly disrupted by the availability of free or low-cost online courses and alternate pathways for acquiring job skills, as we'll see in chapter 7. Business guru Clayton Christensen believes that, because the value proposition for college has declined so radically and the finances of many colleges are so shaky, "15 years from now half of US universities may be in bankruptcy."[5] (We're a little more optimistic than our friend Clayton. We believe that many will become assisted living homes!)

When the two of us went to college decades ago, its combined overall cost (all four years of tuition, room, and board) was generally in line with typical first-year starting salaries. Ted, for instance, paid about $8,000 *in total* for his four years of college—or about $40,000 in today's dollars. (He graduated in 1974 from a state college with low in-state tuition, and modest room and board costs.) His first full-time position (an entry-level position with a high-tech company) paid $32,000 per year. So Ted's ratio was about 4x. Tony chose to go into teaching instead of technology. But even with a much lower-paying initial position, Tony spent about $13,000 for his entire undergraduate education, and he earned $12,500 in his first year, nearly the entire cost of his college degree.

Unfortunately, those days are gone. Long, long gone.

If you're graduating from college today, the cost of your credential averages about $120,000, and can be as high as $250,000 for private colleges.[6] These costs don't include earlier expenses families often incur in preparing their kids for the college admissions war, which can amount to tens of thousands of dollars for test prep and college counselors, and $100,000 or more for private K-12 education. Analysis of survey data from employers tells us that the average starting salary for a new college graduate is $45,000,[7] and fewer than 40 percent of college graduates even manage to find such jobs.[8]

According to a January 2014 report from the Federal Bank of New York, 44 percent of recent graduates—between the ages of twenty-two and twenty-seven with a BA or higher—have a job that does not technically demand a bachelor's degree. What's far worse is that these grads earn far less than in the past. More than 20 percent of recent college graduates are in low-wage jobs, earning $25,000 a year or less.[9]

Real Tuition and Fees at a Public, Four-Year College and Average Earnings for Full-Time Workers Aged 25–34 with Bachelor's Degree Only (Indexed, 2000 = 100)

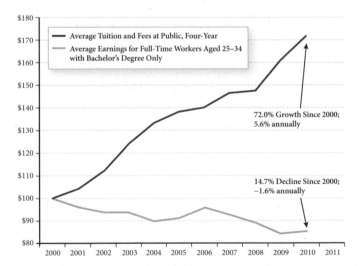

Note: Both tuition and earnings were weighted in 2010 dollars, and tuition and fees were enrollment-weighted.
Sources: College Board, U.S. Department of Education, Census Bureau, and Citi Research.

Debt and Its Collateral Damage

One way that families have tried to close the gap between declining income and increased college costs is to borrow money. We talk a lot about government debt in this country, but the debt we should worry more about is that of college attendees. The emotional toll on these kids is significant because they realize (often too late) that college debt, unlike other forms of debt, cannot be eliminated through bankruptcy. Sadly, our high schools almost never include financial literacy in their curriculum, leaving young adults poorly prepared to assess the long-term ramifications of taking on mounds of college-related debt. According to a 2014 Project on Student Debt report, "In 2013, 7 in 10 (69 percent) graduating seniors at public and private nonprofit colleges had student loans. These borrowers owed an average of $28,400."[10]

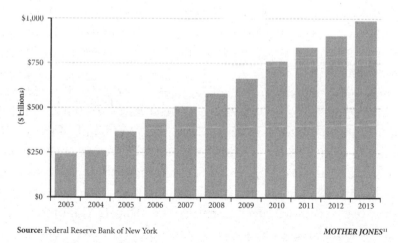

Big Debt on Campus

Student loan debt has nearly quadrupled in the past 10 years.

Source: Federal Reserve Bank of New York   *MOTHER JONES*[11]

Government-backed student debt is out of control, and other forms of debt are also rising exponentially. Private-sector student loans (in constant dollars) ballooned sevenfold, from $2.5 billion to $17.6 billion, from

1997 to 2007.[12] In addition to loans, college students increasingly turn to their credit cards to support themselves. In 2008, undergrads in their senior year had on average $4,100 in credit card debt, at annual interest rates above 15 percent. Some 30 percent of students report using credit cards to pay for tuition costs.[13]

In measuring levels of college-related debt, economists overlook an important hidden source of debt behind funding college tuition bills. Many parents are draining down their retirement savings, taking out second mortgages on their houses, and assuming personal loans to pay for the education of their children. These parents dig deep, expecting that they will somehow retire with enough savings to cover their own expenses until death, and if they do run into financial difficulties, their financially successful children will help them out in their old age.

These assumptions are fraught with risk. As life expectancies stretch out, as the cost of healthcare for the elderly escalates, and as pension fund payouts get restructured or reneged on entirely, more and more adults will struggle to get by in their retirement years. As college grads flounder financially, few will be in a position to pay off their own loans, let alone bail out their parents. For a real wake-up call, consider that some two million adults in the United States over the age of sixty are still paying off student loans—loans generally incurred during times when college tuition was modest.[14]

Because so many young people are deep in debt, far fewer are buying cars, let alone homes. Many have started down a road that is likely to lead to a lifetime struggle to repay debt, instead of building the savings required to retire securely, working long hours as a BArista or a BArtender. Others opt to pursue careers with high starting salaries (e.g., consulting, finance), instead of careers that strengthen the long-term prospects of our country (e.g., community service, entrepreneurship, teaching). Having so many capable young adults pursuing passionless careers is another tragedy caused by the rising costs of college.

The Emotional Costs of College

We note in passing that the financial costs of college, while often debilitating, are not the only toll the college process is taking on young Americans. As the importance of a degree has escalated in the eyes of society, we've managed to turn something that should be a source of joy and empowerment—learning at an advanced level—into a powerful force damaging to emotional health. The victims of this damage aren't confined to the college years. The pressures around college have an impact stretching from middle school through adulthood.

William Deresiewicz's 2014 book *Excellent Sheep* spells out in frightening detail the "epidemic of depression" among America's elite youth. Stanford provost John Etchemendy convened a task force on student mental health issues, reporting that "increasingly, we are seeing students struggling with mental health concerns ranging from self-esteem issues and developmental disorders to depression, anxiety, eating disorders, self-mutilation behaviors, schizophrenia and suicidal behavior."[15] The American Psychological Association released a study, "The Crisis on Campus," pointing to an alarming increase over the past two decades in serious mental health issues on campus.[16] A 2010 survey by the American College Health Association found that some 45.6 percent of college students reported feeling that "things were hopeless," 83 percent felt "overwhelmed" by all they had to do, and some 30.7 percent reported "feeling so depressed that it was difficult to function during the past 12 months."[17]

The emotional damage the hunt for elite college degrees wreaks on kids is important. But we should be every bit as concerned with the damage being done to the kids shut out of this hunt, either because of family poverty, lousy K-12 educations, or a steady stream of mediocre test scores inappropriately equated to inferiority. These are the kids who receive, year after year, the message that they aren't good enough to make it in society. And, with a miserable teach-to-the-test education, the process is now a full-bore self-fulfilling prophecy. Standardized tests based largely on how facile a student is with complex vocabulary or symbolic math manipulation—rather than innovative and resourceful problem-solving—condemn most of these kids to following their parents into the lower brackets of America's caste system. They will largely be shut out of college, face employment challenges stemming from the lack of a college degree, and see their worth to society diminished year after year as advances in automation further marginalize them.

We won't dwell on these emotional costs, as real and troubling as they are. Neither of your authors is a particularly "warm and cozy" type. We know full well that young Americans will live in an intensely dynamic and competitive world. Billions of global workers will compete for a livelihood, with ubiquitous interconnectivity making it possible for hungry young kids in Sri Lanka to take jobs away from complacent young Americans. Given this reality, we can hardly endorse, let alone fathom, movements like "StopHomework.com" or "Ban Busy," which seem to suggest that the way to address the stress in education is to have kids spend more time lounging around. But our issue with education isn't the quantity of time students devote to their development; it's how they are impelled to spend boatloads of time on school-related activities that lead to no real learning. Young Americans live in an increasingly dynamic and competitive world. Billions of global workers will compete for a livelihood, with ubiquitous interconnectivity making it possible for those hungry young kids in Sri Lanka to take jobs away from young Americans who have not had the benefit of an education that fosters creativity and innovation.

Learning in College

College is expensive, more so each year. Applications continue to soar, particularly to elite institutions. So it would seem logical to conclude that colleges do an amazing job of educating students. But do they?

In their groundbreaking book *Academically Adrift*, Richard Arum and Josipa Roksa explore how much students actually learn during their college years. Their conclusions are stunning. They find that the majority of college students learn little or nothing on the important dimensions of critical thinking and analysis, complex reasoning, and writing. Worse, there are indications that, over the past few decades, colleges have actually been teaching students less. In sum, "gains in student performance are disturbingly low; a pattern of limited learning is prevalent on contemporary college campuses."[18]

Arum and Roksa's research is based on a test that gets far less attention than SATs or ACTs: the Collegiate Learning Assessment (CLA), administered by the Council for Aid to Education. Unlike its multiple-choice counterparts, the CLA presents students with open-ended, complex questions, provides them with relevant background materials, and challenges them to formulate a solution or critique alternatives. They are given an hour-long performance task, as well as shorter tests on critical reading and evaluation, scientific and quantitative reasoning, and ability to analyze an argument.

Sample questions from the CLA include:[19]

Example

Scenario

You advise Pat Williams, the president of DynaTech, a company that makes precision electronic instruments and navigational equipment. Sally Evans, a member of DynaTech's sales force, recommended that DynaTech buy a small private plane (a SwiftAir 235) that she and other members of the sales force could use to visit customers. Pat was about to approve the purchase when there was an accident involving a SwiftAir 235.

Document Library

- Newspaper article about the accident
- Federal Accident Report on in flight breakups in single-engine planes
- Internal Correspondence (Pat's email to you & Sally's email to Pat)
- Charts relating to SwiftAir's performance characteristics
- Excerpt from magazine article comparing SwiftAir 235 to similar planes
- Pictures and descriptions of SwiftAir Models 180 and 235

Questions

- Do the available data tend to support or refute the claim that the type of wing on the SwiftAir 235 leads to more in-flight breakups?
- What is the basis for your conclusion?
- What other factors might have contributed to the accident and should be taken into account?
- What is your preliminary recommendation about whether or not DynaTech should buy the plane and what is the basis for this recommendation?

PERFORMANCE TASK

ROLE

You are a staff member for an organization that analyzes the accuracy of policy claims made by political candidates. The organization is nonpartisan, meaning that it is not influenced by, affiliated with, or supportive of any one political party or candidate.

SCENARIO

Leila Jainson is running for reelection as the mayor of Stoneville. Mayor Jainson's opponent in this contest is Dr. Carl Greer. Dr. Greer is a member of the Stoneville City Council. During a recent TV interview about cell phone use, Dr. Greer claimed that these phones interfered with people's ability to operate a motorized vehicle and caused vehicle-related accidents in Stoneville. Dr. Greer said that reducing cell phone usage while driving motorized vehicles would lower the city's vehicle-related accident rate. To support this argument, Dr. Greer presented a chart that compared the percentage of drivers who use cell phones while driving to the number of vehicle-related accidents. Dr. Greer based this chart on cell phone use and community data tables that were provided by the Stoneville Police Department and government population counts.

TASK

Your job is to evaluate Dr. Greer's claims. To do so, please answer the question that follows, using the supporting documents provided (labeled A and B). Your answers should include the appropriate or relevant evidence (drawn from documents A and B) necessary to support your position.

QUESTION

Dr. Greer claims that "reducing cell phone usage while driving motorized vehicles would lower the city's vehicle-related accident rate" (Document B exhibits the chart Dr. Greer used to support this statement).

> 1. What are the strengths and/or limitations of Dr. Greer's position on this matter? What specific information in Documents A and B led you to this conclusion? What additional information, if any, would you like to have had?

In contrast to prevailing standardized tests, CLA measures the skills that higher education claims to teach: critical thinking, analytical reasoning, problem-solving, and writing. While we generally dread the words "teach to the test," kids "taught to the CLA test" will learn skills that are important for careers and citizenship.

Working with a sample of 2,300 students across two dozen universities, Arum and Roksa tracked student results on the CLA over students' entire college experience. They observed no statistically significant gains in critical thinking, complex reasoning, and writing skills for at least 45 percent of the students in their first two years of college, and for 36 percent of students across all four years of college.[20] Overall gains across all students were a scant 7 percent in the first two years and only slightly higher for those completing their graduation requirements.[21] Their conclusions are a sweeping indictment of college education: "[I]n terms of general analytical competencies assessed, large numbers of U.S. college students can be accurately described as academically adrift. They might graduate, but they are failing to develop the higher-order cognitive skills that it is widely assumed college students should master."[22]

Other researchers have examined how little is being learned in college. Keeling and Hersh, in We're Losing Our Minds, conclude that far too many college students graduate without developing the capability to "think critically and creatively, speak and write cogently and clearly, solve problems, comprehend complex issues, accept responsibility and accountability, take the perspective of others, or meet the expectations of employers." They go on to state that "having a bachelor's degree no longer certifies that the graduate has any specific qualifications, is capable of achieving any real intellectual depth, possesses basic workplace skills, or demonstrates personal maturity."[23]

A study by the National Center for Education Statistics found that 20 percent of college *graduates* were completely lost when it came to even the most basic of quantitative skills. They were unable to calculate the total cost of an order of office supplies, compare ticket prices, or arrive at the correct total bill for lunch when given the price of a salad plus a sandwich. The same study found that only one-third of college graduates could read a complex book and comprehend what they were reading.[24]

In his 2006 book *Our Underachieving Colleges*, Derek Bok writes:

Colleges and universities, for all the benefits they bring, accomplish far less for their students than they should. Many seniors graduate without being able to write well enough to satisfy their employers. Many cannot reason clearly or perform competently in analyzing complex, nontechnical problems, even though faculties rank critical thinking as the primary goal of a college education. Few undergraduates receiving a degree are able to speak or read a foreign language. Most have never taken a course in quantitative reasoning or acquired the knowledge needed to be a reasonably informed citizen in a democracy. And those are only some of the problems.[25]

And Bok is not the only college president to hold this view. A recent Gallup poll found that 89 percent of all college presidents think having an emphasis on critical thinking skills in college is "very important," while just 40 percent of these same presidents think colleges are very effective at helping their students develop these skills.[26]

There's a Reason We Use the Phrase "It's Academic"

Colleges view themselves first and foremost as repositories of research and knowledge, with a faculty dedicated to pushing "knowledge boundaries" forward.

It's tempting to gloss over what a university views as "knowledge," but that would be a mistake. Most of us view knowledge as information that is true, insightful, and useful. That's not the way it works in most colleges, though. Academic research generally holds itself to high standards of being truthful and breaking new ground, but the concepts of "insightful" or "useful" don't carry much weight in academia. This outsized emphasis on pushing forward the boundaries in esoteric research is a major factor in why college students learn so little.

An anonymous blog called "100 Reasons NOT to Go to Graduate School" has found a wide audience; it currently has over three million page views. In a post entitled "Virtually No One Reads What You Write," the author points out that the only person you can assume will read your dissertation is your adviser. Not even others on your dissertation committee are likely to read it, let alone anyone else.

The blogger continues: "The same fate awaits the vast majority of published academic writing. Typically, it takes months of research, writing, and revision to produce a journal article that will be seen by fewer people in its author's lifetime than will visit this blog in an hour. Academic presses print as few as 300 copies of the books that their authors have labored over for years. Most journal articles and academic monographs are written because academics need to be published to keep their jobs, not because there is a demand or need for their work."[27]

In Tony's first year of his doctoral program at Harvard, his adviser talked about the nature of a dissertation. She said, "Your dissertation should be an important conversation between yourself and just one or two other people in the world." "Presumably," Tony recalls thinking, "because they'd be the only ones who would either understand or care about the topic." Tony remembers this moment as a turning point for him. He vowed to write a dissertation that practitioners would find useful and that could become his first book—which it did. The book based on his dissertation, *How Schools Change,* was published a year after Tony completed his doctorate.

The dynamics of academic research drive the curriculum and classroom agenda in most of our colleges and universities, with an impact that reaches all of U.S. education. What counts for college faculty members is knowing the most about an obscure facet of an academic discipline, and publishing each incremental finding. Naomi Schaefer Riley, author of *The Faculty Lounges and Other Reasons Why You Won't Get the College Education You Paid For,* cites a study done by the *Journal of Higher Education* that concludes that the more time a college professor spends teaching, the *less* he or she gets paid. These results are true in both big research universities (less surprising) and in small liberal arts colleges (quite surprising). She concludes, "Professors have gotten the message, busily churning out research for a growing number of publications that in most cases are read by next to no one."[28]

If we could do a brain scan of a typical university professor early in her career, here's what we would find. Getting tenure is her sole career priority. Get it and her academic career is set. Being denied tenure is a stigma from which few academics recover. Most departments make tenure decisions on the basis of two criteria: volume of research and politics. Putting your heart and soul into teaching detracts from time spent on research and, all too often, hurts a rising professor politically. Older, tenured professors don't like to get shown up by newbies on teacher evaluations. The net result is that college faculty are not selected, motivated, or incentivized to be inspiring educators.

As Keeling and Hersh write, "Professors do not fail to achieve promotion and tenure because their students did not learn; in fact, few colleges and universities know to what extent, if at all, any professors' students have learned or not. In many universities, for that matter, professors do not fail to achieve promotion and tenure because they do not teach well, either."[29] Some amazing teachers do navigate their way through the tenure process, but they're the exception, not the rule.

And what would a brain scan of tenured faculty look like? Well, they wake up in the morning thinking about their field of focus, and go to bed at night still thinking about it. And their research is channeled at pushing the boundaries of knowledge around this pinpoint focus—whether it's the mating habits of ants in Zimbabwe or why Andorra remained neutral in World War II. So with this mindset, it's more than understandable that tenured faculty feel the most important thing they can do for their students is to cover material they know is significant in their field of study. And, given the average age of tenured faculty, they aren't all that plugged into the world's new reality—namely that facts about ants or Andorra can be readily looked up. The fabric of our university mindset is all about what people know, and nothing about what they can do with what they (or Google!) know.

What You Know (Irrespective of Relevance)	What You Can Do with What You Know
⟵--⟶	
What Colleges Care About	What the World Cares About

> Tony interviewed highly successful young innovators for his book *Creating Innovators*, including some who had graduated from our most prestigious universities—Harvard, MIT, and Stanford. One of his most startling findings was that *none* of the college teachers who'd had the greatest influence on these young people were tenured, nor were they likely to be. They'd made a difference in the lives of their students by being great teachers and mentors. Most also did research, but it wasn't considered "academic" enough to get them tenure.

To paraphrase Abraham Lincoln, colleges are by academics, of academics, and for academics. Academics' passion for narrow areas of content profoundly shapes what is, and what is not, studied in college classrooms. Faculty appointments are based on openings tied to specific areas of expertise, not to teaching skills or experience. As departments construct the requirements for majors, they seek to ensure that all "foundational knowledge pillars" in their discipline are covered. Both faculty and students are strongly discouraged from any form of interdisciplinary studies in the belief that such courses are watered-down academics. Graduation requirements are entirely about seat time, minimum standards of performance, and checking the boxes on "essential" content. You pass forty courses, with a dozen in a department silo that is your declared major, and you're a college graduate. Even at our elite colleges, undergraduate credentials are not based on mastering critical skills, completing complex projects, or demonstrating the ability to work collaboratively.

As David Labaree, author of *How to Succeed in School Without Really Learning*, concludes:

> The payoff for a particular credential is the same no matter how it was acquired, so it is rational behavior to try to strike a good bargain, to work at getting a diploma, like a car, at a substantial discount. The effect on education is to emphasize form over content—to promote an educational system that is willing to reward students for formal compliance with modest

performance requirements rather than for demonstrating operational mastery of skills deemed politically and socially useful.[30]

Keeling and Hersh add:

> Most students graduate from college without having experienced higher learning at all—they gain (but quickly forget) factual knowledge, become adept at giving back rehearsed answers on exams, and, eventually, sporting inflated grade-point averages, find their way into line and shake hands with the president at commencement.[31]

Now don't get us wrong. Many of our friends are academics (or at least they were prior to reading this book!). We cherish their passion, curiosity, rigor, and intellectual values. We fully recognize that many valuable scientific and technical breakthroughs have come as a result of pure research, and sponsorship of research is a valid university purpose. But the arcane research agendas of faculty should not determine the curriculum for undergraduates or our high schools, as is too often the case now.

Assessing College Quality

The most widely cited source of information about the relative quality of U.S. colleges is the *U.S. News and World Report* (USNWR) annual rankings.[32] First issued in 1983 (an auspicious year in the demise of the U.S. education system), these ratings are a fixture in the popular press. As happens for the Super Bowl or election season, attention is riveted each year on whether Harvard has retained its top spot, which schools are on the rise, and which schools are slipping. When released, the new ratings grab headlines everywhere, and college administrators nervously await finding out whether their institution has moved up or down the USNWR ladder.

Leave aside the folly of placing an ordinal ranking on colleges relative to other colleges (a bit like issuing rankings of the greatest all-time artists, with Picasso, Rembrandt, and da Vinci jockeying for the number-one spot). The real shock begins when you look at how USNWR arrives at its rankings. These influential rankings are based on factors like:

- *Acceptance rate.* The more selective a school, the better it just has to be.
- *Perceived reputation.* What do other college administrators and high school guidance counselors think?
- *Average SATs of entering class.* The higher the SATs of its students, the better the college must be.
- *Research budget.* More research equates to a better college, according to USNWR.
- *Graduation and retention rates.* Percentage graduating in six years or less, and percentage of the entering class returning for their second year.

Not one of the criteria used by USNWR to rank colleges reflects how much students learn. The operational consequences of these ratings are immoral. They encourage colleges to direct resources away from true education, and waste lots of their—and their applicants'—time and money. The big winners in this are the multibillion-dollar college prep and higher-ed consulting industries. Here are just some of the ways the USNWR criteria have such an adverse impact:

- *Acceptance rate.* Colleges spend large sums of money to increase the number of applications they receive, so they can reject more and appear more "selective." Don't believe us? Just look at the daily mail any high school junior or senior gets from colleges encouraging them to apply.
- *Perceived reputation.* If there is one thing we've learned, it's that you can't judge a school until you observe classes and review student work and how it's assessed. Basing rankings on "perceived reputation," which is largely formed by past rankings, is circular at best, and encourages colleges hoping to move up in the USNWR ratings to invest in marketing their "brand," not educating their students.
- *Average SATs of entering class.* The higher the SATs of its students,

the better the college must be. Right? So the weight they put on these scores prompts applicants to spend endless hours and money on prep. And many colleges now "super score" the standardized tests of applicants—meaning that an applicant can take the SAT or ACT many times, and the college will cherry-pick the student's best score from each subsection to come up with the highest possible overall score for the applicant. And what score does the college report to the USNWR? The "super score," of course. This policy allows a college to boost its USNWR rankings, while hurting applicants who can't afford endless hours and fees for tutors, test prep, and test-taking.

- *Research budget.* Even though a heavy emphasis on research in universities often comes at the expense of undergraduate learning, more research equates to a better college—according to USNWR.
- *Graduation and retention rates.* Make your school easy and fun, and you'll get a big boost in the ratings. Invest in a fitness center, not better education.

If only more colleges had the courage of Reed College, which pulled out of these rankings in 1995, stating boldly that USNWR's methodology is "hopelessly flawed—a belief widely shared in the education community."[33] We await the day when college presidents start leveling with their community and say, "Our tuition is sky high because we spend a lot of money on things that will make us look better in the rankings—and we're going broke doing it."

Nationally, we spend approximately $500 billion annually to "educate" students at U.S. colleges and universities,[34] but a pitifully small sum assessing how much students actually learn in college. The research for Arum and Roksa's *Academically Adrift* study was funded over a period of six years by four visionary foundations (Lumina, Ford, Carnegie, and Teagle) with a total of just over $1 million. This modest amount, less than what most colleges spend each admission season in marketing dollars to entice more applicants, reflects our lack of investment in assessing colleges that was identified by *The Futures Project: Policy for Higher Education in a Changing World*, which expressed deep concern that our colleges "lack clear measurements for their performance . . . because they are satisfied with the status quo."[35] The Lumina Foundation sums up the assessment of learning that is now happening on most campuses:

> There is too little credible data to justify the quality distinctions that are often made in higher education. We simply aren't doing enough to measure the specific learning that takes place in individual courses and degree programs. In most cases, we can't really tell what value an institution truly adds to its students' lives.[36]

While Arum and Roksa's data is reported on an aggregate basis, it could form the basis for an alternative way of ranking colleges—one based on criteria that actually matter. Imagine how powerful it would be if we had access to longitudinal data, by university, on how students perform on the CLA. Prospective students would use this data to inform their college selection and put priority on colleges that help their students learn, instead of colleges that are hard to get into. Everything in the college world would change. The college experience would be retooled, with far more focus on helping students develop critical skills. Excellent teaching would be considered at least as important as research. Colleges would look to admit students who would benefit the most from their college experience (posting big gains in critical thinking over their four years) instead of picking kids who have been manicured to serve up the perfect résumé *before* they even start.

Alarmed by the rising costs and low graduation rates of many colleges, President Obama recently suggested that the federal government step in and rank colleges on criteria like graduation rates and postgraduation earnings data. While well intentioned, this suggestion is counterproductive. This type of ranking would encourage colleges to be motivated to make it easier to graduate, or concentrate their student bodies on young adults interested in more lucrative careers. One misguided top administration official likens rating colleges to "rating a blender"[37] (which puts a whole new spin on the education phrase "blended learning"). We'd love to see our federal education leaders focus on the central issues around learning and assessment in our education system, instead of proposing yet another flawed rating system.

Employment After College

College graduates are struggling to find decent-paying, meaningful jobs. According to data reported by Hope Yen of the Associated Press, 2011 college graduates "were more likely to be employed as waiters, waitresses, bartenders and food-service helpers than as engineers, physicists, chemists and mathematicians combined (100,000 versus 90,000). There were more working in office-related jobs such as receptionist or payroll clerk than in all computer professional jobs (163,000 versus 100,000). More were also employed as cashiers, retail clerks and customer representatives than engineers (125,000 versus 80,000)."[38]

For the graduating class of 2014, only 17 percent left college with jobs, according to a recent poll by AfterCollege.[39] And many of these kids end up returning home to live with their parents—a stunning 45 percent of recent college grads.[40] Some 60 percent rely on their families for ongoing financial support after graduation.[41]

We hear from employers regularly about how ill prepared graduates are, even graduates from elite colleges, to take on workplace responsibilities. How creativity and imagination have been schooled out of them. How they seem to be allergic to unstructured problems. How they seek constant micromanagement and the workplace equivalent of a daily, or even hourly, grade. Annmarie Neal is the former chief talent officer at Cisco Systems and author of *Leading From the Edge*. She continues to consult to senior leadership in Fortune 100 companies all over the world, and here's what she told us in a recent conversation:

> Even the most elite schools do not prepare students for the reality of work as it is today, let alone what it will become in the future. Most large orga-

nizations are undergoing massive transformations as they move from industrial to innovation-economy business models. The students that thrive within today's education systems are achievement driven, rule-oriented, compliant, linear, singular in focus (i.e., a business or engineering major). The world of work today requires future leaders to be relationship or collaboration driven, rule-defining, creative and innovative, lateral and polymathic in focus. The gap is huge and, sadly, I see only a few progressive schools really stepping up to the transformation required to match that of our businesses.

The Massachusetts Institute of Technology is widely regarded as the world's preeminent engineering educational institution, with a long history of achievement. Of past Nobel Prize winners, some eighty-one have ties to MIT.[42] In a typical year, researchers at MIT file hundreds of patents, start dozens of technology companies, and publish hundreds of scholarly articles.[43] Most people view MIT as being at the pinnacle of engineering education.

A few years ago, an MIT student, Kristen Wolfe, did her thesis on the topic of "Understanding the Careers of the Alumni of the MIT Mechanical Engineering Department." She looked at a wide range of things students could learn and use, whether at MIT or otherwise. She surveyed over three hundred graduates of MIT's Mechanical Engineering Department who were, at the time, about a decade into careers spanning academics, research, business, and nonprofits.

Respondents to Wolfe's survey reported that they spent almost all of their time at MIT on narrow topics that they would not end up using professionally (e.g., fluid mechanics, heat transfer, obscure mathematics), and almost no time at MIT on skills that were essential professionally. Wolfe concludes, "The largest disconnects are in the areas of personal skills, professional skills, independent thinking, teamwork and communication. These areas received the largest scores for proficiency and frequency and the lowest for learning at MIT. For the most part I believe professors assume the students will pick these up by virtue of the MIT experience."[44]

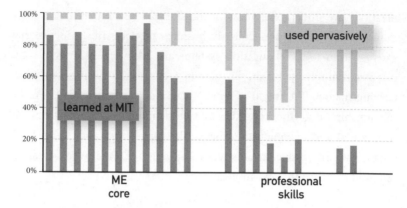

If a blimp flew over our college campuses with a sign saying "You're not preparing your students for careers," it could hardly be more obvious. But has the message reached the academic leaders of our colleges? Apparently not. A recent Gallup survey shows a disconnect that makes the Grand Canyon look like a pothole. Gallup reports: "If provosts could grade themselves on how well they're preparing students for success in the work force, they'd give themselves an A+." They did, sort of, in Inside Higher Ed's 2014 survey of chief academic officers. Some 96 percent said they were doing a good job—but they may have been grading on a curve!

In a new survey by Gallup measuring how business leaders and the American public view the state and value of higher education, just 14 percent of Americans—and only 11 percent of business leaders—strongly agreed that graduates have the necessary skills and competencies to succeed in the workplace. "It's such a shocking gap, it's just hard to even say what's going on here," Brandon Busteed, executive director of Gallup Education, said in an interview before the survey's release.[45]

So 96 percent of provosts—the senior academic officer for a college— believe their institution is effective at preparing students for careers, while just 11 percent of business leaders agree. Whoa! Do these groups ever talk to each other?

The reality is that there is often a disconnect between the academic leadership and those dealing with the outside world (including the president). No matter what academic priorities get set by college presidents, they are largely powerless to do anything about it. The education power at a college lies with its tenured faculty, not its administration. One current college president confided to us, "If I tried to introduce a course here on career readiness, my faculty would revolt." So it's not all that surprising that Gallup found that some 72 percent of college presidents believe it's important that their faculty understand which skills and abilities are needed by employers, but only 22 percent report being effective at communicating these requirements.[46]

What Gallup didn't ask college presidents was the following: "If you spent day after day, month after month, semester after semester, begging your tenured faculty to change their teaching approach to make it more effective, do you think they would pay the slightest bit of attention to you?" We'll go out on a limb and predict that any experienced, truthful college president would respond, "No chance in hell."

Let's be clear on how colleges should prepare students for careers. We don't subscribe to the view that a college needs to revolve around practical courses. Our belief—affirmed by decades of experience in a range of fields— is that the content of a major is, for most college students, less relevant than having an education that develops important skills and reinforces certain character traits. And this shift away from content expertise is accelerating.

In a September 11, 2014, column, *Washington Post* reporter Roberto Ferdman reported on research that compared the starting salaries of recent college graduates with those of mid-career professionals and concluded that "technical abilities are highly valued among recent graduates, which explains why a student who graduates from an engineering program at California Institute of Technology will likely be better compensated, at least at the outset, than a Harvard graduate with an English degree. It also seems that those specialized skills offer a comparative salary edge for only a handful of years before that advantage begins to dissipate—and the salary benefits of a holistic, liberal arts education begin to catch up."[47]

Consider the common misperception that a business degree is better career preparation than a major in the humanities. The reality is that many businesses—especially more innovative ones—aren't interested in hiring graduates for their content expertise, and are particularly skeptical that college business content is relevant to their operations. Of recent college graduates, business majors rank second in unemployment of all majors from college.[48] Today, employers look for graduates who exhibit critical skills, ask great questions, and demonstrate perseverance and grit. These critical skills can be taught in traditional liberal arts pursuits as well or better than in business courses.

Anthony Carnevale, of Georgetown's Center on Education and the Workforce, has produced important, counterintuitive insights about how colleges can best prepare students for careers. One of his center's recent studies found that the unemployment rate among recent information technology graduates is actually twice that of theater majors.[49] Despite the fact that there are a number of IT positions unfilled, majoring in IT at a college may not give you the set of generic skills employers seek. As a recent *Wall Street Journal* story reports, "Courses that teach, say, hospitality management or sports medicine may crowd out a logic class that can help students learn to improve their reasoning or an English class that sharpens their writing. Both of those skills can help in any field, unlike the narrowly focused ones."[50]

John Pryor, a Gallup senior research scientist, summarizes the problem succinctly: "[M]any graduates don't have the job they thought they would get, and many employers have openings for skilled employees they cannot fill. Both are bad for the individuals affected and for the American economy. Changing this needs to be a priority of every college president in the United States."[51] But, unfortunately, this mismatch is widely misunderstood; it's a mismatch of the skills colleges develop in their students, not the content they offer.

The Impact of College on Citizenship and Our Social Fabric

"Education," Horace Mann declared in 1848, "is a great equalizer of the conditions of men, the balance wheel of the social machinery." That was true in our country for a long, long time. But today, the United States faces enormous challenges on the issues of income inequality, social mobility, and our shrinking middle class. Yet, most of the discussion in our country about these issues squarely revolves around tax code policy. On the topic of college's role in leveling the playing field, our leaders espouse platitudes about how we need to help all young Americans obtain a college degree. President Obama recently called a college degree "an economic imperative."[52]

Today, our higher-education system is becoming a *cause* of income inequality in our country, instead of a solution. In a single generation, we've seen college's role in our society and economy change entirely. In the twentieth century, college was instrumental in extending economic opportunity and social integration to millions of young Americans, fueling the rise of a growing, robust middle class. And graduates of our colleges were, by and large, engaged and informed citizens who further strengthened our social fabric. Today, though, college has become our country's very own ivory-tower caste system, penalizing the life prospects of our lower- and middle-income families and locking in advantage for our upper crust, all the while churning out graduates disengaged from their responsibilities as citizens.

A shining example of college's role in promoting social mobility came when President Franklin D. Roosevelt signed the GI Bill into law in 1944. The president's stated goal was to help ensure that all returning military personnel gain "satisfactory employment upon their return to civil life."[53] The legislation's leading provision called for giving "servicemen and women the opportunity of resuming their education or technical training after discharge, or of taking a refresher or retrainer course, not only without tuition charge up to $500 per school year, but with the right to receive a monthly living allowance while pursuing their studies."[54]

The GI Bill educated some 7.8 million veterans of the war, putting in place the foundation for a robust middle class in the postwar manufacturing economy.[55] This was the stuff of the American Dream. When the GI Bill was signed in 1944, just $500 of tuition reimbursement (equivalent to $7,000 today) opened the doors to all U.S. colleges for millions of returning veterans.

Contrast how returning World War II veterans transformed U.S. society with our twenty-first-century experience. The wars in Iraq and Afghanistan were fought by an all-volunteer military drawn largely from lower-income families. Instead of war being the engine of economic growth and social mobility, as it has been in the past, these returning vets have experienced record rates of suicide, post-traumatic stress disorder, addiction, depression, and homelessness.[56] Even with the expanded benefits of the so-called GI Bill 2.0 signed into law by President Obama in 2010, today's returning vets face enormous challenges. Despite their courageous contributions and the critical skills they acquired during their tours of duty, they are likely to struggle at the bottom rungs of our economy and society, instead of fueling the growth of a robust middle class. And many face obstacles because—surprise of all surprises—they don't have the right degree.

The data shows, beyond a shadow of a doubt, that society today is more bifurcated than at any time in U.S. history since the eve of the Great Depression. In a country with a very unlevel playing field, college only serves to tilt this playing field further in favor of the rich. Children from well-off families have numerous advantages in the college admissions process: private K-12 schools that excel at college prep, after-school and standardized test tutors, expensive coaches for elite sports, enrichment programs, et cetera.

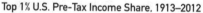

Top 1% U.S. Pre-Tax Income Share, 1913–2012

Source: Piketty and Saez, 2003 updated to 2012. Series based on pre-tax cash market income, including realized capital gains and excluding government transfers.

To compound the imbalance, colleges give explicit preference for legacy applicants, as well as implicit preference for children from families that can be big donors. In *Excellent Sheep*, William Deresiewicz's withering critique of U.S. higher education, he writes that our system of higher education "is exacerbating inequality, retarding social mobility, perpetuating privilege, and creating an elite that is as isolated from the society that it's supposed to lead—and even more smug about its right to its position—as the WASP aristocracy itself."[57]

Deresiewicz adds, "The numbers are undeniable. In 1985, 46 percent of students at the 250 most selective colleges came from the top quarter of the income distribution. By 2000, it was 55 percent. By 2006 (albeit in a somewhat smaller sample), it was 67 percent. Only 15 percent came from the bottom half that year; a slightly older study put the share of the bottom quarter at all of 3 percent." The more prestigious the school, the more unequal is its student body apt to be; Harvard, Yale, and Princeton, writes Jerome Karabel, "are still among the least economically diverse of the nation's major research universities." Public institutions, though, are not much better than the privates. As of 2004, 40 percent of students at the most selective state campuses came from families with incomes over $100,000, up from 32 percent just five years earlier."[58]

The tilting of the playing field isn't just about who gets into our colleges; it permeates all aspects of the experience of students while in college. To be blunt, the dividing line between the rich and the rest on college campuses today is painfully obvious and appalling. Poor kids have limited meal plans and rich kids dine sumptuously. Poor kids can't participate in study groups over dinner with well-off kids who frequent pricier dining spots. Many colleges offer more luxurious dorm rooms to families willing and able to pay more. Rich kids drive BMWs while poor kids walk or ride clunky bikes. When students move off campus (more and more prevalent after freshman year, as enrollments surge), rich kids live in nice apartments and the rest scramble to find substandard housing miles from campus.

Rich kids cruise through their college years with no concern about mounting debt, and no need for a job. Poor kids worry about getting and holding low-level hourly jobs to chip away at college expenses. Rich kids do glamorous internships (arranged through parental connections), while poor kids scramble for any kind of summer employment. And minority students find themselves dealing with the blatant prejudice of some of their peers. A recent op-ed in *The Harvard Crimson* demonstrates this appalling mindset; the author declares that she is a rich legacy, yet sermonizes, "Helping those with primarily low academic qualifications into primarily academic institutions makes as much sense as helping the visually impaired become pilots."[59]

Our colleges no longer level the economic playing field. You might hope that at least colleges excel at producing engaged and informed citizens. Even on the very modest goal of helping its graduates understand the importance of voting, we might hope that colleges are helping in a narrow respect to strengthen our social fabric. Historically, young Americans vote less frequently than older citizens, even though our youth have more at stake in elections about the future of our country. But how has this trended over time? In 1972, the turnout of young voters was about 75 percent of the turnout level of older voters. By 2012, participation rates for young Americans had declined substantially, falling to two-thirds the level of older Americans.[60] Yet, during this period, the percentage of young Americans with a college education soared, from roughly 20 percent to 33 percent.[61] The Campus Vote Project reports that well over a quarter of college students in the United States didn't vote in recent elections because "they did not know where or how to register or they missed the deadline."[62] So rising levels of college education haven't moved the needle in engaging young college-educated adults in our single most important democratic process—voting.

Arum and Roksa comment about the citizenship skills of recent college graduates, noting "a large proportion of college graduates were minimally engaged, with over 30 percent reporting that they read newspapers online or in print once a month or never, and almost 40 percent reporting that they discussed politics and public affairs with family and friends that infrequently."[63] And in *Generation on a Tightrope: A Portrait of Today's College Student*, Arthur Levine and Diane Dean report that 68 percent of students are not politically active or engaged, and 83 percent believe meaningful social change cannot be achieved through traditional American politics.[64]

While voting is an absolutely essential element of citizenship in a democracy, collaboration, communication, critical analysis, creative problem-solving, and problem formulation are even more important. If this list sounds familiar, it's because these are the same skills required for career readiness. The debate about whether colleges should focus on preparing students for careers or for citizenship engages in a false dichotomy. In this world, students need the same core set of critical skills, whether to pursue a career or contribute meaningfully to their community.

Some of our best small liberal arts colleges, where faculty are rewarded for excellent teaching rather than research, do a good job of teaching the skills that matter most for both work and citizenship. Additionally, some are working hard to create a more economically diverse student body, as a recent *New York Times* analysis shows.[65] However, these colleges enroll a tiny percentage of the nation's college population.

In its evaluation of general education requirements in one hundred leading colleges and universities, the American Council of Trustees and Alumni awarded 60 percent of them grades of C, D, and F. The council concluded the following: "What we found is alarming. Even as our students need broad-based skills and knowledge to succeed in the global marketplace, our colleges and universities are failing to deliver. Topics like U.S. government or history, literature, mathematics, and economics have become mere options on far too many campuses. Not surprisingly, students are graduating with great gaps in their knowledge—and employers are noticing. If not remedied, this will have significant consequences for U.S. competitiveness and innovation."[66]

Exploding Myths: The Value of a College Degree

At the beginning of this chapter, Bill Gates, the richest man in the world (which means he must be right), points out that the typical college grad will earn an incremental million dollars more over his or her lifetime compared to someone with just a high school degree. And of course many parents believe that their children won't get a big competitive advantage by attending a "lesser" university, so they push hard for the Harvards of the world.

But recent research suggests that students who graduate from the most highly selective schools do not have the competitive advantage that is widely assumed—even though they likely paid a great deal more for their degree. In a recent National Bureau of Economic Research Working Paper, Stacy Berg Dale and Alan Krueger conclude, "Students who attended more selective colleges do not earn more than other students who were accepted and rejected by comparable schools but attended less selective colleges."[67]

Stating that a college degree leads to an incremental $1 million in life-time earnings appears to be one of those myths that get reported over and over, but without much substantiation. A comprehensive study done by the Pope Center for Higher Education Policy found the earning power difference to be more like $150,000 for most colleges (up to $500,000 for a degree from an elite college).[68] But they point out that this study was based on data from a time when the costs of college were considerably lower.

We have already mentioned that most college-bound high school students are required to take calculus rather than statistics, even though no adult (other than high school calculus teachers) will ever use the calculus taught in high school. But if more of us had taken statistics, we'd understand the distinction between *causal* and *correlated*. So the critical question isn't whether a college degree is *correlated* with higher lifetime earnings (it clearly is); it's whether the degree, and the "education" behind it, actually *causes* graduates to learn and earn more.

Confused about *causal* and *correlated*? Don't worry—you've got lots of company. Here's an example that may help clear things up. You read a study that shows that almost all college squash players attended lots of classical music concerts as kids. The study concludes that listening to classical music when you're young is the key to becoming a college squash player. But do you buy this?

The "variables," or factors, in the study are "time spent listening to classical music up through age twelve" and "playing on your col-lege squash team." And, after collecting lots of data, the study shows that these two factors do indeed go together. That is, they are highly *correlated*. So, by and large, if you interview all college squash players in the United States, they listened on average to lots of classical music growing up. And if you could interview and track all kids in the United States today, those listening to lots of classical music will, years down the road, be far more likely to make their college squash teams.

But does classical music exposure as a child *cause* kids to become top squash players? Or do other factors—parents' income level, parents' education level, attending private schools, parental push—cause both? In this case, our instincts tell us that rich parents tend to take their kids to classical music concerts. And rich parents tend to expose their kids to squash early, fund squash lessons, drive kids to squash tournaments, put their kids in private schools that have squash teams, explain to kids that squash is very helpful in getting into an elite college, et cetera.

So while statisticians can draw on an impressive data set and sophisticated analyses to point to a very significant correlation between two variables (classical music exposure as a child and squash aptitude in college), don't be fooled. Listening to Bach won't help your squash backhand.

The pool of young adults who enter the workforce with just a high school degree tends to come from poor communities, facing a plethora of obstacles and disadvantages in life. And the pool of young adults who graduate from elite colleges generally come from well-educated, high-income families, with a huge running start in life. The differences we see in lifetime earnings for these pools are not due to the college learning experience, but to factors set well before the kids finish high school.

High school kids who get into our elite colleges are invariably smart, driven, and success-oriented. So equating these graduates with "high quality" is efficient. But make no mistake, they're not smart, driven, and success-oriented because they went to the elite school—they got accepted into the elite school because they are smart, driven, and success-oriented.

Young adults with a college credential have other real—though unmerited—advantages in the workplace. Many organizations require a college degree for certain positions or promotions. We often hear about high school grads who, after years of responsible and competent performance, are blocked within their organization from raises and promotions simply because they don't have the right college credential. This bias in the workplace translates into meaningful differentials of lifetime earnings for college grads, due strictly to bureaucratic organization policy.

Ted recently talked to a young man who had worked for years in a Sherwin-Williams paint store. By all measures, he was a spectacular employee—great with customers, knowledgeable about all aspects of the store's operation, strong financial skills, and dedicated and responsible. But he can't ever be promoted to store manager there, unless he gets his college degree.

We live in a world where people use the college credential as a time-efficient sorting tool—a way to "peg" a person. This societal prejudice brings lots of benefits to people with a degree from an elite college. They move to the top of the list for internships and interviews. They appeal to hiring managers for a whole suite of reasons. They get the benefit of the doubt every step of the way. As corporate consultant and human resources expert Jeff Hunter told Tony, "No one in HR ever got fired for hiring a Harvard kid." So in a very real sense, a credential from an elite university is a self-fulfilling prophecy. And parents, sensing these advantages, are desperate to give their children this lifetime advantage.

The good news is that these entrenched societal prejudices are beginning to crumble. Google for years interviewed only kids from elite universities with the highest GPAs and test scores. But when Laszlo Bock, senior vice president of People Operations, analyzed the data, he discovered that these indices were "worthless." He went on to say that the skills needed to succeed in an academic environment had little overlap with what's needed to succeed at Google. So Google no longer asks for an applicant's college transcript, and 15 percent of Google hires today don't have a college degree.[69] The word *college* doesn't even appear in its online guide to hiring.[70]

> Tony thought that Google might be unique in its changes to hiring practices until he was recently invited by Deloitte, the accounting and consulting firm, to speak to business leaders in Vietnam. He had lunch with their regional CEO, who told him, "We used to hire the best students from our best universities, but we've found out that they don't do so well. Now we look for good students from good colleges and invite them to a bootcamp where we observe how they solve problems collaboratively."

New research is starting to reveal that our college emperor has far less clothing than assumed. According to Brandon Busteed, executive director of Gallup Education, "Recent findings from the Gallup-Purdue Index—a massive study of more than 30,000 college graduates in the U.S.—show that few graduates are having experiences in college that are strongly linked to the long-term outcomes that matter most: a great career and great life afterward."[71]

Ben Castleman and Andrew Barr are leading economic and education researchers, with much of their research focused on the value of a college degree. We spoke at length to Castleman, who indicated that the evidence that a college education actually causes (instead of just being correlated with) higher lifetime earnings is "relatively thin."[72] He pointed to a couple of important factors in interpreting studies done on this topic. The studies generally look at averages and mask important variations. A student going to a high-quality college, with lots of support, and getting the most out of a well-chosen major, is likely to experience real, and causal, improvements in earning power. But for many other students, the return on college investment may be far less attractive.

Castleman also pointed out that these studies look at the relative difference between those with a college degree and those without. A big factor in this gap in the United States is that we don't invest in providing good alternatives to college for our young adults. In countries like Finland and Germany, some 45 percent of high school graduates choose not to go to college, but get advanced training in a trade and generally follow attractive career paths. In our country, it's often straight to McDonald's. (More on this subject in chapter 7.)

Here's a research project we'd like to see: Take two groups of comparable kids, give them very different educational experiences, and see what happens over their lifetimes. Consider the following experiment:

Path 1	Path 2
Every spare minute of a four-year high school period dedicated to crafting the perfect college application and/or drilling to improve standardized test performance	Normal, healthy high-school experience with lots of time for play, passion, and purpose

Path 1	Path 2
Four years of college.	Four years of internships and complementary learning experiences. Co-residing with other smart, driven kids. Lots of opportunity for engaged discussion with peers and adults. Periodic outside speakers and background reading.
A degree from an accredited college	Some form of respected alternative credential.
Total cost of $100,000 to $250,000	A four-year experience that doesn't cost much money on a net basis.

As we'll see in chapter 7, exciting and innovative developments now offer a different path forward for young adults. These options enable kids to acquire skills and character traits that lead to successful lives—whether measured by happiness, earning power, ability to make the world better, or informed citizenship—without the psychological and financial toll of Path 1.

PART III

MILLENNIAL INTERVIEWS
(with Tamara Day)

REBECCA

Rebecca was frustrated with high school. Frustrated with the busywork, frustrated with what she felt were arbitrary lesson plans. She grew up in an affluent neighborhood in Massachusetts where college was not only a given, it was in many ways the singular definition of success. "The summary of your worth is what school you get into," Rebecca told us. "Our major detriment is we've designed everything around what school you can get into rather than what niche in our economy you can participate in. That is an evolution since we decided as a nation that everyone should go to college. It used to be everyone should get a job."

Rebecca was a self-starter with extreme focus and tenacity. While in high school, she started her own nonprofit to combat child sex trafficking and was invited to give talks across the country. Over the next three years, she spoke to thousands of people around the globe. While she felt that she was building something exciting and valuable in the world, back at school, she felt bored by a curriculum that seemed to have little relevance to her life and the work she wanted to do. She saw herself as an entrepreneur who excelled at identifying problems and creating innovative solutions to solve them. That was the last thing, however, that high school wanted from her. "I didn't understand why I had to sit in school for eight hours, and not learn anything as efficiently as I could learn it myself, and then sit and do eight hours of homework that was basically just memorizing content," she said. Frustrated and disengaged, Rebecca ended up switching high schools halfway through and even contemplated dropping out.

It wasn't until she found a teacher that championed her creative spirit that things began to shift. With his support, she proposed extending her senior research project (which was supposed to last eight weeks) into her last six months of high school. In order to do this, though, she would have to drop all of her AP classes. Her high school fervently pushed back. They warned her that without taking the AP tests she would never get into a top-tier college. Defiantly, Rebecca wrote letters to the deans of admission at Harvard, Princeton, and Duke. She explained her research project and asked which they would find more valuable in a potential applicant, the AP courses or the research project. They responded unanimously that the research project would make her more competitive. Rebecca moved forward with her plan. She dropped her AP classes and immersed herself in her research project. "It was the best learning experience of my life," she told us. "It was my first exposure in school that involved something beyond the classroom. Go out and try to do something with others in the world."

When it came time to apply to colleges, Rebecca was hesitant. "I didn't want to go to school at that time at all. I was so happy learning and growing and wanted to build my nonprofit. I didn't understand why I would stop doing my nonprofit to go to school." To her community and her parents, though, not going to college seemed unthinkable. "We weren't on the same page," Rebecca told us. "We weren't even reading the same book."

Despite her reservations, Rebecca applied to Harvard, Princeton, Yale, and Duke. She was accepted to all four. She enrolled at Harvard in the fall of 2010 with a full scholarship. As with her high school experience, she was skeptical about what she would gain from earning her degree, but she was also optimistic that she could design an experience around what she wanted to learn.

Rebecca arrived at Harvard in 2010 hopeful that she could tailor her college experience. Shortly into her first semester, though, her concerns about academics began to resurface. She found the coursework irrelevant and felt like a lot of it was just busywork that wouldn't ever be applicable to real life. "Harvard, Princeton, Yale, Columbia are the main perpetrators in destroying our education system now," she told us. "The reason I say that is because they have glorified pure theory-based learning and have dirtied any sentiment of application-based learning, any knowledge that could translate to the real world. They've said that type of academic pursuit is not as 'pure,' 'whole,' 'fill-in-the-blank' as theory-based learning." She continued, "Schools need to stop teaching content because it's all going to be obsolete anyway. They should focus on teaching how to think and connecting the dots between theory and application."

The other nagging concern on Rebecca's mind was that her schoolwork was taking her away from doing the work that she really wanted to do. She found the structure and major requirements rigid and inflexible. She petitioned her university multiple times to be able to design her own major that focused on leadership and organizations. The university denied her requests. Rebecca felt frustrated by the lack of support and the pattern that she saw emerging. She thought, "You did this to Bill Gates, then you did this to Mark Zuckerberg. You have done this to every creative entrepreneur here. All we do is drop out with a bitter taste in our mouth. I am a better bet than my peer that's going to go to Wall Street. There are more and more entrepreneurs, and yes they're risky, but when they win big, they win bigger than everyone else."

Rebecca decided to sit in on a class at the Kennedy School, a school at Harvard that was exclusively for graduate students. She loved it. After class, she approached the professor and made a case for why he should let her enroll. He told her it wasn't possible, it had never been done before, but she was insistent. "I want to learn what you're teaching," she told him. It was in that professor's class that she ended up writing a business plan for what would become her own company. She envisioned designing a youth advisory board for Fortune 500 companies that could connect them with millennials in meaningful ways. To do this, she used experiences from her nonprofit and was, for the first time in school, able to address a real economic issue.

She decided that going forward, she would only take classes in the Kennedy School, Harvard Business School, or as independent study, where she found more creativity and freedom. However, she still needed to look like a sociology major, which meant that she was enrolled in five classes. Juggling so many things began to wear on her. She recalled, "I was so unhappy. I was running my nonprofit, building my company, raising money. I couldn't understand why I was doing busywork, doing something that had no relevance to my life. I didn't have time to do that work. I was physically a mess. I didn't want to see any of my friends. I was at a breaking point, going to bed at 2:30 a.m. getting up at 6:30 a.m. I was really depressed." Still, she was determined to get A's. If she did end up dropping out, she wanted to prove that her decision "wasn't because the curriculum was hard; it was because it was wrong."

Her mentor at the Kennedy School encouraged her to go build her company. Her parents insisted that she stay in school. It was a Harvard Business School trip to Silicon Valley that sealed her fate. Rebecca pitched her business proposal to a few key executives and ended up raising $150,000. "After that, I knew I was going to leave. I had a job; I had plenty of money."

Rebecca finished out her sophomore year and then finally did what she had wanted to all along: She dropped out of Harvard and went to work.

Two years after dropping out of Harvard, Rebecca sold her company at a large profit. She remains working there, dividing her time between Los Angeles, New York, and Boston, and is planning her next entrepreneurial venture. She forged her own pathway to success despite concerns from her parents and community. She has no regrets about dropping out of Harvard: "All it did was provide the network. I needed to be at Harvard because there was no other place where I could one-stop shop for the vast network I garnered while I was there. That's what mattered."

Rebecca has reflected a lot upon the value of her education and has strong ideas about the way in which the system is stunting and discouraging creative problem-solvers. "How many brilliant entrepreneurs are we missing because they've been told no so many times and their risk profile was harder than mine? We're shooting ourselves in the foot." Her concerns extend to the implications that our education system has for the future of our country. "If we continue to manufacture minds that are so stunted at the level of creativity and initiative that our 'best and brightest,' so we claim, are stunted coming out of Harvard, when my Harvard peers can't get a job because they are coming out of Harvard without a marketable skill, or when I wouldn't hire them as an employer and a believer that most of these people are smart, there is something wrong. When the rate is 60 percent going to Wall Street post–financial crisis, something is wrong." She has watched her classmates graduate and go straight into finance or consulting. The most envied of all positions is getting a job at Goldman Sachs or McKinsey. "That's what's prestigious, which is ridiculous. The relative value added to our economy from these jobs is so low compared with what those students could have been doing if they had been exposed and deepened in a particular skill set earlier on."

Rebecca is passionate about fostering environments where other serial entrepreneurs like herself can thrive. She observed, "If we can reach kids earlier and inspire them instead of pushing against them, maybe we could have hundreds of people who would try being entrepreneurs in their early twenties. Whether you're a born entrepreneur or not, these skills are something that everyone's going to need to have. It's not rocket science. When you have a problem, you need to think about different vantage points to solve it."

Ultimately, she believes we can do better. She sees school as being critical for developing empathy and teaching people to be creative problem-solvers. But instead of focusing on real learning and instilling the skills needed to succeed in a twenty-first-century economy, too often, the focus of educational institutions goes to money. Too often the default curriculum becomes rote memorization or drilling outdated standards. Education has become big business, and the priority on teaching skills or knowledge that is actually relevant to work and life has fallen away. "That's really convenient for them, one, because they've invested billions of dollars in these professors that would have nothing to do without their research, and two, the business model is brilliant. You graduate cohorts of students who are intellectually inspired, exploring different subjects, and narrowed into one that doesn't apply to any real-life skill set, so now they need to go to graduate school. Or maybe they'll go into the workforce that will teach them some marketable skills that they didn't have upon graduating. Ultimately, it creates a really convenient pipeline to get more money out of every student. That's the big win. That's an amazing machine."

CHAPTER 6

Teaching, Learning, and Assessing

Teaching

There's an old saying about lectures. A lecture is an event where the notes of the professor pass to the notebooks of the students without going through the brains of either.

The lecture is the workhorse of school instruction. It's how our great-grandparents were taught, how we were taught, and how most students are still taught. The teacher is the subject matter expert who presents material to students taking copious notes. Homework assignments foreshadow tests. Students rarely interact with one another; collaboration with classmates, certainly on tests, is called "cheating." The teacher may pause from time to time to ask students questions. Occasionally, a student asks a question. Often, that question is, "Will this be on the test?"

This model places large demands on our teachers. They have to hold students' attention for lecture after lecture, month after month. They need to know more about the subject than any student. In fielding questions, they need to provide authoritative responses and handle that one student who asks questions designed to embarrass.

In 1893, this lecture model made perfect sense. Students had no other option for acquiring information. Books and libraries were scarce, and the carrier pigeon was still used to transfer important information. Teachers were the definitive source of content. As our education system expanded throughout the twentieth century, the lecture model delivered material efficiently, at scale.

But today students have a vast array of resources at their fingertips. Almost any teacher, on his or her best day, is less effective in presenting material than the best online resource. A science teacher lecturing on black holes is compared to Caltech's Kip Thorne. Someone covering the Civil War competes against Ken Burns. A civics teacher lecturing on justice is up against Michael Sandel. And with mountains of new content posted online every minute, the bar for a teacher's in-class lecture gets higher by the day.

In 1893, students compared their teacher's lecture to a preacher's church sermon. Students in the 1920s contrasted their school experience to gathering around the radio listening to a static-filled broadcast of the Goodrich Silvertown Orchestra. Kids in the 1950s compared it to watching *Leave It to Beaver* on a grainy black-and-white television. And in the 1980s, the bar was still low: low-resolution video targeted mainly at adults or toddlers.

Today's kids live and breathe riveting content. Vivid horror movies or sci-fi thrillers in iMax theaters. Music that is no longer just aural but visually powerful, often provocative. YouTube comedy stars like Smosh and the Fine Brothers. Sports on HD television more real than being there. Addicting video games with stunning graphics. Teenagers now spend hours online watching other young gamers, like PewDiePie, playing video games . . . online. A teacher who can hold the attention of students for a class period, let alone a school year, is performing a minor miracle.

It's of modest academic interest to debate whether a student is better off being lectured by a real person, by an online video, or by a blend. The real question is whether any form of lecture-based education makes sense in today's world. And the evidence says it doesn't.

On the face of it, Joi Ito might seem an odd choice to head MIT's Media Lab, one of our university system's crown jewels. Ito didn't graduate from college. He dropped out. Twice. He started at Tufts, and concluded that the way computer science was taught made no sense. He rebooted at the University of Chicago, studied physics, but concluded that the coursework was largely about memorizing formulas. Ito hasn't done all that poorly in life. He was an early investor in several spectacular start-ups, including Flickr, Kickstarter, and Twitter. He currently sits on the boards of the Sony Corporation, the *New York Times*, the John S. and James L. Knight Foundation, and the John D. and Catherine T. MacArthur Foundation. And he directs one of the world's most innovative research labs.

Recently, Ito recruited a student volunteer to spend a week with sensors monitoring her brain activity. Ito found peaks of activity and troughs of passivity. Most people assume that the near-comatose pattern comes at night when the student is sleeping. But, no. The student's brain is in its most dormant state . . . during lectures.[1]

Sal Khan's views on lectures carry a certain irony. In 2006, he started Khan Academy, an online resource consisting of lectures and quizzes. From initially being used by his cousin, Khan's following has exploded. Each month, well over ten million people listen to his short lectures on math, physics, economics, computing, and art. It's conceivable that we'll reach a point in the future when U.S. kids spend as much time each year listening to this one man's lectures as they spend *in aggregate* listening to lectures from our other four million teachers.

So does Sal think lectures are a good way to learn? In his book *The One World Schoolhouse,* he reflects on his time as an MIT student: "The giant lecture classes were a monumental waste of time. Three hundred students crammed into a stifling lecture hall; one professor droning through a talk he knew by heart and had delivered a hundred times before. The sixty-minute talks were bad enough; the ninety-minute talks were torture. What was the point? Was this education or an endurance contest? Was anybody actually learning anything?" He continues:

> Be that as it may, we couldn't help noticing that many of the students who religiously attended every lecture were the same ones most desperately cramming the night before the exam. Why? The reason, it seemed to me, was that until the cramming phase they'd approached the subject matter only passively. They'd dutifully sat in class and let concepts wash over them; they'd expected to learn by osmosis, but it hadn't quite worked out because they'd never really engaged.[2]

So the most ubiquitous and most successful lecturer in the world thinks lectures are "a monumental waste of time." Content pushed on disengaged students is no better than watching the Home Shopping Network. Khan goes on in his book to describe his ideal education setting. Drawing on lectures would represent a small fraction of the student day, with plenty of time for things like collaboratively doing market simulations to learn economics; working in teams to design robots or develop smartphone apps; working on designs to improve energy efficiency; or working creatively on art, music, or writing projects. And in taking on these creative, unstructured initiatives, students draw on Khan Academy resources to help them accomplish their goals.

Scott Freeman of the University of Washington led a research team that explored 225 studies of undergraduate education. In the *Proceedings of the National Academy of Sciences,* they report that teaching methods that engaged students as active participants, not as passive listeners, "reduced failure rates and boosted scores on exams by almost one-half a standard deviation. The change in the failure rates is whopping."[3,4]

Innovations in Teaching

You've undoubtedly heard about whiz-bang technologies being deployed in our classrooms, especially in affluent schools. As they turn to SMART Boards, iPads, online courses, and flipped classrooms, it would appear our schools are on the cutting edge. These advances prompt some pundits to predict that it's just a matter of time before teachers are obsolete. But these "innovations" are all variants of ineffective passive education. Sure, it's easier to tee up cards on an iPad than have a teacher or tiger parent write them out on index cards. It's easier to have kids do multiple-choice quizzes online with instant feedback than to grade quizzes by hand. It's easier to plop students down in front of an online lecture where their brain waves go dead than to have them attend a live lecture . . . where their brain waves go dead. But passive is still passive.

Our colleague Eric Mazur recounted to us a conversation he once had with a person sitting next to him on a long flight. Seeing some papers that suggested her career involved education, he asked what she did professionally. She pulled out her laptop and showed him a slick application that her start-up was marketing to help kids drill for exams with electronic flash cards. He offered the view that several studies show kids don't retain information they study in this fashion. The education executive responded, "Oh, our goal isn't to help students learn. Our goal is to help them on their tests."

The history of online colleges provides evidence that lectures are ineffective, irrespective of how they are priced and delivered. Founded in 1976, the University of Phoenix is the granddaddy of online education. Its parent company, the Apollo Group, went public in 1994, reaching a market capitalization of $10 billion, with revenue peaking at $4.7 billion in 2011.[5] In "educating" hundreds of thousands of students, it has derived an astounding 90 percent of its revenue from federal student loans.[6] Recently, though, the University of Phoenix and its competitors have fallen on hard times, amid federal investigations of questionable loan practices and scant evidence that their degrees reflect developed competence.

In recent years, interest in online teaching surged to new levels of frenzy. The popular press fell in love with the MOOC (Massive Open Online Course), which sounds a bit like a branch of the CIA. In 2011, Sebastian Thrun, a tenured professor at Stanford University, made his artificial intelligence course available online, and sent out a note to a few friends and forums inviting anyone to sign up, whether enrolled at Stanford or not. He thought he might have a few hundred takers, maybe a thousand. But within weeks, 160,000 people around the globe registered for the course. His, and the world's, eyes were opened to a scalable model—Stanford-quality education . . . for millions . . . for free. And the gold rush was on. Thrun's company, Udacity, moved ahead with some $58 million of venture capital. Two other Stanford professors launched Coursera, raising $65 million in venture funding. Harvard and MIT took edX forward with $100 million of combined institutional support.

These MOOCs employed the same model: videos of "rock star" professors interspersed with multiple-choice quizzes testing recall of what you just heard. As they roared forward, major universities scrambled for a spot on the bandwagon. Early evangelists include all of our most selective universities—Stanford, MIT, and all eight Ivy League colleges. Eighty selective colleges now partner with Coursera. Some forty leading universities have joined the edX consortium. Top colleges, long regarded as our bastions of independent thought, are behaving a bit like . . . well, lemmings. Only a handful resisted the allure. Amherst declined joining edX, concerned that MOOCs "perpetuate the 'information dispensing' model of teaching."[7] But Amherst is the exception, not the rule.

These first-generation MOOCs are a cost-effective substitute for in-class lecture courses—bringing cost efficiencies to a failed model. Kids who learn little from lectures in the classroom can learn just as little watching online lectures from their room. And results to date for MOOCs have been dismal, with completion rates under 5 percent. The promise of democratizing education hasn't been realized, as some 80 percent of MOOC students come from the wealthiest sliver of our population.[8] And MOOC innovation has been caught up on low-level issues like monitoring keystroke patterns to prevent cheating. Sebastian Thrun, Udacity's CEO, offered an honest appraisal of first-generation MOOCs: "We were on the front pages of newspapers and magazines, and at the same time, I was realizing, we don't educate people as others wished, or as I wished. We have a lousy product."[9]

Education is now attracting some of our nation's most talented innovators. Don't sell them short. They are passionate about changing education, and will iterate, refine, and provide, over time, compelling offerings. But the experience to date underscores the need for real innovation, not a hodgepodge of electronic flash cards and canned lectures. In short:

The impact of innovation on education isn't in using technology to deliver obsolete education experiences. It lies in understanding what skills students need in the innovation era, and constructing classroom experiences that promote skills that matter.

THOUGHT EXPERIMENT

Visualize a student you know—a child, relative, family friend, or student. And picture her as an adult in a world where only the most gifted and passionate have successful careers. The rest cobble together a living through part-time gigs. Struggle to pay bills. Hold off on having a family because of financial worries. Never build savings. Can't retire at age sixty-five.

Now imagine this student with her own support team—resources that make her more productive than any adult was in 1980. With this productivity advantage, imagine what she can do—start a nonprofit, invent new products, discover cures, create dazzling art, contribute to her community or employer in myriad ways.

Today, motivated students can become experts on a topic in days, not weeks or years. They can find online the most compelling essays, lectures, videos, and forums. They can ask questions to people all over the world and get answers in minutes. They can ask "dumb" questions without risk of embarrassment. So what kind of classroom experience will be important to kids with this powerful support team? Sitting passively in a chair listening to someone lecture about content? Memorizing math formulas and science definitions? Memorizing names and dates of historical events? Worrying about the placement of accent marks when writing in a foreign language? These century-old classroom tasks are obsolete, and—other than inertia—there's no reason for students to drill endlessly on things when, in the very best case, they'll be "almost as good as a smartphone."

While innovation poses challenges, it creates breathtaking opportunities. Our education system needs to help kids accelerate their potential in the innovation era, not hold them back. With well-designed pedagogy, we can empower kids with critical skills and help them turn passions into decisive life advantages. The role of education is no longer to teach content, but to help our children learn—in a world that rewards the innovative and punishes the formulaic.

Learning

We often ask educators, "Do you think your purpose is to teach students, or to help them learn?" We like to ask this, even though (or maybe because) we invariably get puzzled looks in return. Most educators think that "teaching" and "helping students learn" are synonymous. But, as we shall see, they are often worlds apart. Today, almost all "learning" done by students in our schools is more myth than reality. It's all about short-term memorization, with modest retention at best.

Studies done by Washington University researchers underscore the transient nature of memorization-based "learning." Henry Roediger and Mark McDaniel are cognitive scientists who have dedicated their academic careers to the study of learning and memory. In *Make It Stick*, they report that over 80 percent of college students study by reading and rereading textbooks to memorize content. The authors argue that this approach "has three strikes against it. It is time consuming. It doesn't result in durable memory. And it often involves a kind of unwitting self-deception, as growing familiarity with the text comes to feel like mastery of the content. The hours immersed in rereading can seem like due diligence, but the amount of study time is no measure of mastery." They point out, "In very short order we lose something like 70 percent of what we've just heard or read."[10]

ALTERNATIVES TO THE LECTURE METHOD

The backbone of education in many of the country's leading independent schools is the Harkness method. It was first developed at Phillips Exeter Academy with a gift from oil magnate Edward Harkness in 1930.[11] The ideal is that students and the teacher engage in Socratic discussion in small groups, often around a table. Students form and articulate their own points of view, respond to classmates, and learn to ask good questions and think critically. At its best, the Harkness method is a powerful vehicle for engaging students, helping them develop critical skills, and elevating the education process.

More often than not, though, the Harkness classrooms we've observed fall short. The teacher usually drives the discussion and asks all the questions. In the "discussions," students are playing "guess what's on the teacher's mind" in a hub-and-spoke model, instead of forming and defending their own views. People often wonder why research on class size doesn't show learning improvements in smaller classes, and the answer is simply this: You can as easily lecture fifteen students as fifty—even if you don't call it lecturing.

Even under ideal circumstances, with a dozen students in an hour class, each student speaks for just a few minutes during each period. Kevin Mattingly, dean of faculty for Lawrenceville School, notes, "An adolescent doesn't learn by listening. To really learn, a student needs to be constantly thinking, articulating points of view, and responding to and asking great questions." It's not easy for a teacher to step back and let students control the discussion. But students thrive in settings where their opinion matters and they engage in meaningful debate.

Many people credit Sal Khan with originating the concept of "flipping the classroom." Some teachers have their students watch his lectures at home, and then work on the corresponding multiple-choice questions in class the next school day, getting help as needed. The classroom is "flipped": lectures at home, and "homework" at school. This change, while a modest advance in efficiency, falls far short of the degree of innovation we urgently need.

A pioneer in profoundly "flipping classrooms" is Eric Mazur, area dean of Applied Physics at Harvard. Eric's work on learning is as insightful as any research done around the globe. His classroom hardly resembles the typical college science class. It centers around thought-provoking questions, peer-driven learning, and hands-on projects. During class, students can take on questions like:

An example of a ConcepTest.

Consider a rectangular metal plate with a circular hole in it.

When the plate is uniformly heated, the diameter of the hole

1. increases.
2. stays the same.
3. decreases.

After a few minutes of independent thought, students answer the question individually. The class is then dynamically reconfigured into small groups of students with differing answers. Then, they have several minutes to persuade others as to why they're right. Students resubmit their responses and the class is reassembled, and a few students make their best case for each response. The entire time, Mazur walks around observing but saying nothing—no answers, no hints, no suggestions. Letting the students struggle is a big part of Eric's approach.

We sat in on a talk Eric gave at Google's R&D Center in Cambridge, Massachusetts, to an audience comprised of some of our nation's top technical talent. To illustrate his pedagogy, Eric had participants (with long histories of acing science courses) consider the metal plate question. Given three choices, the distribution of responses was almost a perfect one-third, one-third, one-third. Completely random. But the energy level in the room was electric. Eric noted that if he had lectured on the coefficient of thermal expansion, eyelids would have drooped. Instead, everyone engaged in spirited discussion, as it dawned on "students" that, despite their advanced STEM (science, technology, engineering, and math) degrees, they didn't understand an important aspect of physics that plumbers and electricians know like the back of their hands.

Mazur's classes show the power of the methods described in his book *Peer Instruction: A User's Manual.* We've observed classes where less than 10 percent of the students have the correct initial answer for a Concep-Test. Yet, the student-driven discussion clarifies their thinking and inevitably leads most students to figure it out. In the process, students hone a range of critical skills: forming independent opinions, critically evaluating the logic of others, communicating, collaborating, solving problems creatively, and synthesizing.

During part of Mazur's course, students work in teams on projects. For example, they create, design, and implement a Rube Goldberg contraption, build a musical instrument, plan a mission to Mars, or devise a way to use electrostatics to clean up the environment. In the process, they learn to collaborate as they generate and critique creative solutions to complex problems. These projects bear little resemblance to typical recipe-driven science labs.

In his courses, Mazur tracks students' progress in their conceptual understanding of the physical universe (which is, after all, the point of physics), with striking results. With his peer-driven approach, students show dramatic gains in their conceptual understanding, particularly in contrast to students taught conventionally. And the penalty they pay in performance on more conventional tests of narrow and procedural problem-solving? They actually improve on these measures as well. Mazur comments, "Apparently, and perhaps not surprisingly, a better understanding of the underlying concepts leads to improved performance on conventional problems."[12] And, in stark contrast to lecture courses, students in his classes are having fun, developing a love of science.

Contrast Mazur's class with the typical introductory college physics course, where a professor lectures hundreds of students and tests their ability to plug numbers correctly into memorized formulas. The experiences are night and day. In mainstream science classes, students learn little, retain less, and exit the class with no real understanding of how the world works. Hardly an inspiring way to teach science, and small wonder that so few students end up with STEM degrees.

Mazur gets two complaints about his class. Parents wonder why Harvard charges $60,000 per year for courses with a professor who doesn't lecture. And some students say, "Professor Mazur didn't teach us anything. We have to learn it all ourselves." And that's the point.

We can hear critics saying, "Well, this fellow Mazur sounds unusual.

Maybe his approach works with intelligent, motivated Harvard students. But his class sounds like one of those 'lightning in a bottle' things, not really for the rest of the world."

Ten thousand miles away in India, Akshay Saxena and Krishna Ramkumar started Avanti Fellows to help low-income children access high-quality education. [Full disclosure: Ted is a supporter of Avanti.] They offer dirt-cheap after-school programs in chemistry, physics, and math, with pedagogy based on Mazur's approach. Being highly entrepreneurial, they've enticed retired professors and volunteer students in India to help them construct an extensive library of ConcepTests. Students work collaboratively in small groups, debate concepts, and master the material. So much so that Avanti students taking the Indian Institute of Technology entrance exam (probably the world's hardest entrance exam) score over an order of magnitude higher than the national average—a whopping 40 percent success rate versus less than 1 percent nationally.

These results are stunning, but not as stunning as one of their other discoveries. With scarce budget dollars, Avanti can't afford good teachers. Initially, their students were placed in learning centers with the best teachers they could hire. In centers where they couldn't attract teachers, they hired social workers with no STEM background. They were shocked to find that the students helped by social workers outperformed the students with teachers. How, in a million years, could that be the case? Saxena explained in a recent conversation:

> Teachers, irrespective of how good they are, all want to teach. They assume a certain student level—often skewed towards either the top or bottom of the class—and then lecture to this group. We've found that most students gain very little from the time they spend listening to lectures. The only option our social workers have is to let the group struggle to understand the material. And when we were able to get experts in the classroom a few times a month, every minute of their time was used clarifying misconceptions and not teaching. Where the social workers helped our students most was with their problems outside of the classroom, which for low-income kids in India is the most important thing an adult can do for them.

Avanti's learning centers use minimal technology. ConcepTests are presented on sheets of paper. Students write their answers with old-fashioned pencils. No SMART Boards, iPads, or one-laptop-per-child. Some learning centers offer a few aging computers with Internet access so students can dig for relevant online resources. But the innovation behind Mazur and Avanti's approach isn't using technology to do what's always done, but completely reimagining the classroom to help students learn science and develop essential skills in the process.

On a recent trip to India, Mazur visited the Avanti Learning Centers and saw their peer-driven pedagogy in action. In describing what he saw, he uses superlatives like "Absolutely amazing. Mind-blowing." He explained, "I went to see one of these classrooms in Mumbai. You have to imagine forty kids cramped together, shoulder to shoulder." Avanti uses almost no technology. Students raise color cards depending on the answer that they choose. The instructor then tells them, "Turn to your neighbor." Mazur notes that the instructor "has no idea what the question is or what the right answer is. She would not be able to explain it. Kids start talking, you see this chaos, and then they raise their flash cards again and you see an overwhelming shift to the correct answer." If there are unresolved issues, students see a short video of the instructor explaining the right answer. If some students still don't get it, the instructor asks if any other student can help clear things up. Only then do they note a lack of clarity and send a question to main headquarters for further explanation. Mazur notes that this experience really made him rethink his view that the teacher needs to be far more expert than the most advanced student, as Avanti's centers show just the reverse. "It's really very encouraging."[13]

While the current generation of online offerings has been underwhelming, there are some amazing online courses. Several years ago, Ted's daughter took an inspiring history course offered by Virtual High School with a class of some thirty high school students from all over the country. The "teacher" was an adult supervisor who monitored the forums, but never lectured. The course revolved around intriguing propositions. In one assignment, students read original journals, diaries, and newspaper accounts of the early explorers of Northern Canada—Frobisher, Baffin, and Hudson. They then took on the question, "Were these explorers heroes?" They had to form their own position, articulate it in an essay posted online, read everyone else's contribution, and engage in online debate. The "teacher" observed the forum, made occasional suggestions to students about the importance of being constructive and civil, and pointed out when a question hadn't been fully addressed.

In this online class, each student's work was public. By the end of the course, the class forum was active from before dawn to well past midnight. Because the course was strictly online, social status was invisible—a shy kid with shabby clothes was on a level playing field with an outgoing cheerleader driving a BMW. Students were motivated by peer reaction and intrinsic curiosity, not by the teacher's grade. And the grade given each student was superfluous. By the end of the course, all participants knew who had excelled, having been immersed in so many peer-driven exchanges.

Contrast this VHS online course with a typical history class, with a teacher lecturing on a topic no one cares about. Students take multiple-choice tests to assess their recall of the facts. Occasionally, they write formulaic essays, read only by the teacher. And even though this traditional class focuses on covering facts, students don't remember them. Ironically, students in the VHS program are more likely to remember facts about this period of history because they immersed themselves in it. The mind of an engaged kid is a sponge; a mind that is lectured to is a leaky sieve.

Lynn Stein, associate dean of Olin College, describes the vast majority of coursework as "just in case" education. Students memorize facts and low-level content just in case they remember it, and just in case they ever need it. And almost always, they don't and won't. Her innovative college focuses on "just in time" education—where students get good at learning content and mastering concepts as a means to completing ambitious projects, understanding complex real-world problems, or answering challenging questions.

The opportunity for our education system is to use content, concepts, and real-world phenomena to help our kids develop critical skills and inspire them to pursue challenging career paths. Whether it's a well-implemented Harkness method, an online course on North American explorers, an innovative physics class at Harvard, or learning centers for low-income kids in India, these approaches share core pedagogical principles. Students:

- attack meaningful, engaging challenges
- have open access to resources
- struggle, often for days, and learn how to recover from failure
- form their own points of view
- engage in frequent debate
- learn to ask good questions
- collaborate
- display accomplishments publicly
- work hard because they are intrinsically motivated

We're encouraged by the innovations we see in learning, but these inspiring examples remain outliers. Everything about mainstream education in the United States works against innovation in our classrooms, discouraging our teachers and impairing the futures of our youth. As we shall soon see, our educrats' compulsion to assess every aspect of school, and hold our teachers accountable, will—unless reversed—be our nation's downfall.

Assessment

Throughout history, informed assessment has been the key to determining whether a student has mastered important competencies and integral-to-meaningful learning. Expert craftsmen assessed and guided the training of apprentices. Our Boy Scouts and Girl Scouts use evidence of competence as a means of awarding merit badges and ranks. Our businesses, the envy of the world, make effective decisions on personnel based on collective evaluation of an individual's contributions. And, historically, caring teachers assessed the work of their students. These forms of assessment shared certain principles: trust, a personal connection, an alignment between assessments and purpose, and use of evidence. And they weren't constrained by the need to rank an individual's performance, precisely, against millions of others. Done right, learning and assessing are two sides of the same coin.

Today, assessment in our schools has become the bitter enemy of learning. It is perverting the school agenda. It is killing curiosity and motivation. It is driving our best teachers from the profession. Assessment in our schools has become the single biggest threat to our nation's long-term national security. It is corroding our nation's education and society in the same way invasive species like kudzu or snakehead fish drive healthy species from our environment.

The multiple-choice bubble test wasn't originally designed for school. During World War I, Robert Yerkes, a strong proponent of IQ testing, convinced the U.S. army to let him design a mass test of intelligence for incoming recruits. One of Yerkes's assistants, Carl Brigham, continued this work after the war, modifying it for the purpose of evaluating college applicants. It was first given to a few thousand students in 1926, at a time when our elite colleges were entirely for the upper class.

In 1933, the president of Harvard, James Bryant Conant, courageously pushed to broaden his entering class beyond elite East Coast private boarding schools. He asked his staff to find a test to determine which non-elite scholarship students Harvard should accept. They turned to Brigham's Scholastic Aptitude Test. By 1938, all members of the College Board were using it to test scholarship applicants. By 1942, it was extended to all applicants. The Educational Testing Service was established in 1948 to design these tests for the College Board, and our education landscape would never be the same.[14]

Brigham and his test-designing colleagues held repugnant views on race and intelligence. Brigham said, "Our figures would rather tend to disprove the popular belief that the Jew is highly intelligent," and he described the arrival of African Americans to the United States as "the most sinister development in the history of this continent."[15] It's unfair to associate today's test industry with the century-old views of its founder. Yet the data remain clear that these assessments play to the strengths of kids raised in affluent (generally white and Asian) households.[16]

Average SAT Scores, by Race and Ethnicity, 2012

Group	Reading	Mathematics	Writing
American Indian	482	489	462
Asian American	518	595	528
Black	428	428	417
Mexican American	448	465	443
Puerto Rican	452	452	442
Other Latino	447	461	442
White	527	536	515

SAT: Student Affluence Test

Average scores on each section of SAT (and combined) by parental income

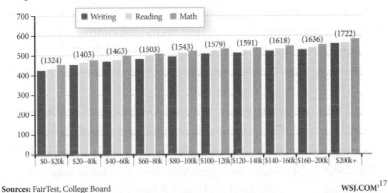

Sources: FairTest, College Board   WSJ.COM[17]

As we've written elsewhere, we believe these patterns would evaporate if we had a way to test traits like resilience, resourcefulness, or perseverance.[18] But, of course, you can't rank-order character traits. So instead of focusing on characteristics that matter, we turn to narrow skills that can be tested. We're a bit like the drunk who loses his keys at night in some distant location, but looks for them under a streetlight since it's a place where he can see. And people who should know better, like Harvard professor of psychology Steven Pinker, argue that the *sole* criteria elite schools should use in selecting their incoming classes is standardized test performance.[19]

The standardized test industry has sprawled to include alternatives to

the SAT (the ACT), subject-matter tests (AP, SAT subject tests), professional school admissions tests (LSAT, MCAT, GRE), and ubiquitous state
standardized tests required by the No Child Left Behind Act—seeping
into every nook and cranny of our schools. There seems to be no limit
to which aspects of school the education industry feels need to be tested.

An executive search professional recently related to us an experience she
found shocking. A money management firm had retained her services
to find a senior executive to manage one of its funds. Its leading candidate had a two-decade track record of unprecedented success, had done
exceptionally well in the interviews, and was close to getting an offer.
Toward the end of the process, though, the employer's human resources
representative requested the candidate's SAT scores, and panicked when
the scores were average. The firm rejected the candidate, prompting the
search executive to say, "We thought we had seen it all . . ."

People believe that test scores are important indicators of academic capability, intelligence, a person's intrinsic worth, parenting skills, a school's quality, or a nation's competitiveness. But they're not. Like kudzu or snakehead
fish, they've taken over our education ecosystem. And those who weigh these
scores so heavily generally don't understand how these tests are designed.

THE LEGENDARY "BELL CURVE"

The SAT is *not* designed to determine whether a student has mastered
important or essential skills. It is designed to generate a bell curve of
results. We're guessing this is a bit confusing because it's likely you—like
almost everyone going through our school system—never took statistics.
The bell curve is a distribution that can be found occasionally in nature.
For instance, the distribution of heights for adult females or males in our
country looks like this:[20]

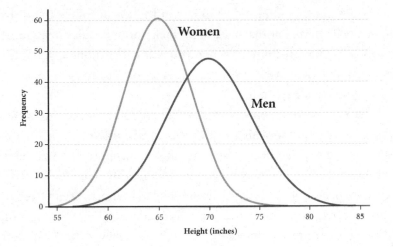

Adult heights for each gender cluster around an average (5'5" for women and 6' for men). As you move further from the average (or mean), you find fewer and fewer outlying data points (people that are extremely tall or short). There's a hairball formula for the bell curve that produces curves with the right shape, telling us things like 68 percent of the population falls within one standard deviation of the mean.[21] But for now, it's okay to note that these curves are shaped like a "bell." We emphasize that the plot above reflects the actual heights of people.

Normal Curve

Standard Deviation

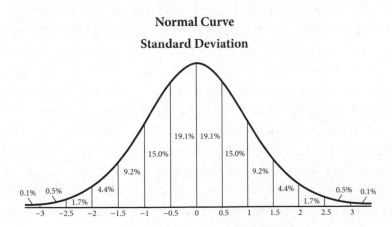

Chart prepared by the NY State Education Department

Besides heights, a few other things in the world follow the distribution of a bell curve. For instance, the velocity of molecules in an ideal gas conforms to this distribution. When you really dig, though, you find that this "normal" distribution really isn't all that normal, and only a few natural phenomena adhere to it.

What's so interesting about the bell curve's role in standardized tests is that it doesn't reflect anything real. *It was chosen arbitrarily by the College Board.* As the College Board itself explains in a report, "So we chose the normal distribution for its symmetry and familiarity. We did *not* choose it because we believe ability is normally distributed [italics in original report]."[22] In other words, the performance scores for students taking the test conform to this shape because a group of Princeton, New Jersey, statisticians decided they liked its look. We'll make the "intelligence," or "aptitude," or "SAT-ness" of our kids look like the heights of adults.[23] We'll have a relatively small number of really dumb and really smart kids, and clump everyone else in the middle. Meanwhile, the rest of us trust that these statisticians know what they're doing, since of course they have PhDs from elite universities.

So here's how these tests are constructed to produce a bell curve distribution. Test designers play with the range of difficulty of a set of questions, as well as how many questions to include in each section. To ensure that few kids end up at the bottom of the distribution, each section includes some really easy questions. Obscure, tricky, or advanced questions are used to thin things out on the high end. To further spread the distribution, they pack in enough questions that many kids will make errors because of time pressure—either by rushing or by not getting to some of the questions. They refine and tune the mix of questions until they get the right distribution, and then roll the test out nationally to millions of kids, whose futures are on the line. And, *voilà*: The results form a bell curve.

What does this shape mean in practice? The good news is that very few kids get a score telling them "You're dumb as a fence post," since only a tiny percentage of scores are near numerical rock bottom. The narrowing of the tail at the upper end means very few students get scores at the high end of the numeric range. And this forced distribution means that for students near either tail, small differences in aggregate test scores translate into large differences in their SAT numeric scores. Missing a few questions can send your score tumbling from the 700s to the 600s—a drop parents assume will cost their child any chance of getting into an elite college. Economists describe the way this dynamic plays out as Prisoner's Dilemma. All kids would be better off taking a relaxed approach to these tests, but when some engage in intense preparation, others are forced to choose between two suboptimal outcomes: waste lots of time preparing, or deal with a demonstrably lower score.

The building blocks of the SAT are short questions, half math and half verbal, each answerable in less than sixty seconds. If you're like us, you took the SAT so long ago that you're hazy on the details. You probably still associate certain words, like *noxious*, *officious*, and *nefarious*, as SAT words—words seldom if ever used in daily conversation, but essential to scoring well on these tests. To prepare for these tests, kids practice questions like:

There is no doubt that Larry is a genuine _____: he excels at telling stories that fascinate his listeners.
    a. braggart
    b. dilettante
    c. pilferer
    d. prevaricator
    e. raconteur

Before escaping the SAT verbal section, you encounter several reading passages, some clear and some cryptic. Part of the challenge is understanding the passage, but a big part of the challenge is taking on head-scratching questions like:

The author's tone in this passage is best characterized by the adjective:
    a. bold
    b. ontogenous
    c. perfidious
    d. voracious
    e. audacious

To parse through these questions, you need a broad vocabulary and the ability to shut down creative ways of interpreting an essay.

When you finally feel like you've found your sea legs on the verbal section, you put down your pencil, take a short break, and head into math-land. There, you'll need to whiz through bunches of short procedural micro-problems like:[24]

If $x > 1$ and $\dfrac{\sqrt{x}}{x^3} = x^m$, what is the value of m?

    (A) $-\dfrac{7}{2}$

    (B) -3

    (C) $-\dfrac{5}{2}$

    (D) -2

    (E) $-\dfrac{3}{2}$

These questions give you a sense of why the SAT is only loosely correlated with anything of consequence, and why mastering the SAT doesn't equate to mastering an important life skill. When was the last time you used the word *raconteur* in your daily conversation? Does coming up with the right cookie-cutter answer about the author's tone reflect anything important? When is the last time you had to solve for the exponent in a higher-order expression?

Time pressure plays a big role in a student's test performance. Yet how often in life are we given forty-five minutes to complete a life-shaping task? In the world of Frederick Winslow Taylor, the industrial engineering pioneer who pushed for enforced standardization of behavior to wring every ounce of efficiency from an assembly line, time constraints mattered. But Taylor is dead, and so is the assembly line. Yet our kids live with the time pressure of these high-stakes tests. Unless, of course, they belong to one of the growing number of affluent families who game the system by investing the resources required to get their child eligible for extended time. The Government Accounting Office study reported that the cost to obtain an exemption runs between $500 and $9,000.[25]

We should see these tests for what they are. Students, under enormous stress, scramble to solve lots of small problems quickly—problems that have almost no connection to life. Even studies performed by the College Board itself conclude that the main value of the SAT is a modest ability to help predict first-year college GPA. That's it.[26]

We'd bet our collective bottom dollars that Sudoku and the *New York Times* Sunday crossword puzzle would be every bit as effective as the SAT math and verbal tests in predicting success in college or career. These puzzles test vocabulary breadth and narrow cognitive skills. If we used puzzles to determine life outcomes, at least the test prep might be fun. And if colleges and employers relied on fun puzzles, instead of SAT scores, society might stop viewing these tests as meaningful reflections of a child's worth.

Imagine if our statisticians hadn't locked in on a bell curve for our standardized tests. Suppose they started by saying, "We'll present students with questions reflecting what we expect competent college students to be able to do. We'll take time pressure off the table and give most test-takers adequate time to complete the test and check their work. And we'll avoid tricky 'gotcha' questions that serve no purpose other than to generate a bell curve distribution." They might structure the test with just three possible scores:

In Good Shape: Nothing about your ability to perform a narrow set of cognitive skills will hold you back in life or impair your ability to complete the work required by a good college.

It Won't Be Easy: Based on how you performed these narrow cognitive skills, aspects of college will require above-and-beyond dedication.

Think Different: Cognitive skills aren't your thing. We'd encourage you to think boldly about life paths that play to your noncognitive strengths.

This scoring approach—no more arbitrary than a bell curve—would completely change the role of standardized tests in society. By reporting only coarse distinctions, scores would legitimately reflect the extent to which SAT test scores predict anything. Sure, kids in the "In Good Shape" category would, on average, have very different life outcomes from those in the "Think Different" pool. But we'd completely eliminate the absurd assumption that a kid who spends a huge amount of time and money on prep to get a score of 760 has any real edge over a kid who can't afford test prep and scores a 630. We could easily argue that the first kid, who docilely follows parents' insistence to drill for months on mind-numbing content, is actually losing his or her entrepreneurial spirit along the way— impairing life prospects.

In the "true confessions" department, Tony was never a good test-taker and scored in the low 500s on his SATs. His Miller Analogies Test score—which was then the only test required to get into the Harvard Graduate School of Education—was similarly mediocre. He was probably admitted because he was a published author by then. But it is not clear that he'd be admitted now, with the increased and more stringent test requirements. (Incidentally, his lowest grade while completing a master's and doctorate at Harvard was an A-. So much for the predictive validity of low test scores!)

In this three-outcome universe, test prep would be irrelevant for most test-takers. Colleges would get the information they should care about. Almost no student would take the test more than once. The pressure and the stakes around these tests would disappear. So who could possibly lose if we moved to more reasoned scoring?

The annual revenue generated by the standardized test preparation industry is roughly $4 billion.[27] The revenue generated by the consortiums of ACT, the College Board, and the Educational Testing Service is comparable in magnitude. This industry actively lobbies federal and state legislatures.[28] With billions of dollars on the line, there are powerful entrenched interests arguing that, in fact, minuscule differences in test scores should be reported, craved, and chased, costing millions of families time, money, and sanity.

In recent years, the ACT has overtaken the SAT in terms of annual tests administered. The ACT is less memorization-based and, in a narrow sense, is a better test. Responding to competitive pressure, the College Board is making the SAT more ACT-like. But in the end, these differences won't turn a snakehead fish into a valued species. As long as these tests are administered on the scale of millions, with robotic questions tailored to robotic grading, and with stakes that far exceed substance, they will remain the enemy of true education.

Advanced Placement (AP)

The Advanced Placement tests were originally championed by our elite private schools to demonstrate to colleges their advanced level of study. But as AP tests became a major revenue driver for test organizations, they took on a life of their own. Designed by bulky committees, heavily dominated by college professors concerned that every speck of precious content get its due, AP exams expanded from a mile wide and an inch deep to ten miles wide and 1/100 of an inch deep. AP world history covers from 8000 BCE to the present. AP biology spans microscopic biological systems to evolution. AP art history covers from ancient to present art, across all continents except — in an admirable display of restraint— the Antarctic. Like any smart business proliferating its product line, the College Board now offers almost forty AP courses and exams, with its $89 test fees contributing substantially to revenue and income.

A number of our top private high schools and some of our most forward-thinking public high schools have dropped AP courses, recognizing that superficial content coverage is antithetical to real learning. And that leaves most of our public and lagging private schools to pick up the AP pieces. Highly regarded public school districts like Wellesley, Massachusetts, do their best to warn families off of AP. A Wellesley parent with education expertise told us, "It was amazing to observe. The chair of the biology department advised parents against enrolling their kids in AP biology. Yet the AP class was crammed, since parents believe that a student who doesn't take the school's AP class (even though the Level 1 biology class is equally 'rigorous') will be penalized severely in the college application process." And they will.

A few years ago, Dartmouth College had incoming freshmen who had scored a 5 on the AP psychology Exam take the final from Dartmouth's introductory psych course. Ninety percent failed. Perhaps even more telling, students who failed the final and then enrolled in the class performed no better than students who hadn't taken AP psychology.[29]

In several productive conversations we had with some of the senior leadership of the College Board, including Trevor Packer, who is head of the AP program, and David Coleman, the College Board's new president, it was clear that they recognize many of the problems with the current generation of tests. Some of the Advanced Placement tests and course syllabi are being rewritten as we write this. But we know that, in the case of the APs, the College Board has run into tremendous resistance from committees of college professors who want to continue to see more academic content knowledge tested and taught. (Read Eric Mazur's experience below.) The vested interests that want the same content knowledge taught and the perfect bell-shaped curve produced stand in the way of meaningful reform.

Tony proposed to David Coleman that as an experiment David poll students, after taking AP courses, to find out if they have more or less interest in the subject after having been tested. (In our experience, most students never want to take any course like the AP again!) David seemed eager to conduct this experiment, and we are looking forward to seeing the results!

Eric Mazur spent several years on the AP physics Advisory Board, where he pushed, and eventually convinced, them to pilot the use of conceptual questions on the exam. They did, but concluded they couldn't use them, since the pool of students who did well on conceptual questions did not correlate well with the pool who did well on questions that involve manipulating formulas. So the AP physics exam continues to be anchored on competencies that have nothing to do with being a world-class scientist, providing further evidence that standardized tests tell us nothing about someone's creative problem-solving, conceptual insight, or ability to design and implement effective experiments.

John Tierney, former government professor at Boston College, wrote in *The Atlantic*, "Fraudulent schemes come in all shapes and sizes. To work, they typically wear a patina of respectability. That's the case with Advanced Placement courses, one of the great frauds currently perpetrated on American high-school students."[30] Tierney, who taught at BC for some twenty-six years, concludes that AP courses represent "a kind of mindless genuflection to a prescribed plan of study that squelches creativity and free inquiry. The courses cover too much material and do so too quickly and superficially. In short, AP courses are a forced march through a preordained subject, leaving no time for a high-school teacher to take her or his students down some path of mutual interest. The AP classroom is where intellectual curiosity goes to die."[31]

State Standardized Tests

Recent education policy has been shaped by a complete lack of trust. The business leaders who influence education feel that teachers, as a group, can't be trusted to evaluate one another or their students. Much of this mistrust stems from the visceral dislike business leaders have for unions. Their thinking goes as follows: If someone has a job for life after just three years of service (not exactly the case in our public schools, but not far off), and there are outrageous examples of teachers abrogating their responsibilities (and there are some), we need to ensure accountability, no matter what.

And the accountability snowball has grown and grown as it—along with our education system—careens downhill. As we continued to post mediocre international standardized test scores, the calls for accountability grew shriller. With bipartisan support, the U.S. Congress enacted landmark legislation, No Child Left Behind, signed into law in 2002 by President George W. Bush. This initiative, at times referred to as "No Child Left Inspired," has failed entirely at its stated goal of improving test scores. But rather than question the basic approach, the accountability voices only grew stronger. In 2008, Barack Obama swept into office on a wave of idealism and a shared belief in our ability to work together as a community. These values didn't quite reach his Department of Education, though, which quickly ratcheted up national priority on test-based teacher accountability through its Race to the Top initiative.

These policy botches have turned education upside down. It is all about the numbers, and nothing about real learning or meaningful assessment. The choice we made? Fill our classroom hours with shallow learning we can readily test, and then drill, baby, drill. If the covered wagon isn't going fast enough, whip the mule train even harder. And if we lose a few teachers along the way, so be it—even if they're some of our very best. So award-winning teachers like Ron Maggiano, a revered social studies teacher at West Springfield High School in Fairfax County, Virginia, resigned after a thirty-three-year career, writing in his letter of resignation:

> Now more than three decades later, I have just spent my last day as a teacher. I resigned my teaching position because I can no longer cooperate with the standardized testing regime that is destroying creativity and stifling imagination in the classroom. I am sad, angry, hurt, and dismayed by what has happened to education and to the teaching profession that I so dearly love.[32]

Valerie Strauss of the *Washington Post* wrote a column a few years ago about a longtime school board member in Florida who took the tenth-grade Florida Comprehensive Assessment Test (FCAT). This man is a senior executive of a $3 billion company, widely respected in his community, and has a BS and two master's degrees. He did what every school board member and state and national legislator should do: took the tests that they require all students to pass to graduate, and which are used to evaluate teacher performance.

He reports that he guessed on every math question, and only got *10 out of 60 correct*. He did better—but poorly—on the reading, scoring at the 62 percent level. According to the FCAT system, he belonged in a remedial program, with jeopardized chances of getting even a high school degree. He described the test to colleagues across a range of professions, and got consistent feedback—no one used any of the test's math. He commented, "It might be argued that I've been out of school too long, that if I'd actually been in the tenth grade prior to taking the test, the material would have been fresh. But doesn't that miss the point? A test that can determine a student's future life chances should surely relate in some practical way to the requirements of life. I can't see how that could possibly be true of the test I took."

What's so powerful about this man's story is his reflection on the experience. He notes that if he had to take these tests as a tenth grader, his life would have been completely different. He would have been told he wasn't up to the standard of going to college, and might have set his life ambitions much lower. He concludes, "It makes no sense to me that a test with the potential for shaping a student's entire future has so little apparent relevance to adult, real-world functioning."[33]

U.S. education is failing because of the misguided belief that it's imperative to test on a massive scale. But to test millions of students every year is expensive—in terms of time, money, and opportunity cost. With the goal of rank-ordering millions of test-takers, assessment inevitably gets reduced to dumbed-down quizzes, with a complete disconnect between what's easy to test and what matters. We need an education system that cares about the success of our kids, not the success of the standardized test industry.

What Can Teachers Do in the Classroom

We hear from teachers, "I am committed to helping my students develop critical skills, but where do I start?" We'd encourage teachers to take the following steps.

1. Find and team up with a trusted colleague. That person's support and objectivity will be invaluable.
2. Review the tests, quizzes, and assignments you give students. Assess them on the basis of how memorization-intensive they are. Could anyone with access to online search have answered the questions? Do these assignments help your students develop critical skills? How?
3. Gauge how much of the "talk time" in your class is your lecturing, compared to student-led discussion. Do students have opportunities to teach and learn from one another? To work in teams? It's easy to have the impression that you're speaking very little, only to find that you're talking most of the time. Use your phone to video one of your typical classes, and be rigorous in determining your percentage of "air time." If it's more than 20 percent, figure out how to restructure your class.
4. Are students assessed on the questions they ask, as well as the answers they provide?
5. Do students have opportunities to create their own projects, define goals, develop their plan, and communicate their achievements to a broader audience? Can a student afford to make mistakes and fail, and still do well in your course? What percentage of the time they spend is on self-defined projects? If it's less than 20 percent, try to get there.

CHAPTER 7

A New Vision for Education

People compare the challenge of changing our education system to taking on global warming. They point to how our education system is so big, so entrenched, with all sorts of vested interests resisting change. And they shrug their shoulders and say, "How much difference can one person make?"

A lot, fortunately.

Unlike global warming, where one person's impact is just a drop in a massive bucket of carbon, education is inherently local. Someone passionate about changing education can make a difference to a child, class, grade, or school. Local change can inspire a national movement. Each of us can contribute to bringing education into the twenty-first century. But, as the saying goes, "If you don't know where you're going, any road will get you there." This chapter will help "get you there."

The road isn't easy. Inertia and centrally mandated dictums gum up the works—and we'll deal with some of those problems in the first part of this chapter so that you'll have a better sense of what education policies to advocate for. Then, in the second part of the chapter, we describe some of the many inspiring new initiatives in both K-12 and higher education that give us reason for hope. In the last part, we'll will talk about ways in which parents, community members, and educators can work together for change in their local communities.

Part 1: Reframing the Problem

We need to start by reframing the problem. If our conversations, school strategic plans, and national policies revolve around how we make the current system better, we are doomed. These reforms are akin to putting all our efforts into making a covered wagon go fast enough to win the Indianapolis 500. And with no discernible progress, our education dialogue ends up devolving into a blame game, with teachers' unions serving as the piñata. We need to be going 225 miles per hour, and no amount of reform will get a covered wagon to go faster than four miles per hour. It ain't happening.

We need to reimagine education. We have to put ourselves in the shoes of the Committee of Ten who, back in 1893, said, "Gee, we need to train millions of kids for a growing number of rote jobs in our burgeoning industrial economy." The Committee of Ten came up with a good solution for their era. Today, we need to educate millions of kids (and adults) for the innovation era. How do we do that?

First, this is our mantra: Our challenge isn't making incremental improvements to an education model designed in 1893. Our opportunity—and our obligation to our youth—is to reimagine our schools, and give all kids an education that will help them thrive in a world that values them for what they can do, not the facts that they know.

What should our education policy-makers do to get our education system on track again? What are the macro issues? Getting anything sensible out of our government these days isn't likely. But we do have election cycles, and we do have ways to petition groups, from the U.S. Department of Education to the local school board. And the more of us who share a common vision, the more impact we will have on national policies that affect our kids' futures.

New Education Outcomes

What does it mean to be an educated adult in the twenty-first century? What are the core competencies that matter most for work, learning, and citizenship today? And how are these skills different from what students needed a century ago? These questions must be the starting point for reimagining education. The first challenge is to clarify the outcomes that matter most for a high school graduate.

Throughout this book, we have described the new skills that matter most today. The world simply no longer cares how much you know, because Google knows everything. What the world cares about—what matters for learning, work, and citizenship—is what you can *do* with what you know. Of course, our students will continue to need content knowledge, but that's the easy part now. As we've seen, content knowledge has become a free commodity—like air or water—growing exponentially, changing constantly, and available on every Internet-connected device. The harder part is helping students develop the skill and the will to ask new questions, solve new problems, and create new knowledge. As we said in chapter 2, we believe that this tripod—content knowledge, skill, and will—is the foundation of all learning in the twenty-first century.

Of the three, we believe that will, or motivation, is the most important, and the one damaged most by our schools today. If students are intrinsically motivated, they will continue to acquire new skills and content knowledge throughout their lives, enabling them to thrive in the innovation era. So the first question we must ask ourselves about any proposed change in education is: Will this "improvement" likely increase or diminish student motivation for learning and how will we know? And, to be clear, we're not just talking about the thrill factor of learning. We are talking about the motivations that include grit, perseverance, and self-discipline.

Then comes the question of skills. In recent years, a number of books have been written about "twenty-first-century skills." While different authors have emphasized particular skills over others, most everyone agrees about the importance of the four C's: critical thinking, communication, collaboration, and creative problem-solving. We believe these skills can and must be taught and assessed every day in every class.

We're not suggesting that these skills be taught instead of content knowledge. You cannot teach critical thinking without engaging students in rich and challenging academic content. The goal must be to choose the academic content selectively so as to create the required foundation for lifelong learning, without letting the quest for content coverage overwhelm the development of core competencies.

Forging a New Consensus on the Purpose of Education

How do we develop greater clarity and consensus on the purposes of education in the twenty-first century? It's not enough to write books. Nor is it enough to organize conferences and listen to compelling speakers. And, fortunately, we're well past the time when any Committee of Ten can dictate an entire country's education policy for a century or more! What is needed to move us forward today is a new kind of dialogue at every level.

Many attribute the last great turning point in our education history to the publication of A Nation at Risk in 1983, which described a "rising tide of mediocrity" in our schools. But, in fact, nothing of any consequence happened for more than a decade after the appearance of this legendary call to action. It took the courageous leadership of a couple of business leaders to create real momentum for change. In 1988, David Kearns, who was then CEO of Xerox Corporation, co-authored a compelling book, Winning the Brain Race, which argued that American workers needed a very different—and dramatically better—education in order to compete in the late twentieth century. And, in 1995, Lou Gerstner, then CEO of IBM Corporation, called for a National Summit on education. Almost all of the nation's governors, many CEOs, and other national and state leaders came to the Palisades, New York, in 1996 and agreed to push for new academic standards and sweeping education reforms. Tellingly, only a handful of educators were invited to the summit—and then only as observers.

So where are the Lou Gerstners and David Kearnses of our era? We've met countless business leaders who decry the lack of real improvement in our education system. Many know that No Child Left Behind and Race to the Top have been abysmal failures. But few are willing to speak out. Their handlers tell them to stay out of the education arena because it's too controversial. So with the future of millions of students on the line, far too many CEOs merely end up tossing some money at STEM initiatives and calling it a day.

Until there is real national leadership, state and local leaders must step into the vacuum. We have met policy makers and education and business leaders in a number of states—including California, Minnesota, Kentucky, New Hampshire, Idaho, and Vermont—who are well aware of the profound failings of our national education policies. Their opportunity going forward lies in taking the initiative, holding their own education summits for the innovation era, and then joining forces to demand that the Department of Education issue the testing waivers that are permitted. It's time for states to set a more inspiring course for their education systems.

New Hampshire recently set an example by being the first state to eliminate the requirement that students amass a specified collection of "credit hours" called the Carnegie Units—in order to graduate from high school. With visionary leadership from Fred Bramante, an entrepreneur who served on the state board of education from 2003 to 2012, New Hampshire is moving forward with the competency-based approach to earning a high school diploma.[1]

And we have seen a bottom-up revolution occurring in local communities, such as in Scarsdale, New York, whose school board became the first to establish a local innovation fund to support teams of teachers in developing new courses and performance-based assessments. In Scarsdale and elsewhere, business leaders understand that they cannot just talk about workplace skills, important though these are. In order to forge new alliances with educators, they also talk about the skills needed for learning and citizenship in the twenty-first century.

Testing and Evaluating

Nothing has been as damaging to the learning prospects of our kids than one seemingly innocuous statement: "Well, of course, we have to measure student progress." When we give our students complex problems that require creativity, it becomes harder to measure their learning precisely. Here's the honest truth: If we want to organize education so a bureaucrat in Washington, DC, can readily monitor the monthly performance of a class in Topeka, Kansas, then we should stick with our current failed model. But if we're committed to meaningful student progress, we need to accept that an entirely different assessment model is required—one that is more qualitative than quantitative, and one that gives up on rank-ordering millions of kids to the nearest tenth of a percentile. Our choice is stark. We can focus classrooms either on what's easy to measure or on what's important to learn. But we can't do both well.

Our Boy Scout and Girl Scout troops provide a role model for evaluating the progress of our youth. Scouts earn merit badges on the basis of demonstrated mastery of competencies, as judged by informed adults directly involved in the experience. To get a camping merit badge, kids practice and master the skills required to camp—they don't jump through hoops by memorizing the names of various tent types. They get a cooking merit badge by learning how to cook—not sitting in a chair watching someone else cook for 150 hours and filling in multiple-choice questions about how long it takes to bake a potato. To become an Eagle Scout, they master core competencies and earn additional merit badges aligned with their interests. They don't just hang around the troop for twelve years and avoid getting kicked out. This system has standards of achievement and accountability. Troop leaders have clarity in determining what constitutes acceptable levels of mastery to earn a merit badge. And their system trusts its adults to render appropriate judgments.

And guess what? No one obsesses about whether the standards for an Eagle Scout in Oklahoma are higher or lower than for an Eagle Scout in California. National Scout organizations don't rank-order the monthly performance of every Scout in the United States on the basis of numbers tied to timed multiple-choice tests. Assessment is based on the judgment of trusted adults observing competencies.

Is the Scout system perfect? No. None is. But would we want our Scout troops taking cheap, dumb tests just to satisfy bureaucrats who don't trust local Scout leaders? History has shown that the merit badge system serves the long-term interests of our youth. But those insights haven't reached those shaping our education system. Maybe Arne Duncan, Joel Klein, Bill Gates, and Michelle Rhee should spend a year in a Scout troop and a year in one of the classrooms they architect, and compare the two experiences. We have a feeling they'd share the perspective of this experienced teacher who shadowed students for two days, and reported feeling that "most of the students' day was spent passively absorbing information." As Grant Wiggins reported, this teacher concluded:

> It was not just the sitting that was draining but that so much of the day was spent absorbing information but not often grappling with it. I asked my tenth-grade host, Cindy, if she felt like she made important contributions to class or if, when she was absent, the class missed out on the benefit of her knowledge or contributions, and she laughed and said no. I was struck by this takeaway in particular because it made me realize how little autonomy students have, how little of their learning they are directing or choosing.[2]

Shifting to a competency-based system would invite the question of what should be the core "merit badges" for kids in school. What competencies would we want all kids to develop? Would we prioritize chemistry over collaboration? Calculus over creative problem-solving? Chaucer over critical thinking? Civil War trivia over communication? A competency-based system would force us to rethink school in terms of two fundamental dimensions. Do we want students' learning to be shallow or deep? And do we want their primary focus to be subject content or critical skills?

Our Scout organizations are clear in their mission: Prepare every youth for citizenship, leadership, and competence in dealing with the wilderness. These goals in turn determine the skills every young Scout needs to master. If the goal of education is to prepare our youth for citizenship, leadership, and competence in dealing with the innovation era, the skills they need to master are self-evident.

A High School Diploma as a Certificate of Mastery

We think a high school diploma should be a certificate of mastery—and not just a certificate of seat time served, as it has been since 1893. We believe local schools and communities should develop merit badges in common—beginning with the four C's of critical thinking, collaboration, communication, and creative problem-solving. There should be clear performance standards established for these core competencies, with input from employers and college teachers. These performance standards can then be backwards mapped to requirements for exiting eighth and fifth graders in order to create an aligned K-12 system.

Students would work on their merit badges by taking a rich assortment of courses—some of which would look like the ones we described in chapter 4—and through independent study, work internships, and service learning projects conducted in the community. Learning would not be confined to the traditional academic calendar or even to school buildings.

In addition, we think students should be required to meet performance standards that are specific to academic modes of inquiry. The New York Performance Standards Consortium is a group of twenty-eight high schools that have collaborated since 1997 to develop and score a series of common performance-based assessments. They require every high school student to complete the following projects to a specified performance standard in order to graduate:[3]

- Analytic literary essay
- Social studies research paper

- Original science experiment
- Application of higher level mathematics

These projects often overlap with work students complete to meet the requirements of the Four C's merit badges outlined earlier, allowing a student to earn a critical thinking merit badge in one of the essays mentioned above. Additionally, local communities may wish to add merit badges that reflect their community's particular priorities. Urban and rural communities might set entrepreneurship as a highly prized skill, since it empowers young people to create jobs enabling them to stay in the community. Schools in some areas might shift emphasis to reflect priorities on things like conflict resolution, self-direction, or advanced manufacturing.

As schools move to a merit badge approach, districts and states could use a small number of very high-quality tests as auditing instruments for overall system accountability. These superior assessments would be given to representative samples of students, primarily for informational purposes. This sampling approach would allow us to perform more careful evaluations of higher-level skill development among students. It would point to schools that are significantly underperforming, and would highlight schools with practices that are leading to exceptional performance.

A thoughtful, sampled approach to assessment could be based on the College and Work Readiness Assessment or the international PISA test. These tests are effective in evaluating critical skills, with a history of successful field deployment. But even these more authentic tests are under pressure to reduce costs through more automated grading mechanisms, enabling them to be administered in bulk. Remember, any solution that can be accurately evaluated by computer is invariably tied to a skill that can be handled by a computer—better than the best human. In a variant of an old saying, we caution, "Be careful what you test for."

How would students demonstrate that they had met the performance standard for a particular merit badge?

First, students would regularly present and defend their work in front of audiences of peers, teachers, parents, and community members, a variation on the dissertation defense common to all doctoral programs and an approach widely used by more than five hundred K-12 schools that belong to the Deeper Learning initiative.[4] (More about this effort in a bit.)

Second, students would have a digital portfolio that follows them through school. The portfolio would represent a collection of the students' best work—papers, speeches, projects, works of art—that would be evidence of mastery of the skills that matter most. Today, a student can use free services from companies like Seesaw, Pathbrite, or Google to construct online portfolios of their work, providing a basis for formative assessments. Pathbrite notes that the vast majority of employers would rather see demonstrated skills in critical thinking, communication, and problem-solving than simply looking at a degree or an undergraduate major. And we'd love to see colleges adopt this view, as a growing number are doing.

On the school level, portfolios could be randomly audited by qualified teams—teachers from other schools, parents, employers, and college teachers. These evaluations would provide an informed sense of teacher and student performance, identify opportunities to improve effectiveness, and begin to align the authentic long-term interests of teachers and students.

Proctored essay exams, widely used throughout Europe instead of computer-scored, standardized tests, may have a place in a robust accountability system as well. But we are strong believers in open-book/open-Internet exams. We admire Denmark's announcement in 2009 that all students would have open access to the Internet on national exams. In 2013, Bertel Haarder, their minister of education, stated, "Our exams have to reflect daily life in the classroom and daily life in the classroom has to reflect life in society."[5] In a world where any test-taker has ready Internet access, most current standardized tests would only assess a student's ability to do quick and effective Internet searches. Testing with Internet access would require massive, and productive, restructuring, and begin to reflect deeper learning and the ability to apply insights to new, often ambiguous, situations.

Teacher Preparation

Most U.S. education schools use obsolete education models to train teachers on obsolete methods. Student teachers spend far too much time listening to boring lectures on education theory and far too little time practicing teaching skills. Most receive token university "supervision" that is totally ineffectual, and they work under so-called master teachers who are anything but. And so we graduate about 100,000 new teachers from our colleges each year, with few prepared to teach in a way that reflects state-of-the-art practices for today's very different world. Add to the mix thousands of Teach For America teachers launched into their assignments with just *five weeks* of training, and it's clear why there's a crisis in teacher preparation in our country.

Finland improved its education system by taking decisive steps. Beginning in the 1970s, it closed down 80 percent of its schools of education, retaining only those associated with its best universities. Every teacher is required to earn a real master's degree, which includes successful completion of a yearlong apprenticeship with some of the best teachers in the country as supervisors. Teachers in Finland start their careers prepared to manage their classes in ways that promote critical skill development. Finally, Finnish teachers average only about 600 hours a year teaching in the classroom, versus American teachers' 1,100 hours, giving them far more time to meet with students and parents, and to learn from colleagues.[6]

With these changes, Finland has thrived. Students are innovative, teachers are respected and fulfilled in their jobs, and learning in schools is effective and student-driven. Finland pulls this off with almost no testing, homework, teaching-to-the-test, or extended school schedules. Yet Finnish students have consistently scored among the top ten countries on international PISA test results since the tests were first administered in 2000.

Some elements of Finland's strategy are relevant to the United States in 2015, but not all. The National Commission on Teaching and America's Future reports that one-third of our nation's four million teachers will be retiring over a four-year period.[7] In an ideal world, we'd fill these openings with amazing and trained teachers, who would live in a country that respects their career choice and compensates them appropriately. Regrettably, this ideal world isn't likely to materialize in the United States anytime soon. And we can't instantly shut down 80 percent of our schools of education and turbo-charge the remaining 20 percent, and still fill a million teaching vacancies. So for planning purposes, we should assume our go-forward teaching force will look much like it does today: dedicated to their mission, disillusioned with our policies, dealing with too many classroom hours, and disadvantaged in professional development.

There is one change we could make that would provide an immediate boost to teacher effectiveness: We could give teachers our trust. We can call off the dogs on nonsensical accountability schemes that are being pushed onto our schools. No businesspeople would accept circumstances where their annual review was determined by how well their direct reports score on multiple-choice tests—let alone under the bizarre circumstance where the direct reports have *no stake whatsoever* in their own performance on this test. Yet businesspeople, who love to talk about the relevance of free-market concepts in reforming education, insist on evaluation practices they'd never impose on themselves. By contrast, the motto for Finland's education system is "Trust through professionalism."

We can begin innovating in teacher professional development. For starters, we should change current policies that reward teachers—in pay and position—for simply putting in a year of seat time to get a master's degree, especially when this advanced training isn't improving learning outcomes. Instead, we should educate, assess, and reward our teachers on the basis of demonstrated mastery of new competencies, leveraging online resources and peer-driven forums. The benefits of this change would be twofold. Teachers would receive superior, more cost-effective professional development. And they'd be exposed to a different learning model—a model they could in turn use in their classes.

We believe teacher effectiveness should be assessed in the same way that students' work should be evaluated, on the basis of digital portfolios. These portfolios should contain videotapes of lessons, examples of the work their students have produced in the class, and videotaped focus groups with students where they'd talk about how they had been engaged as learners. Teacher effectiveness can be assessed according to the evidence of improvement in students' work between September and June. Most teachers we know would eagerly embrace this tailored form of accountability.

Research & Development

The need for radically new and better approaches to assessment and to improved teacher preparation and professional development point to a much larger need in education today. To develop better approaches to accountability and to create laboratory schools for new approaches to learning, teacher training, and assessment, we must have a massive investment in educational R&D.

The U.S. federal budget is awash in spending on research and development. In fiscal year 2013, we spent $72 billion on military R&D. With the exception of Bernie Sanders and Rand Paul, you can't find a politician in our country at the national level who doesn't assert, "State-of-the art military technology is vital to our long-term national security." As a side note, our military spending outpaces the second most aggressive nation, China, by a 4.1-to-1 ratio. The United States spends more on its military than the defense-related expenditures of China, Russia, the United Kingdom, Japan, France, Saudi Arabia, India, Germany, Italy, and Brazil combined.[8]

But can our leaders possibly believe that investing in military R&D is far more important than investing in R&D for educating our youth? Well, the FY2013 U.S. budget for investing in education R&D is just one two-hundredth the size of the federal budget for defense R&D. For every dollar we spend on military R&D, we spend half of a penny on investing in how to improve our kids' futures. Education research is an order of magnitude lower than federal R&D for space or agriculture. There is good news, though. The Office of Management and Budget reports that our R&D budget for education did come in slightly ahead of R&D expenditures for the Smithsonian.[9]

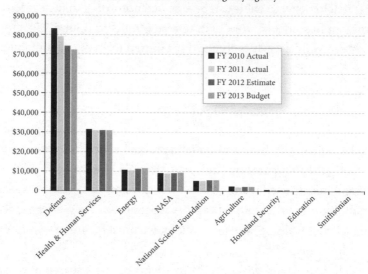

R&D in the FY 2013 Federal Budget by Agency

For the most part, the Department of Education invests small sums in programs doing underwhelming things—initiatives focused on boosting test scores and using data to track results. You can look high and low for something bold, scalable, risky, and disruptive, but you won't find it in our national R&D agenda. Portfolio-based assessment of students' skills? Not there. Non-test-based approaches to evaluating teacher effectiveness? MIA. Support for any of the exciting new initiatives described in the second part of this chapter? Nowhere to be found.

In fact, the overwhelming majority of money given out under the Department of Education's "i3" grants has gone to existing organizations in order to allow them to "scale up." Teach For America and Success for All, an elementary reading program, have been by far the biggest winners. The most important criteria for getting a scale-up grant? A track record of improving student test scores.[10] Rewarding standardized test success is a bit like having the Defense Department fund initiatives that can get muskets and catapults to be used more broadly.

If there's a big shortfall of investing in innovative education at the federal level, it only gets worse at lower levels. Most states spend peanuts on education R&D. District superintendents laugh when we ask them about their budget for R&D. At the school level, finding enough unallocated budget dollars to cover a field trip is often a stretch, let alone to fund outside-the-box initiatives that might transform learning experiences.

The point of R&D is to have a scalability strategy in place from the get-go. A company invests in R&D with a clear path to scaling up breakthroughs and bringing them to market. When our Defense Department invests in new technologies, it has the wherewithal to award contracts to turn innovations into production systems. To date, there's no national strategy for identifying successful innovations in specific schools or networks and determining how they can scale across our 137,000 schools.

Compounding the problem, business leaders generally believe that if we could only introduce free-market dynamics into schools (e.g., charter schools, choice vouchers for parents), our most promising education innovations would thrive. But profound advances in education have impacts that stretch out over lifetimes, not months. Real innovation in education often isn't readily transparent to those funders or politicians who just want to see numbers on paper. As a result, we underfund education R&D, focusing on initiatives that produce near-term results on hollow metrics.

In the 1980s, the nascent U.S. semiconductor industry was worried about falling behind Japan, a world-class manufacturing power. So fourteen U.S. semiconductor companies, with some federal support, formed and funded a pooled R&D initiative called SEMATECH (SEmiconductor MAnufacturing TECHnology) to perform deep R&D on behalf of this strategic industry. SEMATECH was an innovation center for all U.S. semiconductor manufacturers, akin to AT&T's Bell Labs or Xerox's PARC. This consortium brought together top research minds and made decisive contributions to our country's long-term economic interests by helping U.S. technology companies maintain global leadership in semiconductor technology, which in turn enabled our country to lead the entire digital revolution.

U.S. education desperately needs the equivalent of a SEMATECH or Bell Labs. Our top companies, foundations, philanthropists, and government need to step up and fund the R&D needed to modernize education. This center could invent and assess bold new measures, partner with lab schools around the world, and evaluate and endorse innovative practices that are succeeding locally. And by forming the world's center of gravity for education R&D, we would bring a powerful dimension of credibility and scalability to education innovation.

Despite the paucity of real education R&D performed at the federal level, innovations are emerging to improve, or entirely replace, existing models for how kids learn, how they demonstrate competencies, and how they pursue careers. Resources that weren't on the radar screen a decade ago are getting traction, changing the landscape. These advances create opportunity for moving education forward.

Each of us can begin transforming education by taking one simple step: Stop glorifying it. Much of school today involves jumping through pointless hoops with the end goal of a college degree. If we insist that a college degree is mandatory for a high-potential career path, we force many lower- and middle-income families into financial hardship just to get their kids to the starting line. If we require a high school degree or GED for jobs at the bottom of the economic ladder, we punish many resilient young adults desperately trying to escape poverty. When this happens to one of them, it's a tragedy. When it happens to tens of millions, it sows the seeds of national demise.

Ted has worked closely with lots of great technology businesses, each hiring exceptional software developers. For three decades (1981–2011), his Boston-based companies had entry-level recruiting strategies that revolved around college. Some preferred the "raw horsepower" of fresh Harvard graduates. Others recruited MIT grads for their world-class technology education. Still others sought students from Northeastern for its amazing co-op program, or, more recently, Olin College for its transformational project-based experience. While the tactics differed, every recruiting strategy centered on one narrow dimension: college.

In the blink of an eye, academic credentials have become largely irrelevant to innovative software companies, which now tap into online evidence of a candidate's competence. GitHub is a vast repository of software code from millions of developers. An expert can examine someone's GitHub code base and make an informed judgment about coding proficiency—whether it's foundational or derivative. A top venture capital firm, Andreessen Horowitz, believes so strongly in GitHub's potential to disrupt historic hiring practices that it invested $100 million in the company to scale operations.[11]

GitHub isn't alone in reshaping hiring. Online platforms like Elance and oDesk show a person's project track record, work samples, and Yelp-like client reviews. LinkedIn includes employment history, peer endorsements, and access to trusted references. Compelling writing skills are evident on blogs. Creative public speaking shows up in YouTube videos. Technical writing skills are evident in eHow posts. Social media shed light on a candidate's personality and judgment. Increasingly, employers recruit in the same way you'd want to commission an artist to do a portrait—reviewing portfolios of work instead of interviewing Art History majors from Ivy League colleges.

HireArt is a New York City start-up focused on providing employers with authentic ways to assess a candidate's fit for open positions. The company works with employers (e.g., tech companies like Airbnb and Facebook) to craft rigorous and appropriate challenges that in turn gauge an applicant's competence and passion for a position. For example, when applying for a sales role, an applicant might be asked to write an email pitching a product. It's unlikely that someone without real expertise or interest would step up to this challenge. But applicants who can't imagine anything more fun than taking this on have a chance to demonstrate their capabilities, whether they went to an Ivy League college, attended a community college, or dropped out of high school. Hiring practices that assess competence, rather than relying on credentials, give hiring organizations a competitive edge. Elli Sharef, founder of HireArt, commented, "Employers are thrilled to be finding new sources of talent, applicants love being able to demonstrate their talents and passion, and everyone benefits from a more authentic and efficient hiring process."

Koru and Breaker are two new education start-ups that will likely disrupt higher education. Koru offers three-week workshops to recent or soon-to-be college graduates, who work in teams to solve problems in new or fast-growing businesses. Students learn skills that make them immediately employable, with 85 percent of Koru grads landing jobs right out of the program.[12] Koru currently partners with leading colleges and more than thirty fast-growth companies.

Founded by TED Fellow Juliette LaMontagne, Breaker has worked with Stanford's d.school to design and sponsor intensive workshops for young adults who want to create solutions to real problems, while learning the skills needed to succeed in the innovation era.[13] How long will it take for prospective college students to wonder if, maybe, they should just take a few Koru or Breaker workshops and skip college altogether?

Innovation pays no heed to historic practices or boundaries. Innovators like HireArt, Koru, Project Breaker, and GitHub are attacking the traditional credentials-driven hiring process. Beyond hiring, disruption will be widespread. Massive Open Online Courses (MOOCs) are going after the core classroom experience. Other new models make learning more effective, affordable, and aligned with what matters in life. In coming years, innovation will completely restructure higher education, exploiting glaring market inefficiencies.

Innovations in Mainstream Colleges

Our country is fortunate to have a number of colleges that provide students with transformational experiences that go far beyond the normal routine of lectures by day, parties by night. These institutions—some highly regarded, some less heralded—will be an enduring part of our higher education landscape. What distinguishes these colleges is that their history of success doesn't prevent them from constantly looking to reinvent themselves. A particularly inspiring example is Stanford University; its interdisciplinary project-based d.school is having outsized influence all over campus.

Some forward-looking colleges now encourage students to start new enterprises or solve real problems as a regular part of their regular academic coursework. In *Creating Innovators*, Tony profiled three of our favorites: the Olin College of Engineering, the d.school at Stanford, and the MIT Media Lab. In all three, students work on solving real problems in teams, using a multidisciplinary approach. Inspired by these examples, and with strong support from President Mitch Daniels and leadership from faculty members Fatma Mili and Jamie Mohler, Purdue University has established a brand-new, competency-based undergraduate program. According to Gary Bertoline, dean of the College of Technology, "Starting with a competency-based, learn-by-doing degree that is integrated with the humanities, the transformation will soon touch all parts of the college: curricula, learning/teaching methods, learning spaces, student assessments, use-inspired research, community and industry engagement, and nearly every fiber of the college's culture."[14]

Many other universities also sponsor initiatives to encourage students who want to create new businesses or social enterprises, and draw on faculty and community members for support.[15] While well intended, these initiatives generally don't allow students to earn academic course credit for their work, presumably because offering credit threatens tenured faculty fiefdoms. Students' work, which can involve long hours over many months, is entirely extracurricular.

We don't envy the typical college president. In most cases, college presidents can't cut costs because of built-in infrastructures, and they are largely powerless to influence faculty to make meaningful changes in their institution's learning environment. These colleges are sitting ducks in the innovation era. Absent real change, they are likely to either fail over time or become expensive four-year summer camps for rich legacies. As hard as change is within a university, these institutions urgently need to shift their model in important ways, to increase learning and manage costs. Some will, and will go on to survive, even thrive. Many won't, and will fall by the wayside. You will be able to handicap a college's prospects for survival by looking at where it stands on these dimensions:

20th-Century College	21st-Century College
Lectures	Seminars / Group projects / Independent study
Content coverage	Skill development / Learning how to learn

20th-Century College	21st-Century College
Departmental majors	Interdisciplinary / Capstone
Define paths for students	Students create their path
Seat time	Competency-based
Transcripts / Grades	Digital portfolio of accomplishments
Campus-centric experience	Internships / Co-ops / Study away / Virtual
Isolated from real world	Connected to real world
Four consecutive years	On and off campus over longer periods
Large staffs serving students	(All) students take on roles
Numbers-driven admissions	Admissions based on purpose
Unaffordable tuition	Tuition reduced through employment
Obsessed with spurious rankings	Obsessed with authentic learning
Favoring the rich	Helping to level the playing field

Just to make the kind of transformation we're discussing more tangible, consider the following. Most colleges spend large amounts of money on outside consultants who help "market" the school to prospective applicants with videos, web infrastructure, direct mailings, and brochures. And many students at these colleges would love to develop media and marketing skills, irrespective of their major. Why not turn these costly consulting arrangements into student-based projects, with assessments and credits? And if you think it's because outside consultants are far more effective at telling a college's story, just look at a few college videos and brochures—which are generally so "corporate" in nature that they turn off the high school students they target.

While we expect pressure on traditional colleges to increase gradually, there is a scenario where things go south for them quickly. Peter Thiel argues that a diploma from a second-class university has become a "dunce hat in disguise," awarded to graduates foolish enough to spend $100,000 to

$250,000 to brand themselves permanently as mediocre.[16] Thiel's view is far from today's mainstream, but attitudes can shift suddenly in a fickle society. If they do, these colleges will enter a death spiral, with falling demand for an overpriced offering, no ability to cut costs, and eroding public confidence.

As waves of innovation reshape our higher-education landscape, we expect to see a number of radically different models emerge, evolve, and disrupt:

MOOCs: The first wave of Massive Open Online Courses fell short of expectations, but these innovators will keep improving. Some of the most powerful pedagogies we profiled in earlier chapters lend themselves to online implementations. MOOCs have the potential to be effective learning vehicles, posing a real threat to mainstream colleges, and making all in-person lecture courses obsolete.

The Co-op Model: In earning their degree, most Northeastern graduates complete at least one six-month co-op experience, getting their hands dirty with a real job. Many Northeastern undergrads do multiple co-ops, which boost learning *and* give them extended periods when they make money instead of pay tuition. This model reduces the all-in cost of a degree, while giving students decisive career advantages. Other schools, such as Waterloo, use a similar model with equally impressive results.

Internships: A college with meaningful internship opportunities helps students with their learning and careers. A Gallup Education poll confirmed that internships make college experiences more effective in launching careers.[17] The good news? In a world with Internet connectivity, internships no longer require working at the employer's site, but can encompass working on spot projects while on campus. An ongoing challenge is that too often, desirable internships go to students with connected parents, not to students with drive and competence.

Focused Feed-In Programs: IBM's P-TECH program (Pathways in Technology Early College High School) sponsors a growing number of schools teaching grades nine through fourteen. These schools provide students with an applied education, integrated with IBM internships. Students at P-TECH start working on their associate's degree in tenth or eleventh grade and can then get an attractive job with IBM or elsewhere, or matriculate to another college.[18] This focused feed-in model gives IBM a source of diverse talent, with the potential to deliver a superior education. Expect more organizations to adopt this model in sourcing their next generation of leaders.

ALPs: Accelerated Learning Programs, such as General Assembly, Dev Bootcamp, and Flatiron [full disclosure: Ted is an investor in Flatiron], offer short-term programs (three months or so) that equip students with state-of-the-art computer programming skills. At an affordable cost ($5,000 to $10,000), they deliver stunning job placement rates (> 90%) with high starting salaries (> $75K). As applications have surged, leading ALPs have become as selective as Harvard and Stanford. Expect this model to spread rapidly to other fields and locations.

ALPs address a gigantic hidden risk of traditional higher education. Consider a student who goes through four pre-law undergrad years and then three years of law school, at a cost of $400,000. Assuming the student passes the bar, he or she will try to land a solid starting position. A recent *Atlantic* magazine story, "The Jobs Crisis at Our Best Law Schools Is Much, Much Worse Than You Think," reported that some 44 percent of law school grads in 2012 hadn't found stable employment nine months after graduating, with numbers only "marginally better" for those who attended prestigious law schools.[19] The kicker? After going through years of expensive hoops, many who do find employment discover a few months into their career that the last thing they want to be is . . . a lawyer. This same pattern can be found in many fields requiring advanced degrees. Just ask your dentist.

So consider a world where young adults draw on periodic ALPs to develop job-specific (e.g., computer programming, welding, editing) or skill-specific (e.g., communication, leadership, project management, sales) proficiencies. Over time, they interleave ALPs with real work experience, building a portfolio of "merit badges." Through these experiences, they develop a network of professional contacts and lifetime friendships, deepened through ongoing social media engagement. This path would offer better learning outcomes, far more affordability and career flexibility, and reduced career risk.

Hacking Your Own: Imagine a resourceful high school graduate forgoing college for a series of eight six-month internships—internships that they define and obtain. Someone with a passion for nature might work at a biology research station, an REI retail store, a national park maintenance crew, a NOLS (National Outdoor Leadership School), a high school biology class, a company designing camping equipment, a legislative committee on the environment, a studio producing a nature documentary, or an overseas initiative fighting to preserve an endangered species. Compare this experience to an expensive four-year degree in Biology. Should society reward, or penalize, an enterprising young adult who "hacked" (or created) this higher education path? We hope the answer is obvious.

Meaningful Jobs Early: Look no further than Google for insight into the value of college credentials. As discussed in chapter 5, Google has transitioned from recruiting its new employees from elite colleges, focusing on SATs and GPAs, to radically different hiring criteria. For some teams, close to 15 percent of new hires have no college education.[20] This *Moneyball* strategy will give Google a competitive advantage over more narrow-minded competitors, prompting others to rethink hiring criteria.

Hands-On "Advanced Degrees": A preview of coming attractions in advanced degrees can be found in Silicon Valley. For decades, a Stanford or Harvard MBA was pure gold in Valley hiring circles. But today innovative programs, such as Paul Graham's Y Combinator, are giving young entrepreneurs powerful learning experiences and a "brand" as powerful as an elite MBA. Y Combinator is every bit as selective as a top business school, but with admissions criteria focused more on a person's ideas than his or her undergraduate GPA. A young entrepreneur going to business school will study topics, start a business (now mandatory at many programs, including Harvard Business School), develop a network of contacts, and . . . pay substantially more than $100,000 in tuition. At Y Combinator, the student will learn similar topics, start a serious business, develop a powerful network, and get funding for a start-up while paying no tuition. Not surprisingly, Y Combinator and other similar programs are becoming the new "MBA" in the Internet economy, with an emerging sense that spending more than $100,000 for a business credential in 2015 is a bit of a sucker's play.

The field of law provides another example of an apprenticeship-based "surrogate" advanced degree. In some states (California, Virginia, Vermont, and Washington), you can take the bar without attending a single law school class. Instead, aspiring lawyers learn through a multiyear apprenticeship at a law firm. Without mountains of debt, these apprenticed attorneys feel less pressure to seek high-paying positions. As the *New York Times* reported, "[At] a time when many in legal education—including the president, a former law professor—are questioning the value of three years of law study and the staggering debt that saddles many graduates, proponents see apprenticeships as an alternative that makes legal education available and affordable to a more diverse population and could be a boon to underserved communities."[21]

Vocational Training/Community Colleges: Someone in our society who pursues a career in the "trades" faces two obstacles. First, education options are lousy. Second, society looks down on you. In the United States, an adult who becomes an electrician (requiring know-how in applied science, technology, and business) has less social status than an aimless college graduate swimming in debt. Contrast us to Finland and Germany, where some 40 percent of high school graduates pursue a career in the trades, receiving good educations and social respect, and form the basis for a robust middle class. Our country needs to reinvigorate applied learning in our schools and society—and treat acquired competence with respect.

As poorly as we've treated vocational paths in the past, our system has managed to outdo itself in applying Common Core standards to the GED. Many minimum-wage jobs in our country—construction, fast food, retail—require a high school degree or equivalent. In 2013, some 540,000 young Americans earned their GED, giving them a fighting chance to grab the very bottom rung of our economic ladder. With the introduction of Common Core standards to the GED, completion rates have fallen by an order of magnitude. These requirements are shameful. Students are tested on bizarre cognitive tasks. Even worse, they need to pay for laptop access, test fees, and even tutoring—amounts beyond the means of someone trying desperately to escape poverty. To what end? Does anyone in his or her right mind think that a gritty kid should be denied a job in construction because he stumbles in explaining how Thomas Jefferson would feel about a school's expulsion policy? That someone hoping to work in McDonald's needs to be able to interpret, via an equation, whether energy is stored, created, or produced when glucose, water, oxygen, and carbon dioxide are combined?[22] Sadly, these aren't hypothetical examples.

And what, exactly, do our college-obsessed policy leaders think will happen as young adults are shut out of jobs because they can't complete their GED? Well, the answer is obvious to any ten-year-old. Many will end up in jail, at an enormous cost to society. The state of California now spends more money on prisons than on higher education.[23] Wouldn't it make sense to have a GED program that teaches and tests skills that matter—such as financial literacy, sound communication and reading skills, and the obligations of citizenship? But, no, we ask students to calculate the number of angels that can dance on the head of a pin, using precise scientific notation.

The Trap: Bad things happen when a young adult is under- or unemployed for long stretches. Each unproductive month makes it that much harder to secure a good career path. As confidence ebbs and as opportunity remains out of reach, these trapped young adults become a ticking time bomb for our society. Many would thrive in an education system focused on life skills instead of college prep. Today, though, our education system says to our kids, "You can either get your college degree or end up with a menial job." But the reality in America today? Millions of young adults end up with both.

As inescapable economic forces lead to the creative destruction of our higher education system, we'll see the impact as college admissions play a reduced role in shaping our K-12 schools. As long as high school students are measured on criteria like GPA, standardized test scores, and AP courses, anyone trying to change K-12 schools will feel like Don Quixote tilting at ivory windmills. But we're already starting to see innovative changes in the college admissions process. Robert Sternberg, when he was dean of the School of Arts and Sciences at Tufts, pioneered the use of optional YouTube videos and other creative assessments as part of the application process. Bard College accepts four essays in lieu of any information about high school performance. MIT reviews MakerLab portfolios. And more than eight hundred four-year colleges and universities are test optional, meaning applicants no longer need to submit standardized test scores. The list includes top-tier colleges like Middlebury, Bowdoin, Bates, Smith, Hamilton, Bryn Mawr, and Wesleyan.[24]

In the same way employers are finding more effective ways to evaluate a candidate's competencies, colleges will discover that they can review digital portfolios of real achievement as easily as mountains of formulaic applications material. They'll start looking for meaningful indications of an applicant's passion and purpose, instead of dwelling on SATs and GPAs. They'll realize that the success of their admissions strategy shouldn't be measured by an entering class's first-year GPA, but by how many remarkable alumni they produce. When that day comes, we'll see far more real innovation in our K-12 schools—exciting developments along the lines of some of the school networks and individual schools described below.

Innovations in K-12 Public Schools

Charter schools, by themselves, are not a strategy for improving education, as we've seen. Nevertheless, the existence of charter legislation has enabled some truly outstanding school models to come into being. Collectively, they represent the very best educational R&D currently under way. Most incorporate the approaches to learning, teaching, and assessment that we have described throughout this book. Indeed, the reason we are so confident about the approaches we describe is because we've seen them work in hundreds of classes with every kind of kid.

HIGH TECH HIGH, THE DEEPER
LEARNING NETWORK, AND ED LEADER 21

We are big fans of High Tech High (HTH), a network of twelve schools serving five thousand predominantly minority students in grades K-12 in the San Diego region. HTH also has its own graduate school of education. In brief, the school embodies all of the best practices that we've described here: Teachers team-teach interdisciplinary courses where students master core competencies through engagement in challenging projects; students regularly present and defend their work orally and in their digital portfolios, and they complete both a work-based internship and a team-based service-learning project as requirements for graduation. (The documentary film *Most Likely to Succeed*, mentioned previously, features an in-depth look at ninth graders' experiences in High Tech High. Tony also described the school in his book *The Global Achievement Gap*, and HTH's recently established graduate school of education in *Creating Innovators*. Viewers and readers wanting to know more about the school are encouraged to seek out these sources.)

In 1999, when Tony first began working with Tom Vander Ark, who had just been appointed head of education grant-making at the Bill and Melinda Gates Foundation, there were only a handful of schools like High Tech High around the country—and most were affiliated with the network Ted Sizer founded in 1984, called The Coalition of Essential Schools. There was Deborah Meier's legendary Central Park East Secondary School in Harlem and, later, The Mission Hill School in Boston; The Met in Providence, co-founded by Dennis Littky and Elliot Washor; and an alternative high school Ann Cook directed called Urban Academy, as well as some other great small secondary schools in New York City.

Vander Ark, to his great credit, quickly recognized the potential of these schools to transform the high school experience—especially for the most disadvantaged students—and so he set out to aggressively fund expansion of some of these models and the creation of new ones. In New York City, a large number of new small public high schools were created that borrowed heavily from the legacies of the schools mentioned above. Today, students attending these high schools are "15 percent more likely to graduate within four years and 22 percent more likely to enroll in college—that's despite the fact that 3 out of every 4 of these students were behind grade level when they entered the 9th grade."[25] Unfortunately, though, this educational R&D did not produce the kind of immediate test score improvements most valued by Bill Gates, and so Vander Ark and his strategic approach were both replaced in 2006. But many of the school networks have gone on to survive—and to thrive!

In the last few years, The Hewlett Foundation and other funders have played a vital role by convening a larger association of schools under the umbrella of the Deeper Learning Network. The group consists of more than five hundred K-12 schools around the country that are committed to the following principles:[26]

- Mastery of core academic content: Students build their academic foundation in subjects like reading, writing, math, and science. They understand key principles and procedures, recall facts, use the correct language, and draw on their knowledge to complete new tasks.
- Critical thinking and problem-solving: Students think critically, analytically, and creatively. They know how to find, evaluate, and synthesize information to construct arguments. They can design their own solutions to complex problems.
- Collaboration: Collaborative students work well in teams. They communicate and understand multiple points of view and they know how to cooperate to achieve a shared goal.
- Effective communication: Students communicate effectively in writing and in oral presentations. They structure information in meaningful ways, listen to and give feedback, and construct messages for particular audiences.
- Self-directed learning: Students develop an ability to direct their own learning. They set goals, monitor their own progress, and reflect on their own strengths and areas for improvement. They learn to see setbacks as opportunities for feedback and growth. Students who learn through self-direction are more adaptive than their peers.
- An "academic mindset": Students with an academic mindset have a strong belief in themselves. They trust their own abilities and believe their hard work will pay off, so they persist to overcome obstacles. They also learn from and support each other. They see the relevance of their schoolwork to the real world and their own future success.

While most of the schools in the network use the approaches to learning and teaching pioneered by High Tech High and a handful of other pioneers, a number are developing new strategies and resources. For example, the Expeditionary Learning school network has a wealth of student work and projects for grades K-12 on its website to give teachers a better idea of the kinds of performance standards they can and should expect of their students.[27] The six-minute video showing how a first grader incorporates peer reviews to improve his drawings of a butterfly over half a dozen iterations is a modern education classic![28] Expeditionary Learning works with more than 160 schools and 4,000 teachers, serving 53,000 students in thirty-three states, and Expeditionary Learning schools currently outnumber the better-known KIPP network.[29]

Exciting educational R&D is no longer confined to start-up charter schools like the ones just mentioned. Founded and headed by Ken Kay, EdLeader21 is a new association of more than 170 public school districts, plus some international and independent schools, that are committed to teaching and assessing the four C's of critical thinking, collaboration, communication, and creativity. Together, they are doing groundbreaking work in the development of rubrics for assessing these core competencies, and their membership includes some of the most extraordinary public school district leaders with whom we have ever had the pleasure of working—notably Jim Merrill, superintendent of Wake County, North Carolina, and Pam Moran, superintendent of Albemarle County, Virginia.[30]

MALCOLM X SHABAZZ AND THE FUTURE PROJECT

The minute you set foot in Malcolm X Shabazz High School in Newark, New Jersey, you notice something different. In a school that for years held a spot on the list of our country's most troubled high schools, kids walk down halls with confident smiles and a sense of purpose. In the past couple of years, attendance rates have jumped dramatically. Kids now come to school on snow days. And during lunch, groups of kids take their lunch trays to sessions tutoring them on things like writing skills.

The Newark school system has long been viewed as Ground Zero for education reformers. Several, including Bill Gates, Mark Zuckerberg, the Waltons, and Eli Broad, set out to transform Newark schools and make them a national model. Zuckerberg announced a $100 million gift to Newark education on the Oprah Winfrey show, timed to coincide with the documentary *Waiting for Superman*. But, as the *New Yorker* reported, this heavily funded reform initiative accomplished nothing other than lining the pockets of consultants. In a telling line from Vivian Cox Fraser, the president of the Urban League of Essex County, "Everybody's getting paid, but Raheem still can't read."[31]

Gemar Mills, the principal of Shabazz, explains, "When I took over as principal in 2011–2012, I was the fourth principal over the course of four years, the state had recommended the district close the school, and the media dubbed the school 'Baghdad.' I couldn't begin to count the problems at this school. Nothing was working." So what's different now about Malcolm X Shabazz, if reform policies had no impact? Principal Mills teamed up with The Future Project, which hired an extraordinary visionary named Divine Bradley. Bradley is the head Dream Director at Shabazz, and part of the audacious nonprofit called The Future Project. He walks the halls of Shabazz, gets to know the students, and engages them on the question of "What's something big and bold you'd like to do with your life to make your world better? I'm here to help you." Most students have never been asked about life goals before. As a result of this kind of engagement, students at Shabazz rise to challenges, take on ambitious projects, and approach education and life with newfound purpose.

In the 2013–2014 school year, the Shabazz girls' basketball team hadn't lost a home game in thirty years and was ranked number two in the nation by *USA Today*. Though most players had never been on an airplane before, the team dreamed of playing in the national tournament in California, in which they had been invited to compete for two consecutive years. They approached their Dream Director for support, who responded, "I'm here to help, but you need to lead this effort, figure out your plan, and make it happen." Well, they did research and learned that former NBA star Shaquille O'Neal was born in Newark. They found a time he'd be in town. They worked with Bradley and Principal Mills to figure out a way to convince Shaq to come to their school and help them paint a mural. In advance, they prepared their pitch asking him to support their trip, complete with well-written backup. When he was at Shabazz, the team made their case, and O'Neal committed the funds to make the team's dream a reality. Principal Mills explains, "The impact on these girls, and on the rest of the school, was transformational. Under different circumstances, many would have dropped out of high school. However, this team served as an example of what could happen when you dream big and work hard. Of the five seniors on the team, all five graduated from Shabazz with diplomas—three with high honors. Moreover, all five seniors received scholarships to top colleges throughout the country. We now call our school Possibility High."

This school year, The Future Project launched an initiative called FutureU, as it expanded to high schools all over the country. Students spend time during lunch hours, before school, after school, or on Saturdays learning the skills required to accomplish their dreams: effective communication skills, how to manage projects, how to collaborate, and how to critique and exchange feedback. FutureU makes other school classes more compelling for the students and more effective for the teachers, since the link between a class and life is more apparent. Principal Mills reports that The Future Project doesn't just transform his students. He notes, "Our teachers and our staff all have dreams of their own, and Divine and his team help them achieve what they strive for. I knew just how special this program is when one of our security guards put up a huge picture of himself, alongside other students', which said his dream is to be a Newark policeman."

Not yet three years old, The Future Project is one of the fastest-growing and most successful nonprofit start-ups since the founding of Teach For America in 1990. Possibility High? That's the point of The Future Project. If the top priority of our education system were engaging and inspiring kids—not testing and measuring them—all sorts of things would be possible.[32]

Independent and International School Innovations

RIVERDALE COUNTRY SCHOOL

A growing number of independent schools are also engaging in a variety of R&D activities. Several leading schools, including Phillips Andover, Pomfret, and Sidwell Friends, have established Innovation Centers to encourage faculty to develop interdisciplinary courses. Most notable is the varied and interesting work being done at the Riverdale Country School, in New York, where Dominic Randolph has served as head since 2007. Under his leadership, Riverdale has undertaken a number of exciting new initiatives and partnerships.

The first step was to eliminate all Advanced Placement courses. In a December 2014 conversation with Randolph, we asked how this bold step had impacted student admissions to the most selective colleges. "It's actually improved," he said. "Our students are often taking interdisciplinary courses now—like the study of contemporary Latin American politics in a course that is taught in Spanish, or applied calculus combined with advanced physics—and so their transcripts are sometimes much more distinctive than those of other independent schools." Riverdale has also partnered with IDEO, one of the world's most innovative design companies, to teach educators the skills of design thinking and rapid prototyping and to bring more "making" into classrooms.[33]

Randolph has long been interested in the problem of developing character through education. Riverdale's initial work in this area was featured in a September 14, 2011, *New York Times Magazine* article by Paul Tough, and in his subsequent book, *How Children Succeed: Grit, Curiosity, and the Hidden Power of Character*. Later that year, Randolph teamed up with the University of Pennsylvania's Angela Duckworth, a MacArthur award winner in 2014, and KIPP co-founder Dave Levin, to create a new nonprofit called The Character Lab, which sponsors school-based research on topics related to character development.[34] One of their findings was that intellectual-character skills, such as curiosity, are surprisingly anemic predictors of report card grades. "Doing what you need to do to earn high marks on your report card is important. But your grades may not reflect other important qualities, like creativity or the ability to think independently. We have to be careful not to assume that what we know how to measure is all there is that's worth measuring," Randolph told us.

Looking toward 2015 and beyond, Randolph is most excited about the work his teachers are doing to reimagine senior year—and perhaps the junior year, as well. "We've sponsored a number of successful weeklong courses that have used the city as their classroom, and our seniors can now do projects in the spring lasting two months," he explained. "We'd like to push that out so that seniors might entirely reimagine their last year of high school and perhaps work on merit badges, with portfolio documentation."

BEAVER COUNTRY DAY

Peter Hutton has been headmaster of Beaver Country Day, a private school teaching grades six through twelve in Chestnut Hill, Massachusetts, for twenty years. Most longtime school heads get set in their ways. Not Hutton. He has completely reimagined school at Beaver Country Day, with powerful innovations at all levels. For starters, he encourages teams of teachers to innovate. He refuses to let any new idea be shut down because it might create scheduling complications, recognizing how often logistical issues stand in the way of progress.

To give you a feel for just how different things are at Beaver, you won't find a stand-alone computer programming course there. Programming is integrated into all courses, and *every* graduate develops programming competency. Since most teachers aren't programming experts, students serve as resident class-coding experts. At Beaver, you'll see a social studies class with teams of kids collaborating to develop an approach to predict the world's population in the year 2100, drawing on a range of STEM and humanities skills.

History classes involve vigorous debate of thought-provoking questions, not memorization. And when questions come up about how some aspect of Egypt's history affects Egyptian society today, Beaver students resourcefully get direct input from students they find in schools there. In 2013, when most U.S. journalists struggled to bring clarity to what our country should do in Syria, Beaver students interviewed students in Damascus, and discovered that as bad as Assad is, Syrian students—especially the girls—feared the insurgents more.

In 2010, Beaver worked with two MIT Architecture PhDs who wanted to bring the architecture studio approach to teaching to high school classrooms. With NuVu, a "maker's space," students spend ninety days completely away from school at a studio in Cambridge's Central Square. There they work with experts from the MIT Media Lab and from Harvard, with engineers, designers, artists, musicians, and entrepreneurs working in teams on real-world open-ended problems. Projects have included designing the city of the future, creating educational apps for children in the slums of Delhi, building prosthetics with 3D printers, building a bicycle-powered water filtration system, and creating and designing children's books of the future. In all projects there is a heavy emphasis on prototyping. If you got it right the first time, you didn't get it right. A very anti-school attitude! Pure, unadulterated exploration and nonlinear learning.

Hutton is generally dismissive of standardized tests, but does have each student take the College and Work Readiness Assessment twice—as an entering freshman and as a graduating senior. While he feels the CWRA is better than most tests, he is working with ETS to design tests that better assess the effectiveness of what he calls the New Basics: creative problem-solving, collaboration, iteration, empathy, tech and media literacy, visual communication, and presentation skills. He feels that standardized and in-school testing miss the big point—they focus on determining what students don't know. And as a result, they do students a disservice. He feels that learning and assessment should provide students with a range of ways to demonstrate what they know and how they can apply their knowledge. That is the power of NuVu, of those interviews with students in Damascus, of teaching coding the way Beaver does. In an effective classroom students should always be able to answer two questions: "What are you doing?" and "Why are you doing it?" Sadly, most education today remains content with focusing just on the first question.

One recent graduate of Beaver is now a student at MIT, where he meets regularly with MIT president L. Rafael Reif. The topic? What MIT needs to do to make its education more effective and more aligned with developing important life skills. When our K-12 schools deliver meaningful education to students, they go on to be advocates for change, creating a powerful ripple effect.

AFRICAN LEADERSHIP ACADEMY

Ten years ago, two Stanford Graduate School of Business students, Fred Swaniker from Ghana and Chris Bradford from Michigan, set out to establish an accelerated high school with the goal of transforming the continent of Africa. Today, this audacious dream is becoming reality. Their African Leadership Academy, based in Johannesburg, South Africa, draws students from all over the continent to an immersive two-year program combining intense academics (six courses per semester, plus an independent research class), leadership (speakers, seminars, and direct experiences), and entrepreneurship (every student starts and/or manages an entrepreneurial business or social venture). Courses are highly experiential, thought-provoking, and far more compelling than what most elite U.S. high schools offer.

Chris Bradford explains an important aspect of their admissions strategy: "With our applicants coming from a wide range of educational systems, socioeconomic and linguistic backgrounds, we have found that GPAs and test scores are largely irrelevant in our admissions process. Instead, we're looking for underlying character attributes, and we evaluate candidates in their local language of instruction. For example, we've found one question to be a great predictor of student outcomes at ALA: 'Tell us about a problem you observed in your community, and what you did to address it.' Their answers to this question speak volumes about passion, purpose, and resilience."

ALA graduates go on to top universities around the world, performing at levels that would be the envy of our most exclusive private schools. They thrive at over fifty U.S. colleges, including every Ivy League school, Stanford, and MIT. Bradford adds, "We select kids with the passion and drive to make their world better, not with a passion for achieving grades. It just so happens that our kids do really well at university. But we measure our program's success by how our students shape the trajectories of their countries. And it's exciting to report that they already are shaping their communities." The first graduates of ALA finished university in 2014, but have already launched initiatives and organizations that have reached over five million stakeholders, created over two hundred quality full-time jobs, and generated over $1.5 million in investment.

One of ALA's distinctive initiatives is DSC, which stands for "Do Something Cool." During DSC, all other activities at school come to a halt, and students are given forty-eight hours to invent and begin implementing something they're excited about that they feel will make their world better. ALA students go into overdrive with creativity and passion, fueled by the self-directed nature of the activity—and all ALA staff members stop their work to run with their own DSC project. "DSC creates a true community of learners and innovators, and is perhaps the most vibrant and exciting time on our campus," Bradford says. Last fall, a student named Keith from Zimbabwe used his DSC time to write a novella called *Tamu's Purpose*. He had always dreamed of being a writer, but had never had the space or time to write, and he threw himself into his novella. He sought feedback and edited the work in the weeks that followed, and recently learned that the novella he wrote will be published in 2015.

Bradford commented, "When you give students a chance to create something big and audacious, they rise to the occasion. Kids are savvy enough to know how to access what they need to learn to pull off amazing things, and nothing builds their confidence like an authentic accomplishment. At ALA we seek to empower our students with the capacity to learn how to learn throughout their lives, and to realize their capabilities to fulfill a meaningful purpose in life."

Part 3: What Your School Community Can Do . . .

Change processes in schools have a way of going awry. They meander into platitudes, while sparking bitter disagreements over low-level issues like how to deal with hats, gum, and tardiness. Political scientist Wallace Sayre said about academics, "The politics are so vicious because the stakes are so small." But when it comes to the future of our kids and our nation, the stakes are enormous.

Most school planning processes suffer from "driving by looking in the rearview mirror." With historic practices as the baseline, planning revolves around fine-tuning the existing model. It's rare to question underlying assumptions or confront fundamental trade-offs, let alone reimagine the school's core design. Consequently, after months of committee meetings, strategic plans serve up content-free statements like, "In the coming decade, our school will be known, first and foremost, as a vibrant community of educators with an unparalleled commitment to students and to the quality of our work with them." You get the idea.

Successful change processes occur when a respected cross section of the community can:

- Explain the urgency for change;
- Form a shared vision of the priority skills students need in a future world that bears little resemblance to the past;
- Assess the school's effectiveness in helping students develop priority skills;
- Seek student input and identify incremental steps to improve outcomes; and
- Empower teachers and students to design, test, and implement solutions.

Real change won't happen at a school without a sense of urgency and shift in culture. And urgency won't come from top-down edicts, blast emails, or PowerPoint slide decks. Change happens when the community embraces it emotionally and viscerally—in response to hard facts, a compelling speaker, gut-wrenching anecdotes from students and graduates, inspiring successes, or a powerful film bringing the issues to life.

In effecting change, school communities need to think deeply about the skills and characteristics students will need for the world they'll live in as adults. Simple steps can open up the eyes of a community, setting the stage for progress. You can begin this work by considering how the world has changed for your kids and by exploring trends, economic forces, new ways of working, and the impact of technology. For instance, a school community can divide into small working groups who think through:

- What skills did Henry Ford want for his workforce?
- What skills will the organizations of the future want from their employees?
- What skills will society want from its citizens and leaders?

We can't predict the exact words your school will come up with, but there will be consistent, mobilizing themes. Your strategy will be driven by outcomes that reflect your community's aspirations, values, passions, and goals—not obsolete practices forced on you by bureaucrats or inertia.

With this clarity, a school community can assess how school experiences align with desired outcomes. Real work will be required from teams of administrators, teachers, students, and parents, who will evaluate on a sampled basis how classes, tests, graduation requirements, grading mechanisms, and after-school programs affect the development of priority skills. An honest examination of practices exposes what to start, stop, and continue doing in order to produce the outcomes you want.

Finally, with a comprehensive view of effectiveness, a school can identify and implement steps to move forward. It's important not to relegate these steps to the distant future, when a sense of urgency will have dissipated. We suggest building early momentum through some "low-hanging fruit" successes and capitalizing on this momentum in tackling more complex problems. Dislodging entrenched practices is like removing a

Band-Aid—far better to take it off fast. For a great resource encouraging members of a school community to experiment with low-risk "hacks," check our School Retool.

Here's a hypothetical example of how this process might work. A small group of volunteers decides to help move a school forward:

1. They organize a community event around a compelling speaker or powerful film (say, at the risk of being self-serving, the acclaimed documentary *Most Likely to Succeed*). In small groups, they discuss how the world has changed and what skills students need in order to thrive in the future. Such discussions bring urgency to the need to reimagine the school's model for helping students develop essential skills, igniting discussion about community values and aspirations.

2. They conduct focus groups with students and recent graduates to bring the student voice into the conversation. Videotapes of focus groups with recent graduates are discussed by teachers and parents in order to better understand how graduates were most and least well-prepared by their schooling.

3. In response to community input, the team establishes priority skills for students, which could include collaboration, communication, creative problem-solving, and critical analysis. Subcommittees of parents, teachers, and students assess the school's current effectiveness in developing these skills.

As an example, one team takes on collaboration. The collaboration subcommittee reviews school experiences and concludes that classes do little to help students learn collaboration skills. After-school programs, while beneficial, need to be more student-driven. The team recommends near-term action items, including:

- Peer-driven seminars on collaboration, with advice and coaching;
- Professional development for facilitating collaboration among teachers, as well as productive group work with students;
- at least one collaborative assignment in every course;

- at least one major challenge requiring student collaboration as part of every after-school program;
- End-of-semester evaluations (from teachers and peers) on each student's progress in collaboration; and
- Periodic student-produced videos, archived in their digital portfolio, with a self-appraisal of progress and goals for their collaboration skills.

A major failure of education reform has been its exhaustive and exhausting call for doing "more," without identifying what to do less of. Do everything you've been doing, only better, but also prepare your students for state tests. Now make your lessons comply with the Common Core. Now explain to parents why scores are so low. For decades, we've added to the workload of teachers, without strategic clarity. If a school adds new skills for students to master, it has to eliminate less strategic tasks. In shaping these choices, schools need to draw on the people closest to the problem—teachers and students—and empower them to design, innovate, and implement.

These suggestions are based on a depth of experience and expertise. Tony wrote *Change Leadership: A Practical Guide to Transforming Our Schools* in 2010 with his colleagues at Harvard's Change Leadership Group, an organization he founded and co-directed. The book describes methodologies that are based on a decade of research and work with teams of educators who aspired to be change leaders. We worked closely with Stephanie Rogen, CEO of Greenwich Leadership Partners, a national leader in helping schools design and implement effective change processes, whose widely respected work is reflected in these recommendations. Finally, we heartily recommend *The Leader's Guide to 21st Century Education: 7 Steps for Schools and Districts*. Written by Ken Kay and Valerie Greenhill, the book lays out a sequence of steps much like those we've outlined above that many schools districts in EdLeader21 and elsewhere have used as guidelines for change.

Based on this proven body of work, we've invested in the technology to provide every school in our country with an extensive set of resources to help schools move forward, accessible through the website http://www.likelytosucceed.org.

If All Else Fails

It's possible that you've done all you can as a parent or teacher to move your school forward, and you've run into a brick wall. At least in the near term, you want to focus on your own child or class. And success on a smaller scale may, over time, translate into broader change. Take heart. We love the saying, "In the desert, it doesn't take much rain to make the flowers bloom." Whether you're a parent or teacher, you can tap into amazing online resources that help students develop critical skills. For instance, the website http://www.thesparklist.org highlights the very best of what's out there. Rather than listing an overwhelming number of options, the SparkList is highly selective, with the goal of making it easy for you to find engaging challenges aligned with a child's passions. Explore and offer your feedback.

For teachers, there's safety in numbers when it comes to innovating, and your efforts are likely to be more effective if you don't work in isolation. A pair of teachers from different departments can be especially powerful, ensuring an interdisciplinary approach, built-in synergies, and day-to-day support. Over time, your team's success might encourage your school to support additional innovative teaching teams, quickly shifting the school from low to high gear. For innovative teachers running into resistance, encourage skeptics to watch the film *Most Likely to Succeed*, which should provide you with "cover."

A word of caution: Sometimes less is more. Resist the temptation to micromanage every minute of a child's day. Unstructured time can be transformational. Many innovative companies give employees significant blocks of free time for pure exploration. Do the same for a child. And the trade-off between test prep and passion-based exploration? It's a challenge, but engaged students often rise to the occasion on standardized tests, offsetting a lack of direct preparation. Letting kids devour books they care about may not goose SAT verbal scores as much as long hours memorizing SAT vocabulary, but it's better for a child in the long run.

Around the country, teachers are experimenting with what is sometimes called "genius hour" or "Google Time" (named after Google's practice of giving employees time to work on projects of their own choosing). They are often discovering extraordinary things about their kids in the process. Consider this email that Tony recently received from a fifth-grade teacher:

> *Dear Mr. Wagner,*
>
> *I wanted to express my appreciation of your work. This past summer I read* Creating Innovators, *and after also reading Paul Tough's* How Children Succeed, *I spent time reflecting on the types of experiences students have as a result of being in my class. The result of that thinking was that I decided to try an entirely new approach to weekend homework for my fifth grade class this fall.*
>
> *The deal was that, rather than assigning any "regular academic" work on the weekend, they had to create plans for the way(s) in which they would like to spend two hours of their time each weekend. They could use that time in a variety of ways including working to improve an already existing skill, pursuing a passion, or exploring new areas of interest. Each weekend they kept track of how they implemented their plans, and now we are in the process of assessing how they met their goals. They will present to the class next week.*
>
> *Four children in my class used the time to work on writing novels; one learned to play the guitar and to create a soon-to-be-on-the-market book of games; another learned how to do fashion illustration; one learned more about China (as she was adopted into a white family) and learned how to cook a new meal every weekend; and one built and programmed a robot.*
>
> *Many students used the time to practice their instruments, to read for enjoyment, and to improve in their various athletic endeavors.*
>
> *Our students reported that their most significant "take away" from the project was that they learned that if they set and then*

work toward goals, no matter how "hard" or (their word) "crazy" the goals may seem at the start, they can achieve them. I am thrilled by the excitement generated by this assignment and commitment that most had in regard to completing it.

Regards,
Susan Reenan
The Gordon School

What About Parenting?

Now we get to the hard part for parents. At a certain point, your child may lose interest in school—often for the legitimate reason that it's boring. Parents instinctively respond by pushing their child to develop sound work habits, to complete assignments, and to strive for high grades. After all, that's a parent's job. And if children complain that they don't see why they need to study something, parents fall back on the tried-and-true line, "It helps you develop grit." As parents, we are genetically programmed to fight for our child's survival, to go all out to raise a hard-working straight-A child who goes on to a well-known college, and then on to a great life. That's the American Dream, and no self-respecting parent will stand idly by and let his or her child miss out.

But in our current education system, most of what a student does in the higher grades is pointless. So here's the telling question. Is a child trained to plow through day after day of mind-numbing, low-level tasks really better off? What if it just trains your child to accept that life is all about jumping through hoops, following instructions blindly, and responding to approval from others? What if these marching orders are, in fact, killing your child's innovation, creativity, and independence of thought? What if, with the best of intentions, this actually puts your child at risk in the innovation era?

The Future: Innovation versus Education

This book has straddled the worlds of innovation and education. If you want to get inspired about our country's future, look to our inventors, our innovators, our social entrepreneurs, our start-ups. And if you want to get discouraged, look at how we educate our kids. How we treat our teachers. And how we stumble from one failed policy to the next.

Our innovation world reflects the very best of America. Intrepid pioneers pursue bold dreams, in hopes of changing the course of history. Thinking big is a way of life. Failure is embraced, and resilience is rewarded. Out-of-the-box approaches are admired, not marked down. Collective adherence to obsolete methods is a market opportunity, not a reason to give up. The results? In the past five decades, all U.S. economic and job growth has come from innovative start-ups.[35] Our entrepreneurial successes create our jobs, shape our society, define us, inspire us, and are the envy of the world.

But when it comes to education policy, we have lost all sight of what makes our country great. Through a bizarre twist of fate, we have an education system that would make perfect sense in the 1970s U.S.S.R. but is completely out of step with America's core values and strengths. We insist on top-down command-and-control. We micromanage every minute of every lesson plan. Instead of letting a thousand flowers bloom, we replace all flowers with the same lifeless, overtested weed. We take every ounce of bold creativity out of the classroom, replacing it with a soulless march through dull curriculum and test prep decoupled from life skills. We prioritize standardization and accountability, and don't seem to notice or care that students lack engagement and purpose. We rob our kids of their futures.

If we ran our economy the way we run our education system, our GDP would be lower than Haiti's. If our education system reflected America's core entrepreneurial spirit, our youth would create, invent, lead, and contribute. They'd help us understand that their future won't be defined by how they do against kids in China or South Korea on standardized tests, but how they use their talents and passions to forge ways to make the world better.

We wrote this book out of concern. Fear, to be honest. We see brutally efficient innovation accelerating at warp speed. It will do lots of admirable things, for sure. But like Hurricane Katrina bearing down on New Orleans, innovation will wipe out millions of routine jobs, imposing hardship across society. Even if our education system turned on a dime, today's youth are at risk. But our education system won't turn on a dime. Like crew members on the *Titanic* bickering over the dinner menu, our leaders will piss and moan about second-order issues and ignore the opportunity that stares all of us right in the face. Each generation of Americans is capable of doing amazing things, if we just stop putting up irrelevant roadblocks.

It's time.

For most of the last century, U.S. education played a vital role in the American Dream. Irrespective of birth circumstances, Americans could access a sound public education, move into the middle or upper class, and build a better future for their family and community. Our schools extended opportunity to all and made our country great.

Today, our education system has become the American Nightmare. It saps the joy of learning from every child and teacher. Classrooms jump through endless hoops that have nothing to do with life skills. Our education policy-makers lack vision and perspective, and prioritize the need for an outdated version of "accountability," not the long-term interests of our children. For millions of young Americans, school is where their hopes for a meaningful life die, instead of spring into life.

The grandson of two successful engineers and entrepreneurs, Tony grew up in material comfort. He loved reading, but what he was told to learn in school and later what he saw in the world around him began to make no sense. He joined the civil rights movement, then the anti–Vietnam War movement. He dropped out of college twice, finally graduating from a small progressive college, where he studied social problems. He decided to become a teacher—not because he loved school, but because he wanted to reinvent it. Tony managed to get into Harvard for a Master of Arts in Teaching, despite his unconventional transcript, mediocre test scores, and no legacy. He made his way in the education universe by writing about what he was learning in the classroom, eventually earning a Doctorate in Education at Harvard by authoring exactly the kind of dissertation he was told not to write. Tony very much doubts that he would make it starting out in today's world. It's too credentialed, too test-driven. It does not make space for the kind of student that he was or teacher that he became.

Ted grew up in very modest circumstances. His father served on a destroyer in the Pacific Rim in World War II, was in seven bloody encounters, saw midshipmen a few feet away torn to shreds by enemy artillery, and was discharged early because of a nervous breakdown. He never completed his high school requirements, but grabbed the bottom rung of America's economic ladder as a construction worker. He worked overtime each week to put food on his family's table. Ted's mother worked at night as a secretary taking police reports, often for the most gruesome of crimes, to save the extra money required to put her kids through college. And Ted took advantage of an affordable, and fair, education system to realize, in some sense, a version of the American Dream, with a successful career in business and the wherewithal to give back to society.

We now live in a country where these kinds of dreams are so much more difficult to realize. Our education system weeds young Americans out, instead of inspiring them. It makes the bottom rung of the economic ladder more elusive, coating it with academic grease. It has so lost its way that policy leaders can only fumble when asked how school prepares our kids for life in the innovation era.

It's time to reimagine our schools. To return them to an essential role in the American Dream. To do your part.

ACKNOWLEDGMENTS

Several people have made significant contributions to this book. Tamara Day did heroic work in fact-checking the entire manuscript and in researching and writing the powerful student vignettes. These student histories, in their own way, speak volumes about the impact our education system is having on so many young Americans with the potential to make meaningful contributions to their community. We are grateful for the remarkable support provided by our team at Scribner—Shannon Welch, our senior editor; John Glynn; and Lisa Wolff. They jumped right in to this project, providing sound guidance and unwavering support. They helped move our manuscript to a higher level and always offered the most constructive of suggestions. Finally, we wish to thank our literary agent, Esmond Harmsworth of Zachary Shuster Harmsworth, for his wise counsel, assistance in preparing the book proposal, and excellent representation to perspective publishers.

Additionally, we would each like to thank several individuals who have helped us in important ways.

Tony:

I would like to acknowledge the extraordinary work of Ted Dintersmith on this project. The book was Ted's idea from the beginning, and he authored initial drafts of every chapter. His brilliant analysis and bold writing have pushed my thinking and my writing style in very significant ways. Additionally, he brought to the book the invaluable perspective of a true business leader. This book—and the award-winning documentary film of the same title that Ted envisioned and produced—are powerful testimony to Ted's extraordinary talents and commitment to reimagining education for the innovation era. To the extent that this book may offer fresh insights into our education dilemma, Ted deserves the lion's share of the credit.

I would also like to thank my wife, PJ Blankenhorn. She has been my first reader, best critic, and a wonderful thought partner with this, as well as my other books. Her creative and generous spirit infuse all of my work.

Ted

Upon first reading Tony Wagner's *The Global Achievement Gap*, I felt as though a lifetime of anecdotal education experiences suddenly snapped into coherence. It is an inspiring and energizing work, and I only wish that it were required reading for every adult in our country. I jumped at the opportunity to work with him on this book, and can only hope that—in its own way—this new book can approximate the impact that his earlier works had on me and on so many. Tony has been a beacon of insight and hope for a growing number of citizens concerned about the future of education, our youth, and our country. If our country comes to its senses and begins to educate our kids in a way that helps them make the most of life's opportunities, it will be largely because of Tony's lifetime mission to align our schools with bringing purpose and authenticity to the education of millions of students.

I want to thank my wife and children, for all sorts of reasons. For six months, I got up every morning (even on vacations!) at 5 a.m. and wrote for several hours, not particularly interested in talking to anyone else. My supportive wife, Elizabeth, was cool with that and always happy to help. My two kids have taught me more about school than I could ever have learned otherwise. Both are perceptive in distinguishing between meaningful assignments and mindless exercises. I admire them for having the courage to ditch the drivel, and focus on what they are passionate about.

NOTES

Chapter 1. Our Education DNA

1 "America's Call for Higher Education Redesign." The 2012 Lumina Foundation Study of the American Public's Opinion on Higher Education, February 5, 2013.

2 Agresti, James D. "Poll reveals voters misinformed about key issues." *Just Facts Daily*. http://www.justfactsdaily.com/poll-reveals-voters-misinformed-about-key-issues (accessed October 22, 2014).

3 "The Nation's Report Card: Civics 2010." *National Center for Education Statistics*. http://nces.ed.gov/nationsreportcard/pubs/main2010/2011466.asp#section1 (accessed August 16, 2014).

4 "U.S. Suicide Rates, 1950–2003." Suicide.org. http://www.suicide.org/suicide-statistics.html#death-rates (accessed October 22, 2014).

5 Meshchaninov, Yehudi. "The Prussian-industrial history of public schooling." *New American Academy*, April 2012.

6 Goldin, Claudia, and Lawrence F. Katz. *The Race between Education and Technology* (Cambridge, MA: Belknap Press, 2010).

7 "A Nation At Risk: The Imperative For Education Reform." A Report to the Nation and the Secretary of Education, United States Department of Education, by the National Commission on Excellence in Education, April 1983. http://www2.ed.gov/pubs/NatAtRisk/index.html.

8 Busteed, Brandon. "Why the education economy is the next big thing for the American workforce." *Fast Company*, July 29, 2014. http://www.fastcompany.com/3033593/the-future-of-work/why-the-education-economy-is-the-next-big-thing-for-the-american-workforc (accessed August 16, 2014).

Chapter 2. The Purpose of Education

1 Laneri, Raquel. "In pictures: America's best prep schools." Forbes.com, April 29, 2010. http://www.forbes.com/2010/04/29/best-prep-schools-2010-opinions-private-education_slide_15.html (accessed December 30, 2014).

2 Interview and private communication, Kevin Mattingly, Dean of Faculty, Lawrenceville Academy, December 18, 2014.

3   Quigley, Rachel. "What's the Constitution? Don't bother asking 70% of Americans: Alarming number of U.S. citizens don't know basic facts about their own country." *Daily Mail*, March 21, 2011. http://www.dailymail.co.uk/news/article-1368482/How-ignorant-Americans-An-alarming-number-U-S-citizens-dont-know-basic-facts-country.html (accessed December 30, 2014).

4   A number of Tony's keynotes may be viewed at: http://www.tonywagner.com/tag/videos.

5   138,925 schools: NCES 2009-10. http://nces.ed.gov/fastfacts/display.asp?id=84 and 3.7 mil teachers: NCES 2009-10. http://nces.ed.gov/fastfacts/display.asp?id=28 and 83 mill students: U.S. Census Bureau, 2011 (accessed December 30, 2014).

Chapter 3. What's At Stake?

1   Symonds, William C., Robert Schwartz, and Ronald F. Ferguson. 2011. "Pathways to prosperity: Meeting the challenge of preparing young Americans for the 21st century." Cambridge, MA: Pathways to Prosperity Project, Harvard University Graduate School of Education.

2   G.E. "Evaluating Shanghai's high test scores." *The Economist*, January 21, 2014.

3   Zhao, Yong. "How Does PISA Put the World at Risk (Part 1): Romanticizing Misery," *Zhao Learning* (blog), March 9, 2014. http://zhaolearning.com/2014/03/09/how-does-pisa-put-the-world-at-risk-part-1-romanticizing-misery/ (accessed December 30, 2014).

4   The film, *2 Million Minutes*, may be ordered here: https://www.2mminutes.com/films/.

5   Zhao, Yong. "Deja vu: Too Late to Learn from China," *Zhao Learning* (blog), February 22, 2014. http://zhaolearning.com/2014/02/22/deja-vu-too-late-to-learn-from-china/ (accessed December 30, 2014).

6   Zhao, Yong. *Who's Afraid of the Big Bad Dragon: Why China Has the Best (and Worst) Education System in the World* (San Francisco: Jossey-Bass, 2014), 9.

7   Source: Wikipedia. http://en.wikipedia.org/wiki/List_of_Nobel_laureates_by_country (accessed December 30, 2014).

8   Source: Forbes.com http://www.forbes.com/innovative-companies/list/ (accessed December 30, 2014).

9   Source: U.S. Patent Office. http://www.uspto.gov/web/offices/ac/ido/oeip/taf/cst_all.htm (accessed December 30, 2014).

10 "National Charter School Study 2013," Center for Research on Education Outcomes, Stanford University, Palo Alto, CA. https://credo.stanford.edu/index.html (accessed December 5, 2014).

11 Private communication, December 29, 2014.

12 Tough, Paul. *How Children Succeed: Grit, Curiosity, and the Hidden Power of Character* (Mariner Books, reprint edition, July 2, 2013).

13 "Child Poverty," National Center for Children in Poverty. www.nccp.org/topics/childpoverty.html (accessed October 22, 2014).

14 "2013 Ratings of Congress: 113th United States Congress, First Session." The American Conservative Union, 2013. http://www.conservative.org/legislative-ratings/2013-congress (accessed December 30, 2014).

15 Tau, Byron, and Tarini Parti. "How Big Money failed to rescue Eric Cantor." *Politico*, June 11, 2014. http://www.politico.com/story/2014/06/2014-virginia-primary-big-money-eric-cantor-107699.html (accessed December 30, 2014).

16 "Consensus: 97% of climate scientists agree." NASA, *Global Climate Change: Vital Signs on the Planet.* climate.nasa.gov/scientific-consensus/ (accessed October 22, 2014).

17 Saad, Lydia. "A Steady 57% in U.S. Blame Humans for Global Warming." *Gallup*, March 18, 2014. http://www.gallup.com/poll/167972/steady-blame-humans-global-warming.aspx (accessed December 30, 2014).

18 Clement, Scott. "How Americans see global warming—in 8 charts." *Washington Post*, April 22, 2013. http://www.washingtonpost.com/blogs/the-fix/wp/2013/04/22/how-americans-see-global-warming-in-8-charts/ (accessed December 30, 2014).

19 College Board AP biology: Sample Syllabus 4. http://www.collegeboard.com/html/apcourseaudit/courses/pdfs/ap-biology-sample-syllabus-4-id876032v1.pdf (accessed December 30, 2014).

20 Mooney, Chris. "Believe it: Global warming can produce more intense snows." *Mother Jones*, January 21, 2014. http://www.motherjones.com/blue-marble/2014/01/global-warming-janus-snow (accessed December 30, 2014).

21 Clynes, Tom. "The battle over climate science." *Popular Science*, June 21, 2012. http://www.popsci.com/science/article/2012-06/battle-over-climate-change (accessed December 30, 2014).

22 Jacobson, Louis. "Rick Perry says Social Security is a Ponzi scheme." *PolitiFact.com*, September 12, 2011. http://www.politifact.com/truth-o-meter/statements/2011/sep/12/rick-perry/rick-perry-says-social-security-ponzi-scheme/ (accessed December 30, 2014).

23 Baker, Dean, and David Rosnick. "Basic facts on social security and proposed benefit cuts/privatization." Center for Economic and Policy Research, March 2005.

24 Krugman, Paul. "Inventing a crisis." *New York Times* Op-Ed. December 7, 2004. http://www.nytimes.com/2004/12/07/opinion/07krugman.html?scp=539&sq=&st=nyt&_r=1& (accessed October 22, 2014).

25 Meier, Deborah. "Democracy at Risk," *Educational Leadership*, May 2009. http://www.ascd.org/ascd/pdf/journals/ed_lead/el200905_meier.pdf. (accessed December 5, 2014).

Chapter 4. The Formative Years: K–12

1 "Fast Facts," National Center for Education Statistics. http://nces.ed.gov/fastfacts/display.asp?id=66 (accessed December 21, 2014).

2 Sims, Peter. "The Montessori Mafia," *Wall Street Journal*, April 5, 2011. http://blogs.wsj.com/ideas-market/2011/04/05/the-montessori-mafia/ (accessed December 17, 2014).

3 Green, Alex E.S. "How slide rules won a war," *Journal of the Oughtred Society*, June 20, 2005, Vol. 14, No. 1, Spring 2005. http://www2.mae.ufl.edu/sliderule/docs/hsrww-1.pdf (accessed December 31, 2014).

4 Weissmann, Jordan. "Here's how little math Americans actually use at work," *The Atlantic*, April 24, 2013. http://www.theatlantic.com/business/archive/2013/04/heres -how-little-math-americans-actually-use-at-work/275260/ (accessed December 7, 2014).

5 "What Does It Really Mean to Be College and Work Ready?" Executive Summary, National Center on Education and the Economy, May 2013. http://www.ncee.org/ wp-content/uploads/2013/05/NCEE_ExecutiveSummary_May2013.pdf (accessed December 11, 2014).

6 "Can I Use a Calculator?" The ACT, effective September 1, 2014. http://www.act student.org/faq/calculator.html (accessed December 31, 2014).

7 NCEE, op. cit.

8 Lockhart, Paul. *A Mathematician's Lament: How School Cheats Us Out of Our Most Fascinating and Imaginative Art Form.* (New York: Bellevue Literary Press. Kindle Edition, 2009), 20–21.

9 http://www.nwp.org (accessed December 8, 2014).

10 "Writing 2011," The Nation's Report Card. http://www.nationsreportcard.gov/writing _2011/context_1.aspx?tab_id=tab2&subtab_id=Tab_1#chart (accessed December 8, 2014).

11 "NAEP Data Explorer," National Center for Education Statistics. http://nces.ed.gov /nationsreportcard/naepdata/report.aspx (accessed December 8, 2014).

12 "Writing 2011," The Nation's Report Card, National Center for Education Statis-tics. http://nces.ed.gov/nationsreportcard/pdf/main2011/2012470.pdf (accessed December 9, 2014).

13 Ibid.

14 "Sample Questions, Writing 2011," The National Report Card. http://www.nations reportcard.gov/writing_2011/sample_quest.aspx?tab_id=tab3&subtab_id=Tab _1#chart (accessed December 9, 2014).

15 "Education at a Glance 2014," OECD Indicators, 2014, OECD Publishing. http:// dx.doi.org/10.1787/eag-2014-en (accessed December 10, 2014).

16 Wagner, Tony. *Creating Innovators* (New York: Scribner, 2012), 238.

17 More information on the film may be found here: http://www.hbo.com/documen-taries/resolved#/

18 "Why Investments in Early Childhood Work," *The Ounce*. http://www.ounceof prevention.org/about/why-early-childhood-investments-work.php (accessed Decem-ber 21, 2014).

19 Rich, Motoko. "Language gap study bolsters a push for Pre-K," *New York Times*, October 21, 2013. http://www.nytimes.com/2013/10/22/us/language-gap-study -bolsters-a-push-for-pre-k.html?pagewanted=all&_r=0 (accessed December 20, 2014).

20 Private communication, December 29, 2014.

21 "English Language and Composition Course Description," The College Board AP (New York: The College Board, 2014). http://media.collegeboard.com/digital Services/pdf/ap/ap-english-language-and-composition-course-description.pdf (accessed December 31, 2014).

22 "Arts education lacking in low-income areas of New York City, report says," *New York Times*, April 7, 2014. http://www.nytimes.com/2014/04/07/nyregion/arts

-education-lacking-in-low-income-areas-of-new-york-city-report-says.html?_r=0 (accessed December 31, 2014).

23 The video may be found here: https://www.engageny.org/resource/middle-school-ela-curriculum-video-close-reading-of-a-text-mlk-letter-from-birmingham-jail (accessed December 14, 2014).

24 Capps, Kriston. "How Andrew Carnegie built the architecture of American literacy," *Atlantic City Lab*, October 28, 2014. http://www.citylab.com/design/2014/10/how-andrew-carnegie-built-the-architecture-of-american-literacy/381953/ (accessed November 14, 2014).

25 Strauss, Valerie. "Texas GOP rejects 'critical thinking' skills. Really," The Answer Sheet, *Washington Post*, July 9, 2012. http://www.washingtonpost.com/blogs/answer-sheet/post/texas-gop-rejects-critical-thinking-skills-really/2012/07/08/gJQAHNpFXW_blog.html (accessed December 18, 2014).

26 http://thecolbertreport.cc.com/videos/577ry9/the-word---on-the-straight---narrow-minded (accessed December 31, 2014).

27 Stanford History Education Group. http://sheg.stanford.edu/home_page (accessed December 31, 2014).

28 Hestenes, D., Malcolm Wells, and Gregg Swackhamer. "Force concept inventory," *The Physics Teacher*, Vol. 30, March 1992, 141–166.

29 Mazur, Eric. *Peer Instruction* (Boston: Addison-Wesley, 1996), 4.

30 Ibid., 7.

31 Jackson, Anthony. "Global Competence," Asia Society. http://asiasociety.org/global competence (accessed December 18, 2014).

32 https://www.youtube.com/watch?v=kO8x8eoU3L4.

33 Meier, Deborah. *The Power of Their Ideas: Lessons for America from a Small School in Harlem* (Boston: Beacon Press, 2002).

Chapter 5. The Gold Ring: The College Degree

1 Source: Wikipedia. http://en.wikipedia.org/wiki/College_tuition_in_the_United _States (accessed December 30, 2014).

2 Rhoades, Gary. "The Study of American Professions," *Sociology of Higher Education: Contributions and Their Contexts,* ed. Patricia Gumport (Baltimore: Johns Hopkins University Press, 2007).

3 Bok, Derek. *Higher Learning* (Cambridge, MA: Harvard University Press, 1986), 323–24.

4 Keeling, Richard P., and Richard Hersh. *We're Losing Our Minds: Rethinking American Higher Education* (New York: Palgrave Macmillan, 2011), 397–398, Kindle Edition.

5 Mark Suster, videotaped interview at Startup Grind, February 20, 2013. http://www.bothsidesofthetable.com/2013/03/03/in-15-years-from-now-half-of-us-universities-may-be-in-bankruptcy-my-surprise-discussion-with-claychristensen/ (accessed December 8, 2014).

6 "What's the Price Tag for a College Education?" CollegeData. http://www.college data.com/cs/content/content_payarticle_tmpl.jhtml?articleId=10064 (accessed December 30, 2014).

7   "Salary Survey," National Association of Colleges and Employers. http://www
    .naceweb.org/uploadedFiles/Content/static-assets/downloads/executive-summary
    /2014-april-salary-survey-executive-summary.pdf (accessed December 17, 2014).

8   Weissmann, Jordan. "How Bad Is the Job Market for the College Class of 2014,"
    Slate, May 8, 2014. http://www.slate.com/blogs/moneybox/2014/05/08/unemploy-
    ment_and_the_class_of_2014_how_bad_is_the_job_market_for_new_college.
    html (accessed December 8, 2014).

9   Ibid.

10 "Student Debt and the Class of 2003," The Institute for College Access & Success. http://
    projectonstudentdebt.org/files/pub/classof2013.pdf (accessed December 30, 2014).

11 Severns, Maggie, "The Student Loan Debt Crisis in 9 Charts," *Mother Jones*, June
    5, 2013. http://www.motherjones.com/politics/2013/06/student-loan-debt-charts
    (accessed March 31, 2014).

12 *Trends in Student Aid*, College Board (New York: College Board, 2008), 6.

13 *How Undergraduate Students Use Credit Cards: Sallie Mae's National Study of Usage
    Rates and Trends 2009* (Wilkes-Barre, PA: Sallie Mae Foundation, 2009), 3.

14 Olson, Elizabeth. "Student loan debt burdens more than just young people," *New
    York Times*, September 12, 2014. http://www.nytimes.com/2014/09/13/business/
    student-loan-debt-burdens-more-than-just-young-people.html (accessed Novem-
    ber 20, 2014).

15 "Mental Health & Well-Being Task Force issues report," Stanford News Release,
    October 1, 2008. http://news.stanford.edu/pr/2008/pr-mhstory-100108.html
    (accessed December 30, 2014).

16 Eiser, Arielle. "The crisis on campus," *American Psychological Association*, Vol. 42,
    No. 8, September 2011, 18. http://www.apa.org/monitor/2011/09/crisis-campus
    .aspx. (accessed November 20, 2014).

17 "Fall2010ReferenceGroupExecutiveSummary," *AmericanCollegeHealthAssociation*.
    http://www.acha-ncha.org/docs/ACHA-NCHA-II_ReferenceGroup_Executive
    Summary_Fall2010.pdf (accessed December 8, 2014).

18 Arum, Richard, and Josipa Roksa. *Academically Adrift: Limited Learning on College
    Campuse*s (Chicago: University of Chicago Press, 2010), 734–735. Kindle Edition.

19 "College Learning Assessment," City University of New York. http://www.cuny.edu
    /academics/initiatives/cla/sample-tasks.html (accessed December 10, 2014).

20 Arum and Roksa. *Academically Adrift*, 827–829.

21 Arum, Richard, Josipa Roksa, and Esther Cho. "Improving Undergraduate Learn-
    ing: Findings and Policy Recommendations from the SSRC-CLA Longitudinal
    Project" (Brooklyn, NY: Social Science Research Council, 2010).

22 Arum and Roksa. *Academically Adrift*, 2407–2408.

23 Keeling and Hersh. *We're Losing Our Minds*, 171–173, 180–183.

24 "National Assessment of Adult Literacy: The Condition of Education," National
    Center for Education Statistics, 2007. http:// nces.ed.gov/ pubsearch/ pubsinfo.asp
    ?pubid = 2007064 (accessed December 8, 2014).

25 Bok, Derek. *Our Underachieving Colleges: A Candid Look at How Much Students
    Learn and Why They Should Be Learning More* (Princeton, NJ: Princeton Univer-
    sity Press, 2006), 8.

26 Pryor, John H. "College Presidents: Aware of What's Important, Not as Effective

NOTES

at Execution," *The Gallup Blog*, August 28, 2014. http://thegallupblog.gallup.com
/2014/08/college-presidents-aware-of-whats.html.

27 "89. Virtually no one reads what you write," *100 Reasons NOT to Go to Graduate School* blog. http://100rsns.blogspot.com/2013/03/89-virtually-no-one-reads-what-you-write.html (accessed September 22, 2014).

28 "Should tenure for college professors be abolished?" *Wall Street Journal*, updated June 24, 2012. http://online.wsj.com/news/articles/SB10001424052702303610504577418293114042070 (accessed December 8, 2014).

29 Arum and Roksa. *Academically Adrift*, 493–495.

30 Labaree, David F. *How to Succeed in School Without Really Trying: The Credentials Race in American Education* (New Haven: Yale University Press, 1997), 32.

31 Keeling and Hersh. *We're Losing Our Minds*, 308–311.

32 "Education Rankings," *U.S. News & World Report.* http://www.usnews.com/rankings (accessed October 20, 2014).

33 "College Rankings," Reed College. http://www.reed.edu/apply/news_and_articles/college_rankings.html (accessed December 8, 2014).

34 "Fast Facts," National Center for Education Statistics. http://nces.ed.gov/fastfacts/display.asp?id=75 (accessed December 17, 2014).

35 *The Futures Project: Policy for higher education in a changing world* (1999–2005). Note: The Futures Project closed down on March 31, 2005. Information available at http:// www.nerche.org/ futuresproject/ index.html.

36 Merisotis, Jaime P., Lumina Foundation. The Howard R. Bowen Lecture, Claremont Graduate University, Claremont, CA. October 14, 2009.

37 Shear, Michael D. "Colleges rattled as Obama pressures ratings system," *New York Times*, May 25, 2014. http://www.nytimes.com/2014/05/26/us/colleges-rattled-as-obama-presses-rating-system.html?_r=0 (accessed November 18, 2014).

38 Yen, Hope. "Half of new grads are jobless or underemployed." *NBC News*, updated April 24, 2012. http://www.nbcnews.com/id/47141463/ns/business stocks_and _economy/#.V1XZrlux190 (accessed December 8, 2014).

39 Carpenter, Ben. "Is your student prepared for life?" *New York Times* Op-Ed, August 31, 2014. http://www.nytimes.com/2014/09/01/opinion/is-your-student-prepared -for-life.html?_r=0 (accessed September 22, 2014).

40 Weissmann, Jordan. "Here's exactly how many college graduates live back at home," *The Atlantic*, February 26, 2013. http://www.theatlantic.com/business/archive /2013/02/heres-exactly-how-many-college-graduates-live-back-at-home/273529/ (accessed December 8, 2014).

41 Davidson, Adam. "It's official: The boomerang kids won't leave," *New York Times Magazine*, June 20, 2014. http://www.nytimes.com/2014/06/22/magazine/its-official-the-boomerang-kids-wont-leave.html?_r=0 (accessed December 8, 2014).

42 "MIT Nobel Prizes, Institutional Research, Office of the Provost." http://web.mit .edu/ir/pop/awards/nobel.html (accessed December 17, 2014).

43 "MIT TLO: TLO Statistics for Fiscal Year 2013." http://web.mit.edu/tlo/www/ about/office_statistics.html (accessed December 17, 2014).

44 Wolfe, Kristen E. "Understanding the Careers of the Alumni of the MIT Mechanical Engineering Department," MIT senior thesis, June 2004. http://dspace.mit.edu /bitstream/handle/1721.1/32796/57583637.pdf?sequence=1.

45 Grasgreen, Allie. "Ready or not," *Inside Higher Ed*, February 26, 2014. https://www.insidehighered.com/news/2014/02/26/provosts-business-leaders-disagree-graduates-career-readiness (accessed December 8, 2014).

46 Pryor, John H. "College Presidents: Aware of What's Important, Not as Effective at Execution," *The Gallup Blog*, August 28, 2014. http://thegallupblog.gallup.com/2014/08/college-presidents-aware-of-whats.html.

47 Ferdman, Roberto. "Where to go to college if you want the highest starting salary," *Washington Post*, September 11, 2014. http://www.washingtonpost.com/blogs/wonkblog/wp/2014/09/11/where-to-go-to-college-if-you-want-the-highest-starting-salary/ (accessed September 12, 2014).

48 Ingraham, Christopher. "The college majors most likely to lead to underemployment," *Washington Post Wonkblog*, August 26, 2014. http://www.washingtonpost.com/blogs/wonkblog/wp/2014/08/26/the-college-majors-most-and-least-likely-to-lead-to-underemployment/ (accessed December 8, 2014).

49 Capelli, Peter. "Why focusing too narrowly in college could backfire," *Wall Street Journal*, updated November 15, 2014. http://online.wsj.com/news/articles/SB10001424127887324139404579016662718868576 (accessed November 20, 2014).

50 http://thegallupblog.gallup.com/2014/08/college-presidents-aware-of-whats.html.

51 Ibid.

52 Bruce, Mary. "Obama renews push for higher education, hints at Santorum 'snob' comment," *ABC News*, February 27, 2012. http://abcnews.go.com/blogs/politics/2012/02/obama-renews-push-for-higher-education-hints-at-santorum-snob-comment/ (accessed December 8, 2014).

53 "Our Documents: The G.I. Bill," FDR Library. http://docs.fdrlibrary.marist.edu/odgist.html (accessed November 10, 2014).

54 Ibid.

55 Wagner, Meg, Anthony Cave, and Hannah Winston. "GI bill covered tuition for nearly a million post-9/11 veterans without tracking their progress," The Center for Public Integrity, September 3, 2013. http://www.publicintegrity.org/2013/09/03/13297/gi-bill-covered-tuition-nearly-million-post-911-veterans-without-tracking-their (accessed November 20, 2014).

56 "Remembering America's Veterans in 2013," Center for American Progress, November 11, 2013. http://www.americanprogress.org/issues/military/news/2013/11/11/79087/remembering-americas-veterans-in-2013/ (accessed November 20, 2014).

57 Deresiewicz, William. *Excellent Sheep*, 2687–2688.

58 Ibid.

59 Siskind, Sarah R. "Affirmative dissatisfaction," *Harvard Crimson*, November 2, 2012. http://www.thecrimson.com/column/the-snollygoster/article/2012/11/2/Siskind-affirmative-action/ (accessed October 2, 2014).

60 "Voter Turnout by Age." CivicYouth.org (accessed December 8, 2014), http://www.civicyouth.org/wp-content/uploads/2013/07/2012YouthVote.jpg.

61 "Digest of Education Statistics," National Center for Education Statistics, October 2013. http://nces.ed.gov/programs/digest/d13/tables/dt13_104.20.asp.

62 "Statistics," Campus Vote Project, http://www.campusvoteproject.org/statistics.

63 Arum and Roksa, *Academically Adrift*, 1924–1926.

64 Quoted from the summary of the book on amazon.com. http://www.amazon

.com/Generation-Tightrope-Portrait-College-Student-ebook/dp/B008NPSNHQ (accessed December 8, 2014).

65 Leonhardt, David. "Top colleges that enroll rich, middle class and poor," *New York Times*, September 8, 2014. http://www.nytimes.com/2014/09/09/upshot/top-colleges-that-enroll-rich-middle-class-and-poor.html (accessed September 9, 2014).

66 Keeling and Hersh, *We're Losing Our Minds*, 3371–3374.

67 "On the Payoff to Attending an Elite College," National Bureau of Economic Research. http://www.nber.org/digest/dec99/w7322.html (accessed September 9, 2014).

68 Staff, C. J. "Friday Interview: Debunking myths about the college earnings advantage," *Carolina Journal Online*, September 9, 2011. http://www.carolinajournal.com/exclusives/display_exclusive.html?id=8203 (accessed December 8, 2014).

69 *New York Times*, June 19, 2013, interview with Lazlo Bock, http://www.nytimes.com/2013/06/20/business/in-head-hunting-big-data-may-not-be-such-a-big-deal.html?pagewanted=all&_r=0, as well as the April 20, 2013, article by Steve Lohr, "Big data, trying to build better workers," also in the *New York Times*. http://www.nytimes.com/2013/04/21/technology/big-data-trying-to-build-better-workers.html?pagewanted=all. (Both accessed October 3, 2013.) See also Tom Friedman's excellent February 22, 2014 interview with Bock, "How to get a job at Google." http://www.nytimes.com/2014/02/23/opinion/sunday/friedman-how-to-get-a-job-at-google.html?_r=1 (accessed December 8, 2014).

70 "Google: How We Hire." http://www.google.com/about/careers/lifeatgoogle/hiringprocess/ (accessed December 17, 2014).

71 Busteed, Brandon. "College is worth it, but only if we make the most of it," *Gallup*, Opinion Pages, August 14, 2014. http://www.gallup.com/opinion/gallup/176507/college-worth.aspx.

72 Busteed, Brandon. (Executive Director of Gallup Education) in discussion with the author, October 23, 2014.

Chapter 6 Teaching, Learning, and Assessing

1 Ito, Joi. "A week of a student's electrodermal activity," Ito's blog, April 30, 2012. http://joi.ito.com/weblog/2012/04/30/a-week-of-a-stu.html (accessed Decmber 8, 2014).

2 Khan, Salman. *The One World Schoolhouse: Education Reimagined* (New York: Grand Central Publishing, 2012). Kindle Edition. 1985–1989.

3 "Enough with the lecturing," National Science Foundation Press Release 14-064, May 12, 2014. http://nsf.gov/news/news_summ.jsp?cntn_id=131403&org=NSF&from=news (accessed December 17, 2014).

4 Bajak, Aleszu. "Lectures aren't just boring, they're ineffective, too, study finds," *Science Insider*, May 12, 2014. http://news.sciencemag.org/education/2014/05/lectures-arent-just-boring-theyre-ineffective-too-study-finds (accessed December 17, 2014).

5 Source: Wikipedia. http://en.wikipedia.org/wiki/Apollo_Education_Group (accessed December 31, 2014).

6 Cuomo, Chris, Chris Vlasto, Gerry Wagschal, et al. "ABC News Investigates For-Profit

Education: Recruiters at the University of Phoenix," *ABC News*, August 19, 2010. http://abcnews.go.com/TheLaw/profit-education-abc-news-undercover-investigate-recruiters-university/story?id=11411379 (accessed December 17, 2014).

7   Kolowich, Steve. "Why some colleges are saying no to MOOC deals, at least for now," *Chronicle of Higher Education*, December 20, 2014. http://chronicle.com/article/Why-Some-Colleges-Are-Saying/138863/ (accessed December 20, 2014).

8   Daly, Jimmy. "80% of MOOC students already have a college degree," EdTech, December 4, 2013. http://www.edtechmagazine.com/higher/article/2013/12/80-percent-mooc-students-already-have-college-degree (accessed December 8, 2014).

9   Deamicis, Carmel. "A Q&A with 'Godfather of MOOCs' Sebastian Thrun after he disavowed his godchild," May 12, 2014, http://pando.com/2014/05/12/a-qa-with-godfather-of-moocs-sebastian-thrun-after-he-disavowed-his-godchild/ (accessed December 17, 2014).

10 Brown, Peter C. *Make It Stick* (Cambridge, MA: Harvard University Press, 2014). Kindle Edition. 417.

11 Source: Wikipedia. http://en.wikipedia.org/wiki/Harkness_table (accessed December 31, 2014).

12 Mazur, Eric. *Peer Instruction* (Boston: Addison-Wesley, 1996), 16.

13 Private Conversation, December 31, 2014.

14 From the PBS *Frontline* documentary. http://www.pbs.org/wgbh/pages/frontline/shows/sats/where/history.html (accessed December 17, 2014).

15 Owen, David. "Inventing the SAT," The Alicia Patterson Foundation, April 6, 2011. http://aliciapatterson.org/stories/inventing-sat (accessed December 17, 2014).

16 Jaschik, Scott. "SAT Scores Drop Again," *Inside Higher Ed*, September 25, 2012. https://www.insidehighered.com/news/2012/09/25/sat-scores-are-down-and-racial-gaps-remain (accessed December 17, 2014).

17 Zumbrun, Josh. "SAT Scores and Income Inequality: How Wealthier Kids Rank Higher." *Wall Street Journal*, October 7, 2014. http://blogs.wsj.com/economics/2014/10/07/sat-scores-and-income-inequality-how-wealthier-kids-rank-higher/ (accessed March 31, 2015).

18 Strauss, Valerie. "A basic flaw in the argument against affirmative action," *Washington Post*, July 17, 2014. http://www.washingtonpost.com/blogs/answer-sheet/wp/2014/07/17/a-basic-flaw-in-the-argument-against-affirmative-action/ (accessed December 8, 2014).

19 Pinker, Steven. "The trouble with Harvard: The Ivy League is broken and only standardized tests can fix it," *New Republic*, September 4, 2014. http://www.newrepublic.com/article/119321/harvard-ivy-league-should-judge-students-standardized-tests (accessed September 6, 2014).

20 "Fundamentals of Statistics 2: The Normal Distribution." Usable Stats. http://www.usablestats.com/lessons/normal (accessed December 31, 2014).

21 "Normal Distribution: Algebra 2 Trig Lesson Page," Regents Prep. http://www.regentsprep.org/regents/math/algtrig/ats2/normallesson.htm (accessed December 17, 2014).

22 Dorans, Neil J. "The Recentering of SAT Scales and Its Effects on Score Distributions and Score Interpretations," The College Board Research Report No. 2002-11,

NOTES

ETS (New York: College Entrance Examination Board, 2002). https://www.ets.org/Media/Research/pdf/RR-02-04-Dorans.pdf (accessed December 17, 2014).

23 "The SAT Bell Curve," *The Unsilenced Science Blog*, April 25, 2012. http://theunsilenced science.blogspot.com/2012/04/sat-bell-curve.html (accessed December 17, 2014).

24 "SAT Math Practice Tests," College Board. http://sat.collegeboard.org/practice/practice-test-section-start?pageId=practiceMathMultipleChoiceSetup&practice TestSectionIDKey=QuestionType.MULTIPLE_CHOICE&conversationId= ConversationStateUID_2&header=Multiple Choice&subHeader=SAT (accessed December 17, 2014).

25 Shah, Nirvi. "More Students Receiving Accommodations During ACT, SAT," *Education Week Blog*, May 14, 2012. http://blogs.edweek.org/edweek/speced/2012/05/more_students_receiving_accomm.html December 17, 2014 (accessed December 17, 2014).

26 "Validity of the SAT In Predicting First-Year College Grade Point Average." College Board, 2008. https://professionals.collegeboard.com/profdownload/Validity _of_the_SAT_for_Predicting_First_Year_College_Grade_Point_Average.pdf (accessed December 9, 2014).

27 Buskirk, Eliot Van. "Former test-prep exec plots industry makeover," *Wired*, December 3, 2009. http://www.wired.com/2009/12/test-prep-internet/ (accessed December 17, 2014).

28 Miner, Barbara. "Keeping public schools public," *Rethinking Schools*, Winter 2004 /2005. http://www.rethinkingschools.org/special_reports/bushplan/test192.shtml (accessed December 17, 2014).

29 Lewin, Tamar. "Dartmouth stops credits for excelling on A.P. test," *New York Times*, January 17, 2013. http://www.nytimes.com/2013/01/18/education/dartmouth-stops-credits-for-excelling-on-ap-test.html?_r=1& (accessed December 17, 2014).

30 Tierney, John. "AP classes are a scam," *The Atlantic*, October 13, 2012. http://www .theatlantic.com/national/archive/2012/10/ap-classes-are-a-scam/263456/?single _page=true (accessed December 17, 2014).

31 Ibid.

32 Strauss, Valerie. "Life is not a multiple choice test," *Washington Post*, June 24, 2013. http://www.washingtonpost.com/blogs/answer-sheet/wp/2013/06/24/life-is-not-a-multiple-choice-test/ (accessed December 17, 2014).

33 Strauss, Valerie. "When an adult took standardized tests forced on kids," *Washington Post*, updated December 12, 2014. http://www.washingtonpost.com/blogs /answer-sheet/post/when-an-adult-took-standardized-tests-forced-on-kids/2011 /12/05/gIQApTDuUO_blog.html (accessed December 17, 2014).

Chapter 7. A New Vision for Education

1 Stainburn, Samantha. "Taking competency-based learning from policy to reality," *Education Week*, June 3, 2013. http://www.edweek.org/ew/articles/2014/06/04 /33competency.h33.html (accessed December 23, 2014).

2 "Granted and . . . thoughts on education by Grant Wiggins," October 10, 2014.

https://grantwiggins.wordpress.com/2014/10/10/a-veteran-teacher-turned-coach -shadows-2-students-for-2-days-a-sobering-lesson-learned/ (accessed December 17, 2014).

3   More information on the work of the Consortium may be found on its website: http://performanceassessment.org/index.html (accessed December 23, 2014).

4   More information on the initiative can be found on its website: deeper-learning .org (accessed December 23, 2014).

5   "No classrooms and lots of technology: A Danish school's approach," *Globe and Mail*, June 30. 2013. http://www.theglobeandmail.com/report-on-business/econ-omy/canada-competes/no-classrooms-and-lots-of-technology-a-danish-schools-approach/article12688441/ (accessed December 17, 2014).

6   For more information on Finland's extensive education reforms, see the documentary film *The Finland Phenomenon*, and Pasi Sahlberg's excellent book *Finnish Lessons*.

7   The National Commission on Teaching and America's Future. http://nctaf.org /announcements/nations-schools-facing-largest-teacher-retirement-wave-in -history/ (accessed December 15, 2014).

8   http://www.globalissues.org/print/article/75 (accessed December 22, 2014).

9   Adapted from information found at http://www.proposalexponent.com/federal profiles.html (accessed December 23, 2014).

10   More information on the "i3" grant program may be found on the department's web-site: http://www2.ed.gov/programs/innovation/index.html?utm_source=rss&utm _medium=rss&utm_campaign=the-u-s-department-of-education-announced-the-start-of-the-134-million-2014-investing-in-innovation-i3-grant-competition (accessed December 22, 2014).

11   "Forget LinkedIn: Companies turn to GitHub to find tech talent." http://www .cnet.com/news/forget-linkedin-companies-turn-to-github-to-find-tech-talent/ (accessed December 20, 2014).

12   Information taken from the Koru website. Accessed at http://www.joinkoru.com on December 28, 2014

13   More information may be found on its website. Accessed at projectbreaker.org on December 28, 2014

14   As quoted on the Purdue Polytechnic Institute website. https://polytech.purdue .edu/purdue-polytechnic-wins-500000-award-competency-based-degree (accessed December 25, 2014).

15   More information on the initiatives of the two schools mentioned can be found on the respective websites of Davidson and Harvard. Accessed at http://www.davidson .edu/innovation-and-entrepreneurship-initiative/campus-maker-and-innovation -space on December 25, 2014, and https://i-lab.harvard.edu on December 25, 2014.

16   *Time*, "Why College May Be Totally Free in 10 Years," October 12, 2012. http:// business.time.com/2012/10/12/why-college-may-be-totally-free-within-10-years/ (accessed December 21, 2014).

17   Source: Gallup, "Recent Grads More Likely to Have Had Useful Internships." Accessed at http://www.gallup.com/poll/179201/recent-grads-likely-useful-intern ships.aspx on December 23, 2014.

18 More information can be found on their website. Accessed at http://www.ptechnyc .org/Page/1 on December 28, 2014.

19 *The Atlantic*, April 9, 2013, "The Jobs Crisis at Our Best Law Schools Is Much, Much Worse Than You Think." Accessed at http://www.theatlantic.com/business /archive/2013/04/the-jobs-crisis-at-our-best-law-schools-is-much-much-worse- than-you-think/274795/].

20 As quoted in an interview with Thomas Friedman, *New York Times*, "How to Get a Job at Google," February 22, 2104. Accessed at http://www.nytimes.com/2014/02 /23/opinion/sunday/friedman-how-to-get-a-job-at-google.html on December 23, 2014.

21 "The Lawyer's Apprentice," *New York Times*, July 30, 2014. http://www.nytimes .com/2014/08/03/education/edlife/how-to-learn-the-law-without-law-school. html?_r=2 (accessed December 24, 2014).

22 "Nearly 500,000 Fewer Americans Will Pass the GED in 2014 After a Major Overhaul to the Test. Why? And Who's Left Behind?," December 17, 2014, article in *Cleveland Scene*. http://m.clevescene.com/cleveland/after-a-major-overhaul-to-the-ged-test-in- 2014-18000-fewer-ohioans-will-pass-the-exam-this-year-than-last-along-with- nearly 500000 across/Content?oid=4442224&showFullText=true (accessed December 24, 2014).

23 "California Spending More on Prisons Than Colleges, Report Says," *Huffington Post*, September 8, 2012. Accessed at http://www.huffingtonpost.com/2012/09/06 /california-prisons-colleges_n_1863101.html on December 26, 2014.

24 Fairtest.org. Accessed at http://www.fairtest.org/university/optional on December 27, 2014.

25 Zhao, Emmeline. "Small High Schools Post Big Gains." *Real Clear Education*, Octo- ber 16, 2014. http://www.realcleareducation.com/articles/2014/10/16/small_high_ schools_post_huge_gains_in_graduation_college_1117.html (accessed December 24, 2014).

26 More information on the Deeper Learning Initiative can be founded at deeper- learning.org, cited earlier and at the Hewlett Foundation website, http://www hewlett.org/programs/education/deeper-learning (accessed December 23, 2014).

27 Accessed at http://centerforstudentwork.elschools.org on December 25, 2014.

28 Accessed at http://centerforstudentwork.elschools.org/resources/austins-butterfly on December 25, 2014.

29 More information can be found on the Expeditionary Learning website, http:// elschools.org (accessed December 23, 2014).

30 More information about EdLeader21 can be found on its website at http://www .edleader21.com/index.php (accessed December 23, 2014).

31 *The New Yorker*, "Schooled," May 19, 2014. http://www.newyorker.com/magazine /2014/05/19/schooled (accessed December 27, 2014).

32 More information can be found on the TFP website at thefutureproject.org (accessed December 24, 2014).

33 More information on Riverdale's collaboration with IDEO and access to design thinking resources for educators can be found on the school's website at http:// www.riverdale.edu/page.cfm?p=516 (accessed December 24, 2014).

NOTES

34 More information can be found on their website at https://characterlab.org/ (accessed at December 24, 2014).

35 National Venture Capital Association and IHS Global Insight. "Venture Impact: The Economic Importance of Venture Backed Companies to the U.S. Economy, 2012." http://www.slideshare.net/JaanikaMerilo/impact-of-venture-capitalbacked-companies-on-the-us-economy (accessed December 28, 2014).

INDEX

INDEX